Nicholas Hunter and the First Resonance

by

Scott E. Robinson

Dedication

This book is dedicated to my wife and partner for the last 30 years, Jenny. You have stood by me through all the turmoil and helped make this story come to life.

Acknowledgment

This book carries pieces of the people who helped shape the writer I became.

To my high school and college composition instructors—thank you for teaching me how to listen to language, how to trust a sentence, and how to chase the kind of stories that refuse to leave you alone. Your patience, your challenge, and your belief in my voice stayed with me long after the classroom lights went out.

To every teen with ADHD who has ever felt out of time, out of place, or out of sync with the world around them—this story is for you. For the ones who drifted, who daydreamed, who traveled inward when the world demanded they stay still. You are not broken. You are not behind. You are not alone. The way your mind moves is not a flaw; it's a frequency all its own.

And to the readers who step into Nicholas's world—thank you for following the resonance. You're the reason these characters breathe.

Prologue

The dream arrived like a whisper slipping through gears and shadows, a sound too soft to hear yet heavy enough to bend the dark around it.

Nicholas stood alone in a vast cathedral made of clockwork and light. Brass wheels the size of planets turned above him, their teeth catching glimmers of molten gold. Steam curled through the air like ghostly ribbons. Every tick reverberated through the chamber; slow, heavy, alive. It wasn't just sound. It was a pulse. A heartbeat made of metal, steady enough to feel in his bones.

And yet… it wasn't the only heartbeat. Somewhere in the cathedral's endless expanse, he felt another rhythm. Softer. Warmer. A presence he couldn't see but somehow knew. The way you know someone is standing behind you even before they speak. It brushed against him like a memory he'd forgotten to remember.

He reached toward it. Then silence.

A single chime rang out. Deep enough to shake the world, and the floor beneath him cracked like glass under pressure, splintering into a web of light before collapsing into nothingness.

He fell.

Nicholas jolted awake, tangled in his sheets, breathing sharply and ragged. His heart hammered against his ribs like a runaway pendulum. Morning light spilled across his room in soft amber streaks, brushing over the posters on his wall and the cluttered desk he never quite organized. For a moment, he clung to the hope that the dream was just another strange flicker of imagination, nothing more than nerves echoing too loudly in his chest.

Then he saw it.

The old pocket watch on his nightstand. Its hands were ticking backward, each click sending a faint, inexplicable tug through his chest, as if something unseen were calling his attention. Calling him back.

Nicholas Hunter had always been different. Not in the heroic, comic-book way; more in the teachers-whispering-in-the-hallway way. Daydreamer. Distracted. Lost in his own head. He preferred the term visionary, but no one ever asked for his opinion, and he'd long stopped offering it.

But this felt different.

This felt personal.

Nicholas swung his legs out of bed, his wiry frame folding forward as his toes sank into the worn carpet. His dark hair stuck in every direction, a few weeks overdue for a cut, shadowing tired dark eyes. "Great. Another day of being the weird kid," he muttered. He tried to laugh, but the image of that endless clockwork cathedral clung to him like smoke that refused to clear. It's ticking still, faintly echoing in the back of his mind.

And beneath it, that second heartbeat.

Downstairs, the smell of cinnamon toast drifted through the air. His mom hummed softly as she cooked, sunlight catching in her hair. His dad sat at the table, buried in the newspaper, coffee steaming beside him. Nicholas always found it strange that his dad preferred a real newspaper over a tablet. Something about the rustle of the pages, the weight of it, the ink smudges on his fingers—it felt like his dad trusted time more when it came printed on paper. It was the kind of morning that should have felt safe, yet something in the air felt misaligned, like a clock ticking a half beat off.

He hesitated at the bottom of the stairs, hand on the banister, listening to the house breathe around him. The warmth in his chest pulsed once, twice, like a signal waiting for an answer.

But Nicholas knew, deep in his bones, that normal was about to shatter.

School blurred past in a haze of half-heard lectures and restless thoughts, his mind still vibrating with the dream's aftershocks. Then the vision struck.

One moment, he was staring at the whiteboard. Next, he stood in a storm of swirling pink light. Gears massive, impossible turned in the sky above him. A voice threaded through the chaos, stretching his name warm taffy, tugging at him with a pull he felt in his ribs.

"Nicholaaaas…"

But beneath the voice, softer than breath, he felt something else.

A second pull.

A presence reaching toward him through the light.

Not the same as the cathedral's, familiar in a way that made his chest ache.

He blinked, and the classroom snapped back into existence. His pencil clattered to the floor. His pulse thrashed in his ears, as if it had leapt from one timeline into another, leaving a faint shimmer in the air that only he seemed to notice.

By the final bell, Nicholas felt hollowed out, ready to crawl under his bed and never come out. Instead, he trudged home, backpack heavy with books and heavier with questions pressing against his chest like a second heartbeat.

He didn't know that answers were already waiting for him. A girl who wasn't who she claimed to be and who had been watching over him far longer than he knew. A man with a silver watch, capable of tearing reality apart, and bending it toward himself like gravity.

And a destiny that had been ticking toward him since before he was born, waiting for the moment his heart would be loud enough to hear it.

Tonight, time would call his name again: clearer, sharper, impossible to ignore.

And this time, he wouldn't run.

He couldn't. Somewhere, in the quiet space between heartbeats, something waited—listening, patient, already turning toward the boy who had finally begun to hear it.

CHAPTER 1

The day began like any other; chalk dust drifting in thin sunlight, fluorescent lights buzzing like lazy bees, Mrs. Swank diagramming quadratic equations with a squeak that made Nicholas's molars itch.

Nicholas tried to focus. He really did. He'd promised himself again that this year he'd stop zoning out in class. Stop giving teachers more reasons to sigh his name like he was a chore. He'd stop being the kid who drifted.

Anna would've teased him about that gently, with that half-smile that made everything feel a little less sharp. Stay with me, Nicky, she'd say when he spiraled too far into his own head. Just thinking of her steadied him a little, like catching a railing right before a fall.

But the dream clung to him like static, tugging at the edges of his thoughts. He could still feel the gears turning in the dark, a second heartbeat pulsing somewhere just behind his own. It left a hollow ache in his chest, like he'd woken up missing something he couldn't name.

He hated that part most. The missing.

Tap. Tap. Tap. Tap.

His pencil slipped into the rhythm before he realized he was doing it. He froze, cheeks warming, and glanced around to make sure no one noticed. They didn't. They never did.

Anna would've noticed. She always noticed the things he didn't want people to see and somehow made him feel less stupid for them.

He told himself that it should feel embarrassing.

It didn't.

He tried to glue his attention to the board. Mrs. Swank was drawing a parabola that looked more like a wilted flower. The fluorescent lights hummed overhead, but the hum stretched strangely, like someone pulling sound into a thin thread. Chalk dust hung in the air a moment too long before falling.

Nicholas blinked.

The second hand on the classroom clock skipped backward. Just once. A tiny stutter. His stomach dropped. No one else reacted.

He rubbed his eyes hard. "Get it together," he muttered.

Anna's voice echoed in his mind. Hey. Breathe. You're okay.

He clung to that, imagined steadiness like a lifeline. Nicholas glanced across the classroom until he found her. Anna sat two rows over, straight-backed and composed, her dark hair falling in a smooth curtain over one shoulder. Her warm brown skin caught the window light, and her dark eyes were focused on her notebook, calm and intent. As always, she looked a little more put-together than everyone else today in a neat cardigan and pressed skirt instead of the usual hoodies and wrinkled T-shirts. She had a way of seeming older than thirteen, like she had stepped in from a different world where things made sense. Just seeing her there made the pressure in his chest ease a notch.

But the numbers on his worksheet swayed gently, drifting like seaweed under a tide. He blinked again. They snapped back into place—but the chalkboard behind them didn't.

The parabola bent inward, trembling as if resisting some invisible pressure.

The warmth in his chest flickered; soft, steady, familiar in a way that made his breath catch. Not fear. Recognition. And that terrified him more than anything else.

He swallowed. The classroom felt too small, too bright, too loud. Every sound, the scrape of a chair, the whisper of a page turning, echoed with strange clarity, as if the world were amplifying itself around him.

Then the sweetness drifted in again. Chocolate. Warm. Familiar in a way that tugged at something deep in his memory. The tug in his chest tightened. And the world began to tilt, again.

The air thickened, like humidity without heat. The edges of the room softened, as if someone smudged the world with a thumb. The sweetness in the air thickened, as if someone was melting chocolate where they shouldn't.

Then the tug hit him.

Small. Insistent. Familiar.

His ribs tightened around it. A warmth flickered beneath his sternum, steady, grounding, strangely comforting, like something ancient stretching awake.

The hum of the lights deepened into a low, yawning moan. The chalk dust froze midair. The numbers on the board blurred, sliding like wet ink. A faint pink glow seeped into the corners of the room.

Nicholas blinked, and the classroom peeled away like wallpaper. Nicholas's first instinct was not fear. It was a wish.

A stupid, impossible wish that Anna wasn't across the classroom. She always knew how to steady him when the ground went sideways, even when she didn't know why he needed steadying.

The warmth in his chest flickered at the thought of her, like a compass trying to find north.

Then the shimmer swallowed everything.

He was standing inside a clock shop, impossibly real for a daydream.

Two big picture windows. A brass bell over the door. Glass cases lined with watches that caught the light and threw it back in starbursts. The air smelled of oil, varnish, and something sweet … chocolate, maybe.

Nicholas's breath hitched. He wished Anna could see this. Not because he wanted someone to confirm he wasn't losing his mind, though that would've been nice, but because she would've understood the way the place felt. The way it hummed. The way it tugged at something deep in him.

She always understood things he didn't have words for.

The warmth in his chest pulsed once, as if agreeing.

The rhythm was familiar. Half a beat slow.

Just like the mantle clock at home.

He turned toward the sound, but the shimmer faded before he could locate it.

Across the room, a man in black paced the length of the counter like a brewing storm. His coat hung heavy at the shoulders, shadows clinging to its seams, as if reluctant to let go. He didn't look up. He didn't need to; his presence filled the shop, pressurizing the air. A few loose gears on the counter trembled toward him, nudged by an unseen pull.

Rhet.

The name arrived uninvited, whispered from somewhere older than the floorboards.

Nicholas drifted forward. His feet didn't quite touch the ground. The floor felt soft, like walking on thick carpet, though he could see the wooden planks beneath him. The air carried a faint vibration, a hum that wasn't sound so much as sensation, brushing against his skin like static.

A row of pocket watches swung gently as he passed, stirred by a breeze he couldn't feel. One of them ticked in that same half-beat-slow rhythm as the mantle clock at home.

The sound reached into him, syncing with the warmth in his chest.

He thought of Anna again; how she always tapped her foot offbeat when she was thinking, how she'd laugh at him for noticing something so small.

He wished he could hear her laugh now.

Anything human. Anything familiar.

The shop felt alive, but he felt alone inside it.

He reached out instinctively, though he had no hand here. The watch responded anyway. Its cracked face glowed faintly pink, then dimmed, like an eye fluttering open and shut.

Nicholas's breath caught. The warmth in his chest pulsed in answer.

He turned toward a tall grandfather clock in the corner. Its pendulum swung steadily, but the motion wasn't right. It moved too smoothly, too silently, as if gliding through water instead of air. When Rhet shifted his weight, the pendulum stuttered; a tiny hitch, almost imperceptible, but enough to send a ripple through the room.

The shimmer reacted instantly, pulling back from Rhet and curling protectively around the clocks that ticked in the half-beat-slow rhythm.

Nicholas felt the warmth in his chest flare, a protective instinct rising in him so suddenly it startled him.

He didn't know why.

But he knew, without understanding, that the clocks were afraid.

Clocks of every shape and age lined the walls, grandfather clocks with cracked faces, cuckoos with their doors half-open as if afraid to emerge, pocket watches arranged like constellations behind glass. Some ticked forward. Some backward. Some didn't tick at all.

But a few, just a few, ticked in that same half-beat-slow rhythm.

Nicholas felt the tug in his chest answer them.

The shopkeeper appeared through a bead-curtained doorway, tugging at his suspenders, bald head shining under lamplight. He froze when he saw the man in black. Words followed, too quiet to catch, but the tone was unmistakable: warning, defiance, pleading.

The chorus of clocks ticked out of sync, nervous, like a hundred small hearts trying to agree on a rhythm. Even the pink shimmer recoiled slightly from Rhet, shrinking back like prey recognizing a predator.

Rhet placed gloved fingertips on the glass case and leaned forward. The air around his hand warped, bending toward him in a slow, hungry spiral, as though gravity itself had chosen a new center.

"You know what's moving," he said softly. Almost kindly. "You know where it's headed."

The shopkeeper shook his head. "You're in the wrong time."

Rhet smiled. It wasn't a pleasant expression.

Nicholas felt the air tighten, as if the room itself were holding its breath. Rhet's smile didn't reach his eyes; it seemed to drain the light from them, leaving something cold and sharp behind. Rhet's shadow stretched across the floorboards, long and wrong, bending the air around him. The clocks recoiled. The shimmer curled protectively around the half-beat-slow ones.

Nicholas's chest tightened. He wanted Anna.

Not because she could fight this, she couldn't, but because her presence always made him feel like he wasn't facing things alone.

He didn't know why the thought hit him so hard. He just knew the room felt colder without her.

A faint ringing filled Nicholas's ears, high and thin, like the whine of metal under strain. The warmth in his chest recoiled from it, shrinking back instinctively. The two sensations, warmth and cold, collided inside him, leaving him dizzy.

Rhet's presence wasn't just unsettling. It was wrong. Not in a moral sense, but in a structural one, like a load-bearing beam had been removed from a building and the walls hadn't realized it yet. Nicholas didn't know how he knew that. He just did.

Rhet lifted the glass lid with the care of a priest unveiling a relic and reached inside. The pocket watch he drew out was gold, etched with constellations that seemed to shift when the shimmer touched them. Across the back was a strange symbol, three lines crossing in a spine, a star caught mid-breath. The mark hummed faintly, like a memory trying to surface.

Nicholas leaned closer. The watch ticked. Half a beat slow.

His heart lurched. The tug in his chest tightened, sharp and personal, like a thread pulling taut.

The gold watch glowed faintly pink, the symbol on its back humming like a memory trying to surface.

The tug in his chest tightened sharply, personal, almost painful.

He wished Anna could see this. Not the danger, the meaning. The way the watch seemed to recognize him. The way the shimmer pulsed like a heartbeat calling his name. Anna would have believed him. She always did.

A warning.

"Eunomia," Rhet breathed, savoring the word. "Chaos from Order. Imagine it in my hand."

Nicholas tried to move, to shout, to throw himself between them, but he had no body here, only eyes and a pulsing, helpless heart that beat in time with the shimmer's warning rhythm.

The shopkeeper reached beneath the counter. His hand came up with a dagger; short, utilitarian, the edge dull-looking until it found the light. He didn't threaten. He warned.

"You don't understand what you're touching."

"I understand perfectly," Rhet said. He set the watch back in the case, as if baiting fate, then turned the dagger in the shopkeeper's hand with a small, predatory step. The air bent toward him again, subtle but undeniable. "You think time resents being steered. Time resents being owned."

The clocks answered with a fragile chorus. Chimes. One by one, then all together, hour-strikes layered on hour-strikes until the sound braided into a single, trembling note.

The shimmer pulsed sharply, desperately.

Rhet's eyes flicked toward the ceiling, the barest twitch of interest, and returned to the shopkeeper with a look Nicholas would remember forever: a look that promised an ending.

The blade flashed.

Nicholas sucked in air too late, because the scene snapped.

The shopkeeper stumbled backward. The dagger clattered to the floor. Rhet reached into the case and took the watch with a tender, almost reverent grip, like a man lifting a newborn. The air around him warped again, as if the world itself leaned toward the fragment he held.

The shimmer thickened around the watch and licked at Rhet's sleeve, desperate, pleading. He glanced toward the door, toward the street beyond, toward Nicholas, as if he could feel the boy watching.

Nicholas felt the tug again, sharp, personal, like a thread tightening. Then the shimmer folded in on itself like a closing flower, and the shop was gone.

For a split second, both worlds overlapped. The clock shop's pink glow bled into the fluorescent white of the classroom. Rhet's silhouette flickered behind Mrs. Swank's, like a double exposure. The half-beat-slow tick echoed through the room, louder than the hum of the lights, louder than Nicholas's own heartbeat.

Then everything snapped.

The glow vanished. The tick cut off mid-beat. The warmth in his chest collapsed inward, leaving a hollow ache behind.

Nicholas gasped as the world slammed into place.

The classroom snapped back into existence, jarring enough to knock the breath from his lungs.

Nicholas was half-standing, desk legs screeching across the tile. His pencil hit the floor with a crack, echoing louder than it should have. His lungs clawed for air. His heart sprinted. The lights buzzed too brightly. The colors were too sharp. The world felt overexposed, like someone had turned the saturation up on existence.

A faint shimmer clung to the edges of his vision before dissolving, like reality taking a moment to remember its shape.

"Mr. Hunter!" Mrs. Swank's voice snapped like ice. She was crimson, foot tapping a fury staccato. "Would you like to explain why you interrupted my class with your screams?"

He swallowed. Humor, he reminded himself. Humor is a flotation device.

"It's actually a pretty interesting story… actually."

"Office," she said, slicing the air with a palm. "Now! And tell Miss Carter to contact your parents. We will be meeting this afternoon."

Nicholas gathered his books. As he passed Anna in her seat at the front of the room, she leaned in, eyes sparkling with a worry look she tried to hide. She brushed his sleeve with a touch that steadied him more than it should have.

"Tell me about the rest after school," she whispered.

He managed a quick wink and a grin. "You'll never believe…"

"Miss Seward," Mrs. Swank warned, "unless you'd like to join him, silence."

The main office smelled like pencil shavings, warm toner, and the faint citrus cleaner they used every Friday. It was familiar in the way old shoes were familiar, worn, predictable and a little too small.

Nicholas pushed open the door, already rehearsing the speech he'd give Miss Carter. She didn't even look up at first; she just pointed toward the small cluster of chairs against the wall.

"Usual spot, Nicholas," she said, tapping at her keyboard. "I'll call your parents in a minute."

He dropped into the same chair he'd sat in for every detention-adjacent incident since sixth grade. The vinyl cushion wheezed under him like it was tired of his nonsense. He tried to sink into it, make himself small, invisible.

He didn't get the chance.

The door behind him opened with a soft, deliberate click.

A draft swept in, warm, sweet, and unmistakably wrong for a school hallway. Chocolate. Mint. A faint citrus brightness beneath it. The same scent that haunted the clock shop.

Nicholas's breath caught.

Miss Carter finally looked up. "Oh… hello, sir. Can I help you?"

The man who stepped inside didn't belong in a middle school office. He looked like he'd walked out of a different decade, maybe a different century. His overcoat was long and battered, the kind of coat that had seen storms and train stations and places Nicholas didn't have names for. The fabric was frayed at the cuffs, but clean and cared for. His silver hair fell in soft, uneven waves, as if he'd pushed his hands through it one too many times.

He moved with a quiet, deliberate shuffle, but there was nothing frail about him. If anything, the air seemed to shift around him, as if he carried his own gravity. Nicholas froze. The warmth in his chest surged, not sharp, not warning, but recognizing. Like a tuning fork struck the same key.

The man paused mid-step. His eyes, slate blue and sharp as a compass point, flicked toward Nicholas. Not a glance. A search. A measuring. A moment that stretched thin and bright, like a wire pulled taut. For a heartbeat, Nicholas felt seen. Not in the embarrassing, caught doing something the wrong way. In the pattern recognized way. As if the man were reading something written under his skin. A pattern Nicholas did not know he had.

Miss Carter cleared her throat. "Sir? Can I help you?"

The man blinked once, slowly, as if returning from a far distance. "Yes," he murmured, voice low and warm. "I am here for a message."

Nicholas's pulse hammered. The air around the man shimmered, faint and almost invisible, like heat rising off pavement. A soft pink glint clung to the cuffs of his coat before dissolving into the room. His coat ticked. Not loudly. Not like a watch. More like a heartbeat muffled by fabric. Half a beat slow.

Nicholas's skin prickled. His chest answered with a soft, involuntary thrum. The man's gaze flicked to him again, brief but knowing.

Then he turned back to Miss Carter, leaning in just enough for Nicholas to hear the words meant to be private. "…the Council needs confirmation. The artifact is already in motion."

Nicholas's breath hitched. The warmth in his chest pulsed, not fear, not pain, but something startlingly close to relief. Like standing near this man made the world tilt a little less. He did not understand it. But he felt it. Deep. Instinctive. Unavoidable.

The man stepped back, nodded once to Miss Carter, then turned toward the door. Nicholas blurted, "Do you… uh… know a shop called Timely Interventions."

The man paused. Slowly, he looked over his shoulder. His eyes softened, just barely. "Sometimes," he said. "When time is kind."

Then he was gone. The door clicked shut behind him, leaving the scent of chocolate and old clocks hanging in the air like a question Nicholas was not ready to answer.

By the time the bell released the school into the gray afternoon, Nicholas felt as if he had been run through a centrifuge. A faint echo of the shimmer still clung to him, like static. He caught up with Anna at the lockers, side by side in the stream of bodies, their words tucked under the noise.

"That was some daydream," she said, steady but soft, though her eyes searched his face as if she were sensing something deeper.

He tried to grin. "Pink tunnel. Storm. Guy in black. Dagger. Magic watch. You know, Friday."

They walked toward the exit. Nicholas kept glancing at the edges of things, doorframes, lockers, the corners of the ceiling, half expecting the pink shimmer to flicker back into view. It did not. But the world still felt unsettled, like a snow globe that had been shaken and was only now beginning to let the flakes drift down.

Anna walked close enough that their shoulders occasionally brushed. Each time, the warmth in his chest steadied, as if her presence grounded him. He did not understand it, but he clung to it anyway.

He was not sure what scared him more, the vision itself or the strange sense that some part of him had been waiting for it.

Somewhere, a lawn mower droned. A flock of starlings turned as one dark ribbon in the sky. The world looked the same. It just was not.

The room looked solid again, but Nicholas couldn't shake the sense that something remained slightly misaligned, like the world had been put back together a fraction off-center.

"Nicky, what did the watch look like?" Anna asked.

"Gold, clean, etched like stars." He hesitated. "And a symbol. Three lines crossing. And the pink. It reacted to him, and to me."

Anna's grip tightened on her backpack. "Okay," she said, a note of resolve threading through the word. "We should talk. Not here."

The doors opened on the cool air, and the sound of the bell followed them out, the last ordinary chime before the world began to unravel.

Somewhere beyond gears and chimes, Rhet moved through time like a knife through canvas, leaving neat, quiet tears you only noticed when reality started to leak.

CHAPTER 2

Monday afternoon, his parents met with Mrs. Swank, a meeting that did not go well. Nicholas had not been in the room with them, but he did not need to be. He sat outside the office on a wobbly plastic chair, listening to the muted voices drifting through the door, the hallway smelling faintly of dry-erase markers and old carpet. The clock above him ticked in a rhythm that did not match the pulse in his chest.

Inside, Mrs. Swank spoke in the careful, measured tone adults used when they were trying to sound calm about something that was not. "Nicholas is… unusual," she said, and even through the door he could hear the hesitation. "He is bright. Exceptionally bright. But his attention patterns are inconsistent. He will drift off for long stretches, completely unresponsive, and then."

There was a rustle of papers, the soft scrape of a folder being opened.

"…and then he will ace material we have not covered yet."

His mother's voice tightened with confusion. "What do you mean, 'have not covered yet'?"

Mrs. Swank hesitated, as if weighing how ridiculous the truth might sound. "I mean, he scores perfectly on units we have not started. Sometimes weeks ahead. It is almost as if he is…" Another pause, longer this time, as though she were searching for a word she did not want to say.

Nicholas leaned forward, breath held.

"…as if he is a time traveler."

His father let out a startled, awkward laugh, the kind that tried to dismiss the idea without actually addressing it. "Well, he is not."

"Of course not," Mrs. Swank said quickly. "I know. It is just… the pattern is strange. He will miss entire lessons, staring into space like he is somewhere else entirely, and then he will turn in work that suggests he already knew the content before I taught it."

Heat crept up Nicholas's neck. He did not do it on purpose. He did not even realize he was doing it. Sometimes the answers simply arrived in his mind, fully formed, like echoes from a place he could not remember visiting.

Mrs. Swank's voice softened. "I do not think he is trying to be difficult. I do not think he even realizes he is doing it. But it is affecting him socially. The other students notice. They do not know what to make of him."

His mother sighed, a tired, worried sound that made something twist in his chest. "We are doing everything we can. He has been through a lot."

"I can tell," Mrs. Swank replied gently. "And I am not criticizing. I just want to understand him. He is a good kid. A kind kid. But something is pulling him away from the present. Something he is not ready to talk about."

Nicholas stared at the floor tiles, tracing the cracks between them with his eyes. He wished she were wrong. He wished he were not slipping. He wished he were not being pulled. But the truth sat inside him like a second heartbeat, uneven, insistent, impossible to ignore.

When the door finally opened, Mrs. Swank stepped out with a warm, practiced smile, the kind meant to reassure without promising anything. "We will figure it out," she said.

But Nicholas could see the worry behind her eyes.

And he could tell she did not believe her own words.

Not really.

And neither did he.

The warmth in his chest had not faded on the drive home. If anything, it had grown heavier, as if it were waiting for the basement to notice him. He paused at the top of the stairs, hand on the railing, the air shifting in that familiar, almost hopeful way.

He hoped Anna would be down there.

He did not know what he would say, or how he would explain the way the world had been bending around him, but he knew one thing with absolute certainty: he could not face whatever this was alone. Not anymore. Not with the warmth in his chest pulsing like a second heartbeat, trying to sync with something it recognized.

The basement smelled of old wood, chocolate chip cookies, and secrets. Dust motes drifted in the lamplight like tiny planets, slow and stubborn, refusing to fall. Pipes ticked, the house breathed, and somewhere above, a clock marked time a half beat slow, as if pacing itself for bad news.

Nicholas took the stairs two at a time, then slowed, one hand tight on the railing. Each step groaned like an old violin. The sound vibrated through his bones, familiar and unsettling at the same time. He had run up and down these stairs a thousand times as a kid, but tonight they felt different, as if they were warning him to turn back.

Halfway down, the lights flickered, not off, just sideways, as if the glow shifted a fraction of an inch before snapping back. The air felt thicker down here, warmer, as if the house had exhaled and forgotten to inhale again.

He swallowed, the warmth in his chest tightening as if bracing against the hollow inside him. He needed Anna's steadiness, the quiet, anchoring presence she carried without trying, the way she could make a room stop spinning just by being in it. With her, the world always felt like it had a center. Without her, everything tilted too easily, as if he were walking on a floor that shifted under his feet.

He had always loved this basement. It was where he and Anna had built forts out of blankets and cardboard, where they had hidden from thunderstorms and parents and the world. But tonight, the familiar clutter felt charged, as if every object was holding its breath.

The pipes overhead ticked in a rhythm that almost matched the warmth in his chest. Almost. The half-beat slow tick from upstairs echoed faintly through the floorboards, threading itself through the basement's sounds like a quiet warning.

The basement seemed to lean in around him. He had spent half his childhood down here, among the old workbench, shelves of tools, and the familiar smell of oil and dust, but tonight the room felt subtly wrong. Shadows pooled thicker in the corners. The air held the metallic tang of a coming storm, cool near the workbench and strangely warm near the couch, as if the basement had developed its own weather. The familiar space no longer felt like a refuge. It felt like a threshold.

And he was not sure what was waiting on the other side.

Anna was already there, crouched near the workbench, her silhouette sharp against the clutter of gears, brass fittings, and halfbuilt contraptions. Relief hit him so hard it almost buckled his knees. The warmth in his chest pulsed, steadying and grateful, as if it recognized her presence.

When she looked up, the lamplight caught in her eyes, copper bright and purposeful. She looked older at that moment, not in years, but in weight.

"You have been having more visions, have you not?" she asked softly.

Nicholas tried for humor, but it came out thin. "Visions, daydreams, cosmic horror shows, take your pick." He raked a hand through his hair, sending a puff of dust swirling. "Anna, what is happening to me?"

She hesitated, fingers tracing the edge of a brass gear. Her touch lingered longer than necessary, tracing the teeth with a precision that felt more like stalling than curiosity. Nicholas watched her shoulders rise and fall in a slow, deliberate breath. She was not just choosing her words; she was choosing which truths she could afford to let slip.

He had seen Anna scared before, spiders, thunderstorms, that time they got lost in the corn maze, but this was not fear. This was something heavier. A kind of grief. Like she was mourning something that had not happened yet.

"Anna," he said softly.

She did not look up. "I knew this was coming," she whispered. "I just did not think it would be this soon."

Nicholas's stomach dropped. "What does that mean?"

She only shook her head, jaw tightening as if she was holding back a flood.

"You are changing," she said finally. "Becoming what you were meant to be."

"Cryptic much," Nicholas muttered, but his pulse quickened. "You sound like a fortune cookie."

Anna smiled faintly, but the smile did not reach her eyes. "There are things I cannot tell you yet. Not until you are ready."

Nicholas barked a laugh, too sharp. "Ready? What am I, an oven timer? Ding, I am done? Or a microwave, beep beep, your time traveler is hot and bubbly." He flopped onto the couch. "Dibs," he said, like always.

Anna smirked, but only a little. "You always take the couch."

"Tradition," he said. "Like the pizza box fort. Queen of Pepperoni decrees that all citizens must pay one slice per hour."

She laughed, soft, reluctant, but real, and the sound eased something tight in his chest. He had not realized how badly he needed to hear it. For a moment, the half-beat wrongness of the world faded, and he felt like he could breathe again.

"You still remember that," she asked.

"Of course I remember," Nicholas said. "This place was our kingdom." He gestured around the basement, the sagging couch, the paint-splattered rug, the shelves crammed with half-finished inventions and forgotten science fair disasters. "We built entire worlds down here. Remember the cardboard city? The one with the zipline for action figures."

Anna's smile warmed. "You burned half of it down with a magnifying glass."

"It was an accident," he protested. "The sun was at a weird angle."

"You were inside," she reminded him.

Nicholas snorted. "Okay, fine. Maybe it was not my best plan." His expression softened. "But you stayed with me. Even when I messed everything up."

Anna looked away, her voice barely above a breath. "I always will."

Something in her tone unsettled him in a way he did not yet understand. Her presence steadied him in a way nothing else did; it always had, even before he knew why. Being near her felt like stepping back into a rhythm he had forgotten he knew, a rhythm his body recognized before his mind could catch up. He studied her face, searching for the girl he remembered and the guardian she had become. There was a tightness at her jaw, a tension she could not quite hide, and her shoulders sat a fraction too straight, as if she had been carrying a secret so heavy it bent her smile out of shape. She looked older, sharper, pulled taut by something she was not saying.

"Anna," he said softly, trying to catch her eyes, "if you know what is happening to me… You would tell me, right?"

The question hung between them like a held breath, fragile and dangerous, the kind of truth that could change everything if she answered it. And he was not sure which scared him more, her telling him, or her not.

Her pause was a crack in the air. "When you are ready," she whispered. "Not before."

He held up both hands in mock surrender. "Great. So I am cake batter. Let me know when I pass the toothpick test." The grin faltered when she did not join him. He tried again, softer. "Ready for what?"

Anna's gaze slid past him, measuring rather than evasive, toward the far corner where their clubhouse trophies lived. The lamp with the house-shaped base cast a warm cone of light across the rug. On the shelf, the bird statue perched alert, its wings forever slightly crooked. Opposite it, the miniature grandfather clock ticked with stubborn certainty. Together, the three pieces formed a triangle, lamp to bird, bird to clock, clock back to lamp, an easy geometry Nicholas had always assumed was accidental. Tonight, it felt deliberate. Ritual. Like a shape meant to hold something. Or someone.

He followed her gaze and frowned. "Since when do our junk treasures line up like a secret pentagram? Should I start chanting? Do we need candles? I can grab tea lights from the Christmas box."

"It is not a pentagram," she said, almost laughing. Almost. "Triangles are stable. They hold."

"As in, do not fall over? Or as in, keep out monsters."

She did not answer.

The silence pressed at Nicholas's ribs until he had to move. He crossed to the lamp and adjusted the shade, pretending to fuss. The light slid, and shadows redrew themselves, bird to clock, clock to lamp, like a compass finding north. The space inside the triangle seemed to be quiet, as if the room itself had been asked to pay attention.

"Okay, this is officially weird," he said, but his voice came out hushed. "You put these here on purpose, did you not?"

Anna's throat bobbed once. "Years ago."

Nicholas stared. "Years ago? Anna, we were kids."

"I know," she said. "That is why it worked."

"What worked."

She stepped closer to the triangle, her fingers brushing the edge of the bird statue. "You do not remember, but you used to have… episodes. Not like the visions now. Smaller. Flickers. You would stare at nothing and say things that did not make sense. Names. Places. Questions you should not have known to ask."

Nicholas's unease sharpened.

"You were eight," she continued. "And every time it happened, the clocks in the house would stutter. The lights would dim. Once, the radio turned itself on and played the same three seconds of a song over and over."

Nicholas swallowed hard. "Why do I not remember any of that?"

"You do," she said gently. "Just not with your head."

She tapped her chest. "You remember here."

Nicholas pressed a hand to his sternum. The warmth answered, a soft thrum beneath his ribs. It steadied when she stood close. It always did.

"And the triangle," he asked.

"It kept you grounded," Anna said. "It kept the visions from pulling you too far."

Nicholas stared at the triangle, suddenly aware of how carefully it had been arranged. How intentional.

"How did you know to do that?" he whispered.

Anna's eyes flicked away. "Someone told me."

"Who?"

She did not answer. A faint shimmer of gold flickered at her collarbone, there and gone in an instant, before she folded her arms across her chest, protectively, as if she was holding something back for his sake. Her jaw tightened in a small, involuntary clench, and she looked away with deliberate care, choosing a point on the wall instead of his eyes. It was not avoidance. It was a restraint. The kind that came from knowing the truth and believing it might hurt him more than silence.

Nicholas sank onto the couch again, elbows on knees. "Anna… I am scared."

The words surprised him. They felt too honest, too exposed. But once they were out, he could not take them back.

Anna's expression softened, the tension in her shoulders easing just a fraction. She sat beside him, close enough that their knees brushed. The contact grounded him, pulling him back from the edge of whatever storm was gathering inside his chest.

"You do not have to be brave right now," she murmured.

"I am not," he said. "I am barely holding it together."

"That is okay."

He let out a shaky breath. "I do not understand what is happening. I do not understand why it is happening to me."

Anna hesitated, then reached out and took his hand. Her grip was warm and steady. The warmth in his chest synced with her touch, settling into a rhythm that felt almost peaceful.

Almost.

He opened his eyes. "It happened again today in class… Everything went weird. The lights stretched. The air bent. And then…" He hesitated. "The clock shop again."

Anna's breath hitched. "What did you see?"

"Rhet," Nicholas said. The name tasted like metal. "And the watch. The one with the symbol. And the pink shimmer, it reacted to me. Like it knew me."

Anna's fingers curled into her palms, the movement small and sharp, as if she was bracing against her own thoughts. "It does," she said, the words slipping out before she could catch them. The moment they left her mouth, her eyes widened just slightly, a flicker of regret tightening the corners. She drew in a quiet breath, shoulders tensing as if she wished she could pull the admission back into her chest and lock it away where it could not hurt him.

Nicholas stared. "What does that mean?"

She did not answer.

He stood abruptly, pacing. "Anna, I am losing it. I am seeing things that are not there. Hearing things. Feeling…" He pressed a hand to his chest. "This warmth. This pull. Like something is waking up inside me."

Anna rose slowly. "It is." He froze.

She stepped closer, voice low. "Nicholas… you are not imagining this. You are not broken. You are not sick. You are changing because you are supposed to."

"Supposed to," he echoed. "By who? By what?"

Anna looked at the triangle again. "By everything."

Nicholas opened his mouth to argue, but the world tilted.

The basement blurred, colors bleeding like wet paint. The air thickened, humming with a low, resonant vibration that made the hair on his arms stand up. The warmth in his chest surged, then pulled hard.

For a heartbeat, he was somewhere else.

A vaulted hall lined with clocks, pendulums swinging in eerie unison. Light spilled from high windows and turned the air into watered gold. The hall stretched impossibly far, disappearing into a haze of gold and shadow. Some clocks had faces with no numbers, only shifting constellations. Others had hands that spun in slow, deliberate circles, reversing direction every few seconds. One enormous clock near the far end had no hands at all, only a single glowing line that pulsed like a heartbeat.

Nicholas felt drawn to it, the warmth in his chest tugging him forward. But he could not move. His feet were rooted to the marble floor, heavy as stone.

Three figures stood before a long table, cloaked in twilight. Power radiated from them, not loud or flashy, but deep and ancient, like tectonic plates shifting beneath the earth.

"The boy has seen too much," the first hissed, voice like cut crystal.

"He carries the mark," said the second, presence like a draft through a keyhole.

The third figure stepped forward, and the hall seemed to bow around it. "He is awakening," it said. "And the world will feel it."

Nicholas's heart pounded. The warmth in his chest flared, bright and hot, as if responding to the figure's words.

"Rhet moves quickly," the first figure said. "He senses the shift."

"If he reaches the boy first," the second whispered, "the balance shatters."

The third figure turned, and Nicholas felt its gaze land on him.

"You must choose your path," it said.

The hall trembled. Nicholas gasped. And the vision shattered.

For a long moment, he could not move. The basement swam in and out of focus, the edges of objects blurring like wet watercolor. His heartbeat thundered in his ears, too loud, too slow, too heavy. He pressed a hand to his chest, half expecting to feel the marble floor of the hall beneath his palm instead of worn cotton. The warmth inside him flickered wildly, like a candle fighting a draft. He could still hear the echo of the third figure's voice, not the words, but the weight of them, the way they settled into his bones like a truth he was not ready to face.

The triangle's shadows seemed sharper now, more defined, as if the vision had awakened a watchful presence in the corners of the room.

He was back in the basement, palms flat to the workbench, knuckles white. The triangle's shadows lay quiet, like a puzzle waiting for the last piece. Anna stood between him and the couch, small and fierce, hands ready but gentle.

"You saw something," she whispered.

"Council meeting," Nicholas said hoarsely. "They know about me."

Anna's expression hardened, fear and resolve braided together. "Then we are out of time."

Nicholas sank onto the couch, head in his hands. His pulse thundered in his ears, each beat echoing the half-beat slow rhythm from upstairs. The warmth in his chest had not faded; it had intensified, spreading through his ribs like a slow-burning ember.

"I do not want this," he whispered. "I did not ask for any of this."

"I know," Anna said softly. "But it is here anyway."

He looked up at her, eyes burning. "Why me?"

Anna hesitated. "Because you are connected. To things you do not remember. To people you have never met. To a history that is waking up, whether you are ready or not."

Nicholas swallowed hard. "And Rhet."

Anna's jaw tightened, and the faintest tremor moved through her shoulders, as if she was bracing for the weight of her own words. "He is connected too. But not the way you are." She did not look at him when she said it; her eyes stayed fixed on the floor, her fingers curling into her palms until her knuckles blanched, every line of her body pulled taut with apprehension.

Nicholas felt a chill crawl down his spine, the kind that made his breath catch and his hands go cold. "What does he want?" he asked, though part of him already feared the answer.

Anna's voice dropped to a whisper, barely more than breath. "You."

The word seemed to hollow out the space between them. Nicholas's stomach tightened, and he took a small step back without meaning to, his pulse thudding unevenly in his throat. The basement lights flickered overhead, and the house creaked as if shifting under the pressure of something unseen. In that moment, with Anna standing rigid and watchful and Nicholas fighting the urge to run, he realized with a clarity that stole the air from his lungs that whatever was coming for him was not far away.

It was already moving.

Anna stepped closer, her movements careful and instinctive, as if she was positioning herself between him and something she could sense but he could not. Her voice softened until it was barely more than a breath. "Whatever happens next… You will not face it alone." The promise trembled at the edges, not from uncertainty, but from the weight of everything she was not saying.

Nicholas swallowed hard, his throat tight, his pulse thudding unevenly in his ears. He searched her face, needing something solid to hold onto. "Promise."

She nodded once, slow and deliberate, her eyes steady on his. "Promise."

The basement shifted around them. Shadows stretched toward the familiar triangle, and the warmth in Nicholas's chest answered with a single steady pulse.

Above them, the miniature grandfather clock ticked once, half a beat slow.

And somewhere beyond the walls, in the thin spaces between worlds, a presence stirred. Faint. Distant. Not fully awake, but listening.

Whatever had begun between them was not complete.
But it was waking.
And whatever waited in the dark had already begun to move.

Chapter 2.5 Interlude

Before the fracture. Before the spring. Before the first thread trembled in the loom of time, there was a man. And he wore a hat.

Not just any hat, but a round-brimmed, dust-worn thing that cast a crescent of shadow across his face, the kind you see in faded frontier photographs where the men look carved from sun and grit. It was the kind of hat worn by those who lived by their reflexes and died by their choices, the kind that made strangers step aside without knowing why.

His name wasn't Rhet then. Not yet.

Back in those days, he went by Rhettson Hale, though most folks in the mining town of Red Hollow just called him Rhet Hale, the way you'd say a single word you weren't sure you should speak too loudly. He was quick with a smile, quicker with a card trick, and quicker still with the twin revolvers holstered at his hips. Tall, lanky, all long shadows and coiled potential, he moved with a loose, predatory ease. His deep-set eyes missed nothing and forgave even less.

Red Hollow knew him as a man who could read a room before he stepped through the door. A man who sensed trouble the way others sensed weather. A man who walked like he was listening to something no one else could hear, a rhythm under the world, a pulse in the dust, a whisper in the seams of reality.

They didn't know what that meant.

Neither did he.

Not yet.

But the world around him did. The wind held its breath when he passed. The dust curled at his boots as if it recognized him. And the shadows stretched just a little too far, as if making room for a future that hadn't arrived.

Rhettson Hale was still human then, mostly.

But the fracture was coming.

And the man in the round-brimmed hat was already leaning toward it.

He didn't drink much. He didn't talk much. But he watched everything. And the world watched him back.

The night it happened, Red Hollow was quiet. Too quiet.

Rhet stepped out of the saloon, boots whispering across the dust. The moon hung low, swollen and red, casting the town in a strange, rust-colored glow. His fingers tapped absently against his hips—a habit he'd never been able to break.

Tap. Tap. Tap.

Phantom rhythm. Phantom readiness.

He paused at the edge of the street. Something was wrong. The air felt thin, like a breath held too long, as a string pulled too tight.

Rhet lifted his head.

The sky split along a seam that had been waiting for him. Not with lightning. Not with thunder.

With light.

A thin, blinding line tore open above the town, pulsing like a heartbeat out of rhythm. The horses screamed in their stalls. The saloon windows shattered. Dust rose in a swirling column around him, pulled upward as though the sky were inhaling.

Rhet didn't run. He never ran.

He stepped forward, hand hovering near his holster.

"What in God's name…" he whispered.

The seam widened.

And something stepped through.

Not a creature. Not a man. Not anything the world had language for. It was a ripple in reality; a distortion, a shimmer, a fracture wearing the shape of a person. Its edges flickered like torn film, stuttering in and out of existence. Its presence bent the air around it, warping lantern light into trembling shapes.

When it spoke, its voice came in layered echoes, each one slightly out of sync with the last.

Rhettson Hale.

Rhet froze.

No one knew his full name. No one.

The figure tilted its head, movements jerking like a broken puppet trying to mimic life.

"You stand at the hinge. You stand at the break. You stand at the moment that decides the rest.:

Rhet's hand hovered over his revolver, fingers twitching with instinct, but instinct meant nothing here. The dust hung suspended. The wind refused to move. The world waited.

And the man who one day would be called Rhet felt the first thread of his fate pull taut.

Rhet's voice came out low, roughened by dust and disbelief. "What are you?"

The figure flickered, its outline stuttering like a lantern flame in a storm. When it answered, the sound wasn't a voice so much as a resonance, a vibration that seemed to come from the air itself. A messenger. A warning. A mirror.

Rhet's jaw tightened. He didn't like riddles. He didn't like things he couldn't shoot. "Speak plain."

The figure raised a hand.

The world obeyed.

The wind froze mid-gust, dust suspended in the air like grains of amber caught in resin. The saloon doors halted mid-swing, stuck between open and closed. Even the horses stood locked in place, their cries trapped in their throats. Only Rhet could move. Only Rhet could breathe. The sudden stillness pressed against him, thick and unnatural, as if time itself had been folded and pinned.

The figure stepped closer, its form glitching with every shift, each movement breaking and reforming like a reflection in shattered glass. The spring is weakening. The timeline is fraying. And you… You are the one who will break it. Every version of you ends here.

Rhet's breath hitched, a sharp intake he couldn't control. "I don't understand."

You will.

The figure touched his chest.

The world detonated behind his eyes.

His vision burst open into a thousand shards, each one a future, each one a ruin. He saw himself again and again, older, younger, twisted, hollow, monstrous, unrecognizable. He saw a boy with frightened eyes reaching for help. A girl with wings folded beneath her skin. A woman made of mist dissolving into light. A Council standing in a circle of brilliance. A world collapsing inward like a dying star.

And at the center of every vision, every ruin, every ending…

Him.

Rhet screamed, the sound ripped from somewhere deep and terrified, a place he'd never let anyone see. The seam snapped shut with a violent crack, and the world lurched back into motion. Wind slammed into him. Dust fell. The saloon doors banged open. The horses reared.

Rhet collapsed to his knees, gasping, clutching his chest as if trying to hold himself together. His revolvers lay in the dirt beside him. He didn't remember dropping them. He didn't remember standing. He didn't remember anything except the voice echoing through the hollow places inside him.

It always comes back to you.

When he finally rose, the revolvers stayed where they were. He didn't look back at them. He didn't look back at Red Hollow. He simply turned and walked into the desert, into the dark, into the thinning edges of the world where the air shimmered, and the fracture waited for him like an open door.

When he emerged, he was no longer Rhettson Hale.

He was something else. Something the world had made. Something the fracture had claimed. Something the timeline feared.

He was Rhet.

And though his holsters were empty, the phantom weight of the six-shooters he no longer carried still tapped against his hips with every step, a ghost of the man he had been.

Tap. Tap. Tap.

A gunslinger without guns. A ghost without a grave. A fracture wearing a man's name.

And somewhere far beyond the desert, the timeline shuddered, as if it knew its end had just begun to walk.

CHAPTER 3

The afternoon hallway smelled like floor wax and paper, a river of students pushing toward the exits. Nicholas and Anna walked shoulder to shoulder, words tucked beneath the noise. He wanted jokes, anchovies and demons, Queen of Pepperoni decrees, but they thinned on his tongue.

He kept glancing at her, hoping she would look back and make the world feel normal again. She always could. One smile from her and the day usually snapped back into place.

But today, she felt distant. Sharper. As if she was listening to something he could not hear.

"You are different today," he said. "Not bad, different. Just… sharper. Like you swallowed a secret and it grew corners."

Anna's smile was soft and brief. "I wish I could tell you everything. I have told you as much as I can without breaking things."

"Breaking what, time? The club rules?" He tried for lightness and could not hold it. "I keep thinking about the triangle in the basement. Lamp, bird, clock. It felt like it was… holding. Us. Me."

She glanced at him, quick, bright, unguarded. "It was."

The word landed like a promise and a warning.

Nicholas swallowed. "Okay. Then promise me something. When I am 'ready'—and I will be, apparently, I bake fast—do not keep me out. Do not leave me standing on the wrong side of the triangle."

Anna's fingers brushed his, a flash of contact like a small spark. The warmth in his chest steadied instantly, as if her touch flipped a switch he did not know he had.

"I will not leave you," she said. She hesitated, then added, "Even if it looks like I do."

Nicholas opened his mouth to ask what that meant, but something in her posture shifted, subtle and instinctive. Her head tilted slightly, as if she was listening to a sound he could not hear. A faint tension rippled through her shoulders, the kind he had seen in birds right before they took flight.

"Anna," he whispered.

She did not answer. Her eyes flicked toward the far end of the hallway, pupils narrowing as if tracking movement no one else noticed. The fluorescent lights overhead flickered, and for a heartbeat, Nicholas thought he heard a faint flutter, like wings brushing air.

The warmth in his chest pulsed in response, syncing with the rhythm of her steps. It was subtle but unmistakable, like their heartbeats were trying to find the same tempo. The air between them felt charged, stretched thin.

"Anna," he said again, softer. "You are scaring me."

"I am not trying to," she murmured. "I am trying to keep you steady."

"Steady for what?"

Her jaw flexed. She opened her mouth to say something, something important, but the bell rang, slicing the moment in half.

And then the hallway shivered.

A heat ripple rolled through the lockers. The hum of the building stretched into a low, thrumming chord. Gravity slipped its leash. Nicholas felt the pull hook him behind the ribs and yank.

"Not here," he thought, reaching for Anna's hand.

His fingers brushed something warm and electric, but it was not her hand.

The floor folded away like a dropped map.

Color bloomed, violet, rose, gold, threads weaving into a tunnel that smelled faintly of brass and peppermint. Sound rounded off; his own gasp stretched thin, swallowed by the hum. He spun without moving, weightless and pinned. Bells chimed, not the school bell, but older, deeper, cathedral tones beating through water.

Symbols flickered in the walls, triangles, constellations, gears turning in impossible directions. The hum deepened into a chord that vibrated through his ribs, syncing with the warmth in his chest.

For a heartbeat, he felt two pulses beside his own, one sharp, one steady, like three rhythms trying to braid themselves together. A whisper brushed his ear, too soft to understand, too familiar to ignore.

Nicholas…

Then the tunnel snapped.

He landed hard on polished wood, air gone, knees stinging. Clocks crowded the narrow room—grandfather, mantel, carriage—ticking in fractured harmony. Some ran fast, some slow, some backward; others had stopped entirely. Shelves packed with tools and brass pressed in around him, and oil and varnish scented the air. A heavy door stood ajar, a bright wedge of lamplight slicing the floor. Voices murmured beyond.

Nicholas edged forward, heart sprinting.

"…safe house will not hold if Rhet moves tonight," a voice said, sharp, gear teeth on bone.

Another answered, smoother, threaded with steel. "Then we move the artifact now. The boy is awake. That changes everything."

He pushed the door, and light washed over him. Three figures stood around a table strewn with maps and brass instruments. Their coats were long; their faces, half shadow. On the table lay a watch like no watch, case etched with constellations, hands spinning in opposing directions, its seam breathing pink.

The tallest figure turned as if they had felt him arrive. "You should not be here," they said, calm and heavy with meaning. "And yet… here you are."

Nicholas found his voice by accident. "Hello. I… um… got lost in a very shiny hallway."

"No one ever means to," said the second figure, stepping closer. Their eyes caught lamplight like polished brass. "Come in, Nicholas. Questions first. Panic later."

He stepped inside. The door clicked shut behind him with the finality of a vault sealing.

Nicholas's breath fogged faintly though the room was not cold, as if the world were still adjusting to his presence.

He stepped closer to a small brass carriage clock. Its glass face was cracked, but the crack pulsed faintly with pink light, like a heartbeat trapped beneath the surface. When Nicholas leaned in, the warmth in his chest answered, soft, steady, curious.

The tallest figure watched him carefully. "You feel it."

Nicholas swallowed. "I do not know what I feel."

"That is the beginning," the figure said. "Confusion is the doorway. You have stepped through it."

Nicholas tore his gaze from the clock. "Why does everything feel like it is… looking at me?"

"Because it is," the brass-eyed figure said. "Time recognizes its own."

Nicholas's pulse stumbled. "I am not… whatever you think I am."

"Not yet," the third figure murmured.

He hated the way they said that, like he was a recipe still in the oven. Like he was a storm cloud waiting to break.

He backed away from the clocks, suddenly aware of how small the room felt. The air hummed around him, vibrating in his bones. He pressed a hand to his chest, trying to steady the warmth there, but it only pulsed harder, as if it was answering something he could not hear.

"Anna," he whispered without meaning to.

The brass-eyed figure tilted its head. "She steadies you."

Nicholas blinked. "How do you…"

"You said her name," they said simply. "And your pulse changed."

Nicholas felt heat rise in his face. "She is my friend."

"Friends do not anchor each other like that," the tallest figure said. "Not unless something deeper is at work."

Nicholas did not know what that meant. He was not sure he wanted to.

"You felt the pull earlier than expected," the tallest figure continued. "That complicates things."

"Complicates what?" Nicholas asked.

The brass-eyed figure tapped the map with a gloved finger. "Paths. Timelines. Choices. Yours intersected with Rhet's on Friday. That was not supposed to happen."

Nicholas swallowed. "So… what does that mean?"

"It means," the third figure said, voice low and resonant, "that the world noticed you."

The watch on the table pulsed again, brighter this time. Nicholas felt the warmth in his chest flare in response, as if the two were calling to each other.

The brass-eyed figure stepped between him and the watch. "Not yet," they murmured. "You are not ready to touch it."

Nicholas bristled. "Everyone keeps saying that. Ready for what?"

"For who you are," the tallest figure said simply.

Nicholas's breath caught. "And who is that?"

The three figures exchanged a look, silent, weighted, unanimous.

"That," the brass-eyed one said, "is the question the world has been waiting for you to answer."

The figures spoke to Nicholas in calm, measured pieces, as if feeding him time by the spoonful. He learned three things fast: the artifact was moving; Rhet was hunting; and the words "Council" and "safe" did not always belong in the same sentence.

"You are going to hear more than you can hold," said the brass-eyed figure. "You may not believe it. That is fine. Believing is a later skill."

Nicholas nodded because his mouth had not decided what to do. "Is Anna okay?" The question galloped out of him.

"For the moment," the tallest figure said. "She knows how to stand in storms."

Nicholas exhaled. "Good. Because I owe her an apology. And about twelve bad jokes."

The brass-eyed figure's mouth twitched. "She will appreciate the jokes more than the apology."

Nicholas blinked. "Why?"

"Because she has been preparing for this longer than you think."

A chill crawled up his spine. "Preparing for what?"

"For you."

Nicholas's breath hitched. "What does that mean?"

The third figure stepped forward. "It means you are not alone in this. You never were."

Something in Nicholas's chest tightened, not fear, not exactly. More like recognition. A sense of being seen in a way he did not understand.

Somewhere beyond the walls, a chime sounded, a single, deep note, answering itself. The watch on the table breathed a thin halo of pink, then went still.

"Time to move," the steel-throated voice said. "If Rhet shifts tonight, we want to be gone before he knows which hour we used."

They folded maps, capped lamps, and the door to the narrow room swallowed its wedge of light. Nicholas followed because forward was easier than thinking. The safe house smelled like leaving.

As they walked, the brass-eyed figure spoke quietly. "Nicholas… when the pull comes again, do not fight it."

"Why?"

"Because it is not just calling you."

Nicholas frowned. "Then who…"

A sound cut him off. A heartbeat. Not his. Not Anna's.

A third rhythm, faint and distant, threading through the walls like a promise.

The brass-eyed figure smiled, sad and knowing. "You will understand soon. When you leave us, you will be at home, and Anna will be there to help fill in the blanks."

Nicholas swallowed hard.

The picture was not clear yet.

But the pieces were starting to fit.

And somewhere, in the unseen spaces between worlds, someone else was waking.

CHAPTER 4

Nicholas pushed through the back door shoulder first. After detention for drifting off in history class, he was too tired to bother with doorknobs. The house breathed its warm, familiar breath—cinnamon, old wood, a thread of laundry soap—but everything felt a half step distant, as if he were listening through water. His nerves were exhausted from bracing all day for pink light and gears every time he blinked. Even the flicker of fluorescent bulbs made his heart lurch.

The hallway clock ticked a half beat slow.

Tick… pause… tock.

The sound hooked into his breathing, dragging it off rhythm. He pressed a hand to the wall and waited for his chest to remember how to rise and fall.

Down the stairs, the basement waited.

Anna met him halfway, her feet light on the steps, her arms around him before he could speak. "Nicky." His name left her mouth like it had been waiting there all day. Her heartbeat fluttered against his chest, quick and precise, making the half beat slow clock behind them sound even more wrong.

He sagged into the hug. They'd hugged before, but never like this; full body, no space left, as if she were bracing him and anchoring herself at the same time. The warmth in his chest shifted, sliding into place against hers, and for a heartbeat he felt less like one person and more like one third of something remembering its shape.

Tick… pause… tock.

His breathing failed to match the clock, but Anna's rhythm was quick, sure, it gave his lungs something steadier. He synced to her without thinking.

"Please tell me the oven timer says I'm ready," he tried, but the joke scraped out thin.

Anna pulled back just enough to see his face, her hands still on his shoulders. "I owe you the truth," she said. "Some of it."

Her eyes flicked toward the clubhouse, and the warmth in his chest answered with a soft thrum. The air between them shifted, a faint rustle like feathers brushing wood.

Nicholas stepped deeper into the basement. The air felt heavier, like it remembered things. His gaze drifted toward the triangle, drawn by a soft, insistent tug behind his ribs.

The shadows bent toward the triangle, swelling and thinning with each half-beat-slow tick. The warmth in Nicholas's chest tightened in answer.

The lamp's light narrowed onto the crooked-winged bird. Its wings shifted—barely, but undeniably.

He stepped closer. Heat radiated from the triangle, prickling his skin and tightening the pull behind his ribs.

The air hummed. The miniature grandfather clock ticked stubbornly, each slow tock landing like a footstep in his chest.

"Everything is moving," he whispered.

Anna stepped closer, her presence soft but urgent. Her hand hovered near his arm, close enough that the warmth in his chest leaned toward her.

"Nicky…" Her voice cracked. "I should have told you sooner."

Nicholas turned toward her, breath uneven. "Five years," he said. "You've been here five years."

Guilt flickered across her face. "I know. And I'm sorry. I never wanted you to find out like this."

The clock ticked. Pause. Tock.

"Why now?" he asked.

Anna stepped into the triangle with him, closing the space between them. Her hands found his shoulders again, steadier this time. "Because you're waking up. Because Rhet felt you on Friday. And because I can't protect you unless you know who I am."

Nicholas's breath hitched. The triangle hummed beneath them.

"I am your guardian," she said softly. "I have always been your guardian."

The words hit him like a blow. Five years of friendship. Five years of trust. Five years of thinking she had chosen him.

"You should have told me," he said, voice raw.

"I know," she whispered. "But if I had told you too soon, you wouldn't have been ready."

"So what am I?" he asked. "An anchor? A prophecy? A confused kid who screams in class?"

"You are you," she said first. "And you are the Equal. The one who balances what is breaking."

"Balances what?"

"Time," she said. "The real thing. The threads that hold everything together."

"And you knew this."

"Yes."

"And you didn't tell me."

"I couldn't."

"You chose not to."

The triangle pulsed between them.

"Nicky," she said, voice trembling, "our friendship is real. Every moment. Every joke. Every late night. That was me. Not the assignment."

"You were supposed to protect me," he said quietly. "But you were also supposed to tell me the truth."

"I was trying to protect both."

The shadows leaned closer.

"Rhet has been searching for a way to cut the rope that holds time," she said. "All timelines. All versions. Everything."

"That's insane."

"It is. And he's close."

She hesitated. "We think the man you saw in the clock shop was Rhet."

Nicholas's breath caught. "He saw me."

"He shouldn't have. You weren't supposed to jump yet. But the pull is waking up faster than we expected."

"So he knows I exist."

"He suspects. And that's enough."

Nicholas rubbed his face. "So I'm a target."

"You're more than that," Anna said. "You're the one thing he can't predict."

Nicholas laughed weakly. "No pressure."

Anna didn't smile. "Nicky, you're not a prophecy. You're not a weapon. You're a person. A good one. And that's why this matters."

"But I don't know how to do any of this."

"You don't have to. Not yet. You only have to stay alive long enough to learn."

He looked at her, the hurt loosening slightly. She had lied. But she had also stayed.

"And Rhet wants to erase all of time."

"Every version," Anna said. "He wants a clean slate."

"Why?"

"Because he thinks he's the only one who deserves to decide what time should be."

"And I'm supposed to stop him."

"Not alone. Never alone."

Nicholas swallowed. "So what makes me different?"

"You don't break," she said. "Most jumpers fracture. You hold. Even when you shouldn't."

"That doesn't make me special. That makes me stubborn."

"Maybe. But the Council saw something in you long before I did."

Nicholas looked away. "So I'm a theory."

"You're a possibility," Anna said. "A rare one."

"And you stayed with me for five years because of that possibility."

"I stayed because I wanted to," she said, pain flickering across her face. "You mattered to me long before I understood why."

The distrust loosened again.

"You're not alone in this," she said. "And you're not something Rhet gets to define."

Nicholas's hands curled into fists. "I'm not ready."

"No one ever is," Anna said. "But you're not alone."

She reached for his hand, steady and deliberate. The warmth in his chest steadied instantly.

"We leave tonight," she said. "Before the next pull hits."

Nicholas looked around the basement—the triangle, the shadows, the crooked winged bird. Everything felt suspended, waiting.

"Okay," he whispered. "I'll go."

Anna exhaled, relief and sorrow braided together. "Good. Then we need to move."

She grabbed the duffel. "Stay close to me," she said. "No matter what happens."

The triangle hummed one last time as he stepped out of it, the shadows stretching after him like they didn't want to let him go. The basement seemed to fold in on itself, already part of a life he was leaving behind.

And with that, the basement,
their clubhouse,
their childhood,
their before,
fell away behind them.

CHAPTER 5

The den felt smaller than usual, as if the walls had leaned in to listen. Firelight flickered across the mantle, catching the brass trim of the old clock that ticked its stubborn half-beat slow. The sound threaded through the room like a second pulse, steady and insistent, as if it belonged to something older than the house itself.

Chase stood in front of it. He didn't sit. He didn't even glance at the couch Mr. and Mrs. Hunter had motioned toward. His attention was fixed entirely on the clock, the way a man might stare at a ghost he had hoped never to see again.

"May I?" he asked quietly.

Mr. Hunter nodded, though his jaw was tight. "If it helps you explain what's going on with my son, then yes. Please."

Chase lifted the clock with both hands, as gently as if he were lifting a sleeping child. He turned it over, thumb brushing the worn grooves in the wood. The ticking did not falter. It never did. He opened the back panel with a soft click.

Mrs. Hunter leaned forward. "Is something wrong with it?"

Chase didn't answer at first. His breath caught, just slightly, as he traced the inner workings with a fingertip. The gears gleamed faintly in the firelight, each tooth cut with impossible precision. And there, stamped into the largest wheel, was a tiny sigil: a looping, interlocking pattern like a knot that refused to come undone.

Chase exhaled. "I have not seen this mark in decades."

Mr. Hunter frowned. "You recognize it."

Chase nodded slowly. "It is my great-grandfather's signet. He carved it into every piece he made. Every gear, every spring, every casing. He was particular about his craft."

Mrs. Hunter blinked. "Your great-grandfather made this clock."

Chase shook his head. "No. He made the gear inside it." He tapped the sigil gently. "This piece does not belong to the rest of the mechanism. It was added later. Hidden."

A silence settled over the room, heavy and expectant, as if the fire itself were waiting for the next word.

Chase looked up, eyes sharp. "Where did you get this clock?"

Mr. Hunter rubbed the back of his neck. "It has been in my family for generations. Five, at least. My grandmother said her grandmother brought it over from the old country. We have always kept it on the mantle."

Chase's expression tightened, not with fear but with recognition, the kind that comes from seeing a pattern you hoped you were wrong about. "Then it has been with your family longer than I realized."

Mrs. Hunter's voice trembled. "What does that mean?"

Chase closed the back of the clock with a soft click. The half-beat slow ticking resumed, steady and stubborn, as if it had been waiting for the conversation to catch up.

"It means," Chase said carefully, "that your family has been tied to this longer than any of us understood. And that Nicholas's awakening was never random."

He set the clock back on the mantle, but his gaze lingered on it, troubled. "There are jumpers who drift into the pull by accident. There are those who inherit the sensitivity. But this…" He nodded toward the sigil hidden inside the mechanism. "This suggests something older. Something deliberate. Something that chose your family long before Nicholas was born."

The fire popped softly, sending sparks up the chimney.

Mrs. Hunter's hands tightened in her lap. "Are you saying he was meant for this?"

Chase hesitated, weighing the truth. "I am saying he was marked by it. And whatever is waking up in him now, it has been waiting a very long time."

Mr. Hunter stood straighter, as if bracing himself. "Awakening."

Chase met his eyes. "Your son is in danger."

The words dropped into the room with the weight of something irreversible. Mrs. Hunter's hand flew to her mouth, her teacup rattling against its saucer. Mr. Hunter's face went pale, the color draining from him as if the truth had reached straight through his ribs.

Chase continued, his voice low but urgent. "Nicholas jumped on Friday. Too early. Too far. And someone felt it."

Mr. Hunter's voice was barely steady. "Someone."

"Rhet," Chase said. The name seemed to dim the firelight, as if the room itself recoiled. "A man who has spent years trying to tear apart the threads that hold time together. If he sensed Nicholas then, and I believe he did, then he will come looking."

Mrs. Hunter's breath hitched. "But Nicholas is just a boy."

Chase shook his head slowly. "He is more than that. And Rhet knows it."

Mr. Hunter stepped forward, fists clenched, the fear in his eyes sharpening into something protective and fierce. "What do we do?"

Chase hesitated only long enough to choose the gentlest version of the truth. "We move him. Tonight. Anna already packed a bag for him."

Mrs. Hunter's voice cracked. "Tonight."

"It is the only way to keep him safe," Chase said. "If Rhet felt him once, he will feel him again. And the next time, he will not hesitate."

The fire popped sharply, sending sparks up the chimney. The room felt smaller, tighter, as if the walls themselves understood what was at stake. The air thickened with fear and urgency, and the Hunters' quiet den; warm, familiar, safe suddenly felt like the last place Nicholas should be.

Mr. Hunter swallowed hard. "Tell us what we need to do."

Chase nodded; the decision was already made. "We get him out before the next pull hits. Before Rhet shifts again. Before Nicholas becomes a beacon, he cannot control."

Mrs. Hunter reached for her husband's hand, gripping it tightly. The untouched shortbread sat cooling on the table, forgotten.

Their world had just split cleanly into before and after.

Tick… pause… tock.

Chase set the clock back on the mantle with careful hands. "He will be safer than he is here."

The fire popped, sending a brief flare of light across the room. The clock continued its slow, stubborn rhythm, each beat settling deeper into the silence. The world, once steady and familiar, seemed to shift beneath their feet, as if the house itself understood what was coming.

The den felt even smaller when Nicholas and Anna stepped inside, the air thickening around them as if it had been waiting for their return. The old clock waited above the mantle, its brass trim glowing in the firelight.

Tick… pause… tock.

Mr. Hunter stood in front of it, shoulders rigid, eyes fixed on the clock's face like he was trying to decipher a message hidden in its rhythm. Mrs. Hunter sat on the edge of the couch, hands pressed to her mouth, tears slipping silently down her cheeks.

Chase turned as they entered, relief and urgency flickering across his features, two emotions fighting for the same space.

"Nicholas," Mrs. Hunter whispered, her voice breaking. She reached for him, but her hand hovered halfway, suspended between wanting to pull him close and fearing that holding on might make letting go impossible.

Nicholas's chest tightened. He had never seen her cry like this. The warmth in his chest fluttered, then twisted, caught between fear and guilt and something he could not name.

Anna stepped forward, her voice steady in a way that made the room feel even more fragile. "Chase. We need to go."

Tick… pause… tock.

The sound pressed into the moment, marking it, measuring it, as if counting down to something none of them could stop. The firelight dimmed for a heartbeat, shadows stretching along the walls, and the den, once their safe place, felt like the edge of a threshold they had already crossed.

Nicholas swallowed hard. The room seemed to lean toward him, urging him forward, urging him out. He looked at his parents, at the fear in their eyes, at the way his mother's hand trembled in the space between them.

He understood then that staying was no longer an option.

And the clock kept ticking, steady and patient, as if it had known this moment was coming all along.

Tick… pause… tock.

Tick… pause… tock.

Mr. Hunter tore his gaze from the clock and looked at his son, really looked at him, as if seeing him through a lens he had never needed before. Something in his expression shifted. Fear, yes, but also a hardening resolve, the same quiet determination Nicholas had seen only once before, the day his father taught him to ride a bike and refused to let go even when Nicholas begged him to stop.

"You will need a vehicle," Mr. Hunter said quietly. "Something sturdy. Something that will not draw attention." He reached into his pocket and pulled out a set of keys, the metal worn smooth from years of use. "Take my Bronco."

Nicholas blinked, caught between confusion and dread. "Dad…"

"It is old," Mr. Hunter said, forcing a small, tight smile that didn't reach his eyes. "But it will get you where you need to go."

Chase accepted the keys with a nod of gratitude. "Thank you. We will take good care of him."

Mrs. Hunter rose from the couch with a trembling breath, her hands shaking as she crossed the room. The firelight caught the tears on her cheeks, turning them into thin, glistening trails. She reached for Nicholas and pulled him into a hug that was both fierce and fragile, as if she were trying to memorize the shape of him.

"Come back to us," she whispered into his hair. "Please. Just come back."

Nicholas swallowed hard, the warmth in his chest tightening until it almost hurt. "I will."

But even as he said it, he felt the room shifting around them, the air thickening with the weight of everything unspoken. His mother's breath hitched against his shoulder, a quiet, broken sound that made the moment feel unbearably real. She clung to him for a heartbeat longer, then let go with visible reluctance, her fingers trailing down his sleeve as if releasing him cost her something she could never get back.

Anna moved to Nicholas's side and rested a hand on his shoulder. "Come on. Whatever happens next, we face it together."

Tick… pause… tock.

The clock's rhythm pressed into the silence, marking the moment their world shifted, marking the moment childhood ended, marking the moment Nicholas stepped into something far older and far more dangerous than any of them had ever imagined.

Together, they stepped out of the den and into the night, leaving behind the warmth of the fire, the trembling hands of a mother who could not protect her son, and the steady tick of a clock that had measured their lives until now.

Tick… pause… tock.

The night air hit Nicholas like a cold hand to the chest; sharp, bracing, real. The Bronco sat in the driveway like a stubborn old beast, paint dulled by years of sun and winters, chrome bumpers catching the porch light in tired glints. Anna guided him toward it with a hand at his back, gentle but insistent.

Chase unlocked the driver's door, muttering something under his breath about vintage engineering as he climbed in. The Bronco greeted him with a sigh of old hinges and the smell of dust, cracked leather, and the faint ghost of pine air freshener that had long since given up. It felt like stepping into a relic that had been waiting for them, a machine built in a quieter era that somehow still remembered how to move through the world.

Nicholas slid into the back seat, the vinyl creaking beneath him. Anna took the passenger side, dropping the duffel at her feet, her breath still unsteady from the goodbye inside. The air in the Bronco felt different from the house they had just left, less fragile, more expectant, as if the vehicle itself sensed the urgency pressing in on them.

Chase turned the key. The engine coughed awake, rumbling like it was clearing its throat after a long sleep. The dashboard lights flickered in uneven pulses, and the radio crackled with static before settling into a heavy silence. Chase stared at the center console with the expression of a man who had seen too many timelines and not enough working machinery.

"Oh, for the love of…" He jabbed a finger at the slot beneath the radio. "An eight-track player. An actual eight-track player. I swear, if time ever gives me a do-over, I am coming back here and deleting eight-tracks from existence."

Anna snorted, the sound small but real. "You are not allowed to delete entire formats. That is how you get paradoxes. And angry music historians."

Chase groaned, but there was a smile tugging at the corner of his mouth. "Fine. But I reserve the right to judge this vehicle's life choices."

He ran a hand over the cracked dashboard, almost fondly, as if greeting an old soul. There was something reverent in the gesture, something that made Nicholas realize Chase wasn't just mocking the Bronco. He was listening to it, the way he listened to clocks and threads and the quiet hum of things that mattered.

Chase shifted into gear, the engine grumbling its protest, and the Bronco rolled forward into the dark.

Anna reached into her bag with a magician's flourish, the movement quick and practiced, as if she had been waiting for the right moment to pull the world back into something familiar. "Lucky for you, this century has better tools."

She pulled out her iPhone and a compact Bluetooth speaker. The speaker blinked awake with a soft chime, its tiny light pulsing like a heartbeat as it paired. The Bronco's interior glowed faintly with the reflection, the old leather catching the modern blue tint in a way that made the moment feel strangely symbolic, like two eras brushing shoulders.

"No complaining about the playlist," she warned, pointing at Chase with a look that dared him to try.

Chase held up both hands, palms open in a gesture that was half surrender, half monk-like serenity. "I would not dream of it." His tone carried that easy, wandering-sage warmth he always seemed to slip into when the world grew too sharp.

Anna tapped her screen.

A soft, dreamy synth chord drifted through the Bronco, curling into the corners of the cabin like a slow exhale. The sound felt out of place and perfectly right at the same time, a surreal lullaby threading through the tension.

Nicholas groaned. "Oh no. Not this again."

Anna grinned, smug and unrepentant. "Dream Weaver is a classic."

"It is ancient," Nicholas muttered, sinking into his seat. "You love your oldies way too much."

"It is called taste," Anna said, flipping her hair with exaggerated elegance. "You should try it sometime."

Chase chuckled as he turned the street corner, the Bronco rumbling beneath them like an old beast waking up. "If we survive the night, I am buying you both a crash course in modern music."

Anna gasped, hand to her chest. "Blasphemy."

Nicholas rolled his eyes, but the corner of his mouth tugged upward despite everything. The warmth in his chest pulsed, still anxious, still unsettled, but steadier with Anna beside him, with Chase's dry humor filling the space, with Dream Weaver floating through the Bronco like a soft, surreal promise.

Outside, the night pressed close around them. Inside, the Bronco felt like a fragile sanctuary stitched together by old leather, warm voices, and a song that somehow made the world feel just a little less terrifying.

The house shrank in the rearview mirror, its windows glowing faintly against the dark. Inside, the mantle clock kept its stubborn rhythm, measuring the moment their lives split apart.

Tick… pause… tock.

And the Bronco carried them into the night.

The engine rumbled down the quiet street, headlights carving soft tunnels through the dark. Dream Weaver drifted through the cabin like a strange lullaby, the synth chords shimmering against the windows. Nicholas leaned his forehead to the cool glass, watching the houses slide past, each one ordinary and peaceful and completely unaware of the world he had just stepped out of.

His chest still felt too warm. Too full. Like the triangle had left a handprint inside him.

The grocery store's neon sign flickered as they pulled into the nearly empty lot. Chase parked crookedly across two spaces, muttering something about temporal emergencies trumping parking etiquette. The Bronco shuddered to a stop, headlights washing over the blank storefront.

Anna looked at Chase "Great idea. Ice Cream is what we need."

Nicholas frowned. "Why are we getting ice cream? Shouldn't we be… I don't know… running for our lives."

Neither of them answered.

Anna hopped out first, tugging her hoodie tight around her. "Come on," she said, nodding toward the sliding doors. "Sugar therapy awaits."

Chase was already halfway across the lot, moving with the brisk determination of a man who had decided the universe could wait five minutes while he found frozen desserts.

Nicholas followed, legs still shaky. The automatic doors whooshed open, releasing a wave of cold, over-conditioned air that smelled like citrus cleaner and freezer frost. The fluorescent lights buzzed overhead, too bright and too sharp, and for a moment his vision wavered. The aisles bent at the edges, the same way the basement had bent around the triangle.

Anna noticed immediately. She stepped closer, brushing his shoulder. "Hey. Stay with me."

The warmth in his chest steadied, the world snapping back into place.

Chase grabbed a basket and headed straight for the frozen aisle, his stride purposeful. "Didn't know your favorite," he called over his shoulder, "so I'm buying everything."

Nicholas blinked. "Seriously. Why ice cream? What does this have to do with anything?"

Anna and Chase ignored him completely.

Anna snorted as she followed Chase. "You say that like it's a threat."

Nicholas trailed behind them, watching Chase load pints into the basket with reckless abandon. Cherry Garcia. Mint Chip. Double Chocolate. Something with a name that sounded like a dare. The basket sagged under the weight, and Chase didn't slow down.

Nicholas rubbed his forehead. "Guys. I'm being serious."

Anna plucked a pint from Chase's growing collection and held it up to the light. "This one has caramel swirls shaped like galaxies. That feels appropriate."

Chase nodded solemnly. "Cosmic nourishment."

Nicholas stared at them, bewildered. "Are you two okay?"

Anna finally looked back at him, her expression softening. "Nicky, we're doing this because you need something normal. Something grounding. Something that reminds you you're still you."

Chase added another pint to the basket. "And because ice cream is the closest thing this timeline has to a stabilizer."

Nicholas blinked. "A what?"

But they were already moving again, the basket clinking with pints, the fluorescent lights humming overhead, the night pressing close outside.

And for the first time since the basement, Nicholas felt the faintest thread of normalcy tug at him, thin and fragile, but real.

Anna dove into the freezer like a pirate claiming treasure. "Cherry Garcia." She held the pint aloft, triumphant. "Mine. Forever."

Nicholas groaned. "You and your oldies."

Anna's eyes widened in theatrical betrayal. "Excuse me. Cherry Garcia is a cultural landmark."

"It is ice cream," Nicholas said. "Not a museum exhibit."

"It is both," Anna insisted, clutching the pint to her chest. "It is history and dessert."

Nicholas shook his head. "You love your oldies way too much."

Anna's grin sharpened. "You say that like it is a flaw."

"It is," Nicholas said. "You made me listen to that seventies playlist for an entire road trip."

"That playlist was a gift," Anna said, offended. "A curated experience."

"It was torture."

"You survived."

"Barely."

She gasped, delighted. "You are dramatic."

Nicholas grabbed a Double Chocolate with Heath Bar and held it up. "This one. This is the only correct choice."

Anna rolled her eyes. "You say that like you have tried anything else."

"I have," Nicholas said. "Once. You made me try that weird lavender thing."

"It was artisanal," Anna said, genuinely wounded.

"It tasted like soap."

Chase cleared his throat, the sound carrying the weary authority of a man who had shepherded too many teenagers through too many crises. "Children. Focus. We are on a schedule."

They made their way to the self-checkout, the basket clinking with pints like a collection of tiny frozen planets. Nicholas scanned items while Anna bagged them with the efficiency of someone who had definitely done this during emergencies before. Chase paid in cash, crisp bills that looked too new, too untouched, as if they had slipped through time rather than a wallet.

Outside, the cold air hit Nicholas again, sharper this time. The warmth in his chest pulsed in response, trying to balance the temperature difference, trying to anchor him in a world that kept shifting at the edges.

Anna nudged him with her elbow. "Eat. It helps."

Nicholas peeled open his pint and took a spoonful. The sweetness hit his tongue, grounding him. The edges of the world softened, not much, but enough to breathe again.

"Better," Anna asked.

He nodded. "Yeah. A little."

Chase unlocked the Bronco. "Good. Because the next part gets weird."

Nicholas froze halfway into the back seat. "Weirder than the basement."

Chase gave him a look that was equal parts sage wisdom and exhausted hippie patience. "Nicholas, the basement was the warm-up."

Anna climbed into the back seat beside Nicholas instead of taking the front, settling close enough that their shoulders brushed. She tucked her legs up, opened her own pint, and nudged him again.

"Keep eating," she said softly. "It keeps you here."

Nicholas took another spoonful. The warmth in his chest steadied, pulsing in time with her presence.

Outside, the parking lot lights flickered. Nicholas took another spoonful of ice cream and let the familiar sounds of the Bronco settle around him. For a few minutes, with Anna beside him and Chase behind the wheel, the impossible parts of the night seemed farther away.

Pink Floyd's "Time" started playing the moment the doors shut, the opening chimes drifting through the Bronco like distant bells echoing across a long hallway.

The Bronco rumbled out of the grocery store lot, the bags of ice cream clinking softly in the back. The music settled into the cabin, low and atmospheric, the kind of sound that made the night feel deeper than it was. Nicholas leaned back, spoon still in hand, the cold sweetness grounding him. But the warmth in his chest pulsed beneath it, steady and insistent, like a second heartbeat trying to sync with something he could not see.

Anna slid around the back seat beside him, close enough that their knees brushed. She angled herself toward him, watching him more than the road. "Keep eating," she said gently. "It helps."

Nicholas took another spoonful. "You keep saying that."

"Because it keeps working," Anna said. "You're less floaty when you're chewing."

Chase snorted from the driver's seat. "Helps is a generous interpretation. More like delays the inevitable."

Anna shot him a look that could have melted the windshield. "Optimism, Chase. Try it sometime."

Chase grinned, but the expression didn't reach his eyes. "Optimism is for people who don't know what's coming."

Nicholas shifted, uneasy. "You two are not helping."

Anna nudged his shoulder with hers, grounding him again. "Ignore him. He gets dramatic when he's stressed."

"I am not dramatic," Chase said, guiding the Bronco onto the main road with the solemnity of a monk steering a sacred relic. "I am realistic."

"You're a realist with a flair for doom," Anna said.

Chase lifted a hand in a vague gesture. "Doom is a spectrum."

Nicholas let out a shaky laugh despite himself. The warmth in his chest steadied again, pulsing in time with the music, in time with Anna's presence beside him. The night outside the windows felt vast and strange, but inside the Bronco, the world narrowed to the soft hum of the engine, the low thrum of Pink Floyd, and the quiet certainty that he wasn't facing any of this alone.

Anna tapped his pint with her spoon. "Another bite."

Nicholas obeyed, the sweetness grounding him again.

Outside, the road stretched ahead, dark and waiting.

Inside, the Bronco carried them forward, the music threading through the moment like a warning and a promise.

The Bronco turned off the main road and onto a narrow gravel path that cut into the woods. The trees rose around them like tall, silent witnesses, their branches arching overhead until the sky disappeared entirely. The headlights carved thin tunnels of light through the darkness, illuminating drifting leaves and the occasional startled rabbit. Nicholas shivered and asked why it felt colder here, but Anna only stared ahead, her jaw tight, before answering that they were getting close. Chase added that they were approaching the seam, the place where the worlds thinned, and Nirvana could reach them. Nicholas tried to joke about how safe that sounded, but Anna's quiet reply made it clear that this was safer than the alternative.

The Bronco bumped over a root, the suspension groaning in protest. The deeper they drove, the stranger the woods felt. The air thickened with a faint hum, the same vibration that had filled the basement, and the shadows between the trees seemed to stretch and contract with a rhythm Nicholas recognized. The branches leaned inward as if listening, the warmth in his chest tightened in response, and the shadows thinned again as though exhaling. He gripped the seat and asked if it was supposed to feel like this. Anna told him yes and no, that the woods were reacting to his resonance, and that he was becoming sensitive enough to feel the reaction.

Chase slowed the Bronco as the trees thickened into a wall of dark trunks and tangled roots. He told them to hang on and reached into his coat, pulling out a pocket watch eerily similar to the one Nicholas had seen in the clock shop, its face catching the same strange pink light. When Chase snapped it open, color spilled out in soft waves of violet, blue, and rose, unfurling into the cabin like warm smoke. The Bronco's headlights flickered, the engine rumbled unevenly, then steadied, then rumbled again. Anna tightened her grip on Nicholas's hand, grounding him as Chase muttered that he knew and told them to hold on.

The colors thickened, swirling around them like a living fog. The Bronco lifted just enough for Nicholas's stomach to drop, and the gravel road beneath them blurred, melted, and vanished entirely. Nicholas gasped that they were floating, and Chase admitted it was temporary, hopefully. Nicholas's voice cracked at the word, but Anna squeezed his hand and told him to breathe, her presence anchoring him as the warmth in his chest surged in time with the swirling colors and the faint, impossible chime that echoed through the Bronco like a bell underwater.

Outside the windows, the world dissolved into shimmering mist that wrapped around the Bronco in slow spirals. It brushed the glass, curled around the tires, and lifted them higher. The Bronco settled onto something that was not quite ground, a surface soft beneath the tires but firm enough to hold them.

Nicholas stared out the window, breath caught in his throat, watching the mist pulse in gentle waves of white, blue, and pink. It responded to the warmth in his chest, brightening when his heartbeat quickened, dimming when he steadied. Chase exhaled, tension leaving his shoulders as he looked out at the shifting landscape.

"Welcome to Nirvana," he said, and the mist curled closer, as if greeting them.

And that was the moment Nicholas understood that the world he knew had already let go of him.

Chapter 5.5 Interlude

The grocery store parking lot sat empty now, the neon sign buzzing faintly in the frosty night air. A stray receipt skittered across the asphalt, catching on a shopping cart wheel before settling in a limp curl. The quiet felt ordinary at first, the kind of stillness that belonged to small towns after midnight. Then the air shifted. It didn't crack or flash or announce itself with spectacle. It folded inward, the way fabric does when pinched by invisible fingers, quiet and deliberate, as if the night itself were being turned inside out.

A seam opened, thin as a paper cut.

Rhet stepped through.

The world reacted before he did. Shadows bent toward him, stretching across the pavement like thirsty roots seeking water. The neon sign flickered twice, then fell into a slow, stubborn rhythm, its pulse slipping into the same half-beat cadence that had haunted the Hunter den. The entire parking lot seemed to breathe in time with it, as though the night recognized him and adjusted itself accordingly.

Rhet inhaled.

The air resisted him for a moment, trembling at the edges, then surrendered as he drew it in. He tasted it the way a musician tastes a note, letting it vibrate across the back of his tongue, letting it settle into the hollow places inside him. Warmth. Sugar. A faint echo of chocolate-chip cookies. Nicholas's signature clung to the molecules like a fingerprint, bright and young and painfully alive.

Rhet closed his eyes, savoring it.

He had always been a man who appreciated the small details of a world he intended to break. There was something almost tender in the way he stood there, boots planted on cracked asphalt, head tilted as if listening to a song only he could hear. The mist that clung to him—thin, pale, and restless—shifted with his breath, curling around his shoulders like a living scarf. It made him look almost human. Almost.

He opened his eyes again, and the illusion slipped.

There was hunger in him, but not the kind that could be fed. It was older, deeper, threaded through with a strange, fractured longing. He carried himself with the easy confidence of someone who had once been charming, once admired, once been loved. The echo of that man still lived in his posture, in the faint smile tugging at the corner of his mouth. But the rest of him, the part shaped by the seam, by the tearing, by the endless pursuit of what he had lost—was something else entirely.

He took a step forward. The shadows followed.

Nicholas had been here minutes ago. The air still hummed with him, warm and bright, a resonance that made Rhet's pulse stutter in recognition. It was the same spark he had felt across the seam, the same flare that had pulled him from whatever fractured place he had been drifting through. The boy didn't know what he carried. He didn't know what he was waking up. But Rhet did. Nicholas's signature trailed away from the parking lot, faint but unmistakable, leaving an invisible path through the night.

And he wanted it.

He brushed his fingers along the side of a shopping cart, the metal warping slightly beneath his touch, bending toward him like it wanted to be remade. The mist around him thickened, swirling in slow, deliberate patterns that mirrored the rhythm of the neon sign. Tick, pause, tock. The world was aligning itself, preparing for him, recognizing him the way prey recognizes a predator.

Rhet smiled, soft and almost fond.

Nicholas was close.

And the night, loyal as ever, was already guiding him toward the boy.

Rhet rose slowly, his coat whispering against the night as he straightened. There was a strange elegance to the way he moved, too smooth and too precise, like a puppet guided by something that understood anatomy but had long forgotten humanity. The parking lot seemed to hold its breath as he turned toward the direction the Bronco had gone, his gaze sharpening with a predator's focus. Nicholas's resonance lingered in the air as a fading afterimage, a soft pink trace stretching away from the lot and into the darkness.

Rhet reached into the fading trace with his senses. The resonance distorted around him, thinning wherever his own signature touched it. He chuckled under his breath. "Still shy," he murmured, his voice warm enough to sound almost kind. The pink shimmer caught in his living eye and flashed across the jagged glass of the other. Through the fading signature, he could follow the path Nicholas had taken. The boy's pull was loud and untrained, spilling into the world like a cracked bell that rang whether it meant to or not.

Rhet breathed in again, letting the taste of Nicholas settle deeper. There was something almost affectionate in the way he savored it, as if he were appreciating a rare wine rather than tracking a frightened teenager. "Run, little man," he said softly. "Run while you still can." The words carried no malice, only a quiet certainty, the tone of someone who had chased many things and caught most of them.

He stepped forward, and the air folded around him with the smooth inevitability of a closing wound. The seam sealed behind him with a soft, reluctant sigh, as though the world itself disliked letting him pass through it. The parking lot fell silent again, the shadows returning to their natural shapes, the mist settling back into the corners where it belonged. Only the neon sign continued to buzz, unaware that time had just flinched, unaware that something old and hungry had slipped through its quiet domain.

Rhet was gone, but the night remembered him.

And somewhere ahead, Nicholas's resonance called to him like a distant, trembling star.

CHAPTER 6

The air in Nirvana felt different the moment Nicholas stepped out of the Bronco. It was cooler than the night they'd left behind, but threaded with a strange warmth that curled around his skin like a welcome. The ground beneath his shoes gave slightly, springy and soft, like stepping onto a cloud that had decided to pretend it was solid. It firmed a little under his weight than it did for the others, as if Nirvana was adjusting itself to him.

Colors drifted through the air in slow, lazy currents, pale pinks and soft blues and milky whites that shimmered as stone and sky woven together. The mist curled and uncurled in slow patterns that felt almost like breath. Nicholas stepped out of the Bronco and felt the ground give slightly beneath his shoes. It wasn't soil or rock or anything he recognized. It felt like standing on a mattress made of cloud, firm enough to hold him but soft enough to shift under his weight, as if the world were adjusting itself to him.

He turned in a slow circle, breath caught somewhere between awe and disbelief. The air tasted faintly sweet, like the moment before snowfall, and the drifting colors brushed against his arms with the lightness of silk. "Is this real?" he asked, his voice barely above a whisper.

Anna stepped beside him, her shoulder brushing his as she took in the landscape with familiarity that made the moment feel even stranger. "Very real," she said, her tone soft but steady, as if she were welcoming him into a place she had always known.

Chase shut the Bronco door with a quiet thud that seemed to echo longer than it should have. The sound rippled through the mist, sending a faint shimmer across the ground. "And very safe," he said, watching the colors shift around them. "For now."

A warm chime drifted through the air, resonant and deep, like a bell ringing underwater. The drifting colors paused for a heartbeat, then parted in a slow spiral, opening a path that hadn't existed a moment before. The mist pulled back with a kind of reverence, revealing a figure walking toward them.

She wore robes with the color of sunrise, gold and rose and pale blue woven together in a way that made the fabric seem alive. Her hair fell in dark waves down her back, and her eyes glowed with a warmth that made Nicholas's chest loosen. Even the mist seemed to still be around her, settling into soft folds at her feet as if acknowledging her presence.

"Nicholas Hunter," she said, her voice carrying the calm comfort of warm tea on a cold morning. "Welcome to Nirvana."

Nicholas blinked, his mind scrambling to place her face. "Miss Carter," he said, the name slipping out before he could stop it.

She smiled. "Call me Bharati," she said. "Miss Carter was my cover." The name settled over Nicholas with a strange weight. Pale pink mist curled around his ankles, warm and curious, and for one impossible moment he had the feeling Nirvana itself had leaned closer. As he looked at Bharati, really looked at her, the memory of Friday afternoon surfaced with sudden clarity: the school office, the hum of the old fluorescent lights, Miss Carter at her desk pretending to sort attendance slips while Chase stood across from her, speaking in a low, urgent voice. Nicholas had been in detention then, sitting just outside the doorway, close enough to hear the tension in their words but not close enough to understand them. He remembered the way Miss Carter's eyes had flicked toward him when she thought he wasn't looking, the way Chase's voice had tightened when he said someone was "shifting too early," the way both had fallen silent the moment he stepped into view. He had assumed they were talking about another student; some unseen kid caught in trouble he didn't understand. But standing here now, with the mist responding to his heartbeat and Bharati watching him with familiarity that went far deeper than a school receptionist should ever have had, he understood the truth. They hadn't been talking about someone else. They had been talking about him. The realization settled into his chest with a weight that felt both terrifying and inevitable, and the mist pulsed in quiet agreement, as if acknowledging the truth he had finally caught up to. Nirvana wasn't just alive. It had been waiting for him, and everyone in that school office knew it long before he did.

Nicholas stared. "So, you… you were at my school? So, you are…"

"One of them," Bharati said. "Though I suspect you learned more from Anna than from me."

Anna flushed. "He learned plenty from you."

A soft rustle sounded behind Bharati, like leaves brushing silk. Two more figures emerged, one tall and slender, the other compact and sharp-eyed.

The shorter one bowed slightly, movements stiff and deliberate, as if his body were following choreography learned long before he ever wore the shape of a teenager. His scruffy face, the too-short frame, the messy hair that refused to lie flat. All of it made him look like a kid who had sprinted out of a school hallway rather than stepped out of a world made of mist. But his eyes told a different story. They held depth, age, and a kind of weathered patience that didn't belong to someone who looked barely sixteen.

"Chanotedah," he said, his voice deep and resonant, carrying the low rumble of distant thunder. "It is an honor to meet you at last."

Nicholas swallowed, unsure whether to step forward or hide behind Anna. "At last," he echoed, trying to understand the weight behind the words.

Chanotedah's smile was small but undeniably kind, the sort of expression that softened the sharpness of his features without ever quite erasing the exhaustion behind his eyes. "You have been expected," he said, and the mist around his ankles stirred as if agreeing with him. The pale pink tendrils curled toward Nicholas again, brushing lightly against his shoes before retreating, curious but cautious.

Nicholas glanced at Anna, then at Chase, searching for some explanation, but both of them watched Chanotedah with the familiarity of people who had known him far longer than his youthful appearance suggested. Chase gave a slight nod, a quiet acknowledgment that this meeting mattered. Anna's hand brushed Nicholas's arm, steadying him, but her gaze stayed fixed on Chanotedah, as if waiting for him to reveal something only he could say.

Chanotedah stepped closer, the mist parting around him with a subtle deference. Up close, Nicholas could see the faint shadows under his eyes, the kind that came from too many sleepless nights or too many lifetimes lived in a body that didn't quite fit. His voice softened, losing some of its thunder but none of its gravity. "You have crossed a threshold most never reach," he said. "And Nirvana has felt you for a long time."

Nicholas's chest tightened, the warmth inside him pulsing in a slow, steady rhythm that matched the shifting colors in the air. Chanotedah watched that pulse with quiet understanding, as if he could see the resonance beneath Nicholas's skin.

"You are not what you think you are," Chanotedah said gently. "And you are not alone."

The mist brightened around them, responding to the truth in his

Before Nicholas could ask what Chanotedah meant, a cluster of tiny lights zipped past his ear with a sound like tinkling laughter. He flinched, instinctively ducking, and Anna's grin widened with unmistakable delight. "Fairies," she said, as if that were the most normal thing in the world.

The lights circled him in a widening spiral, three at first, then five, then a dozen, each no bigger than a firefly but glowing with soft, shifting colors that rippled across their tiny forms. They darted around him in curious loops, leaving faint trails of light that lingered in the air like brushstrokes on an invisible canvas. Three of them hovered near his shoulder, pulsing in a slow, synchronized rhythm that felt almost like breathing. Their glow warmed the air around him, brushing against his skin with a feather-light touch that made the hairs on his arms rise.

One fairy drifted directly in front of his face, its wings a blur of shimmering pink and blue. It hovered there, studying him with a focus that felt far too intelligent for something so small. Nicholas blinked, unsure whether to speak or swat it away. "Uh… hi," he managed, his voice cracking slightly.

The sprite chimed in response, a delighted, crystalline sound, and zipped away to rejoin the others. They swirled around him again, weaving patterns he couldn't decipher, their movements too coordinated to be random. It was like watching a school of fish made of light, each one responding to something he couldn't see.

"They like you," Bharati said, her voice warm with approval. "That is a good sign."

Nicholas stared at her, then at the fairies, then at the mist curling around his ankles. His mind scrambled to make sense of any of it. "This can't be real," he said, the words slipping out before he could stop them. "I have to be dreaming. Or hallucinating. Or… something."

The fairies pulsed brighter at his confusion, as if reacting to the spike in his heartbeat. One brushed against his cheek, leaving a faint warmth behind, and another settled briefly on his shoulder before darting away again. They didn't feel imaginary. They didn't feel like anything his brain could have invented.

Anna stepped closer, her presence steady beside him. "You are not dreaming," she said gently. "They are real. All of this is real."

Nicholas shook his head, trying to reconcile the impossible softness of the ground beneath him, the living mist curling around his legs, the fairies humming in the air, and the fact that Miss Carter from the school office was now wearing sunrise-colored robes and greeting him like she had been waiting for this moment for years. "This is insane," he whispered. "I was in detention this afternoon. I was doing algebra. Now I'm… here."

Chanotedah watched him with quiet understanding, his scruffy teenage face softened by the ancient patience in his eyes. "Nirvana reveals itself only to those it chooses," he said. "And it has chosen you."

Nicholas swallowed hard, the fairies circling him in gentle, glowing arcs. The mist pulsed at his feet. The world leaned in again, listening.

And he had no idea why.

Bharati stepped closer, the sunrise colors of her robes shifting gently with the mist. "Most worlds tell stories about creatures that do not belong to them," she said. "Fairies, wood sprites, giants, river spirits, guardians of forests and storms. They appear in legends, in bedtime tales, in warnings whispered to children. But they were never born in those worlds. They came from here."

Nicholas stared at the drifting lights still circling him, trying to reconcile the idea that the things he had grown up hearing about, things he had assumed were metaphors or exaggerations or outright inventions, were standing inches from his face. "You're saying they're real," he said, his voice thin. "All of them."

"Real," Bharati said, "and purposeful." She lifted her hand, and the mist curled around her fingers like a living ribbon. "When a timeline fractures, when a moment goes wrong, when a thread begins to unravel, Nirvana sends its inhabitants to mend it. Some worlds call them myths. Others call them miracles. But they are simply our people doing their work."

Nicholas felt the ground shift beneath him again, soft and responsive, like the world was adjusting to his weight. The fairies pulsed brighter, drifting closer as if drawn to the confusion rolling off him. He shook his head, overwhelmed. "This is too much. I don't even know what I'm supposed to be doing here."

"You are not supposed to know yet," Bharati said gently. "Understanding comes later. For now, you only need to walk."

Chase stepped to her side, his expression more serious than Nicholas had ever seen it. "The Council will want to see him before the next pull," he said. "We don't have long."

The warmth in Nicholas's chest pulsed again, stronger this time, as if the word itself tugged at something deep inside him. He pressed a hand to his sternum, startled by the sensation. Anna moved closer, her touch steady on his arm. "You're safe here," she said. "I promise."

Nicholas nodded, though his legs felt unsteady, as if the soft ground might swallow him or lift him at any moment. "Okay," he said quietly. "Lead the way."

Bharati smiled, turning toward the shimmering horizon where the mist parted in a slow, graceful arc. "Welcome home, Nicholas."

The mist brightened at the words, curling around his ankles like a greeting.

And for the first time, he felt the faint, impossible truth of it.

And with that, they walked deeper into Nirvana, the fairies trailing behind them like a constellation learning how to follow. They walked.

At first, there was no path: just the endless cotton-candy atmosphere stretching in every direction, swirling in soft currents of pink, blue, and white. The ground beneath Nicholas's feet felt springy and warm, like memory foam made of light. The air hummed faintly, vibrating against his skin.

But the longer they walked, the more Nicholas's stomach tightened.

"Is it supposed to look like this?" he asked, voice small in the vastness. "Like… nothing?"

Bharati smiled gently. "It looks like everything."

Nicholas frowned. "That's not comforting."

"It isn't meant to be," Chanotedah said, his short stride broken. "Not yet."

The mist curled around Nicholas's ankles, brushing against him like curious fingers. He shivered. "It feels like it's watching me."

"It is," Bharati said simply.

Nicholas stumbled. "What?"

Anna stepped closer, her shoulder brushing his. "It's okay. The mist is alive. Sort of."

"Alive?" Nicholas echoed.

"Alive enough," Chase muttered.

Bharati slowed her pace, turning so she could walk backward and face Nicholas. The mist parted around her like it respected her space. "The mist is the foundation of Nirvana. It is the raw material of every world, every possibility, every timeline. It is everything and nothing. Formless and infinite."

Nicholas swallowed. "That's… a lot."

"It is," Bharati agreed. "But you won't always see it like this."

"What do you mean?"

Chanotedah's voice rumbled like distant thunder. "When you learn control, the mist will respond to you. It will take the shape you need. The shape you ask for. The shape you feel."

Nicholas blinked. "It can do that?"

"It already is," Bharati said softly.

Nicholas opened his mouth to ask what she meant and the world shifted. Not violently. Not with a jolt. Just a soft, rippling exhale.

The cotton-candy pink folded inward, swirling around them like a curtain being drawn. The ground firmed beneath Nicholas's feet. The air cooled. The hum faded.

And suddenly, he was standing in the town square of his hometown.

The brick paths. The fountain with the chipped lion statue. The benches where he and Anna used to eat ice cream on summer nights.

The lampposts with their warm, amber glow.

Nicholas's breath caught. "This is… home."

Anna smiled softly. "The mist is trying to comfort you."

Nicholas turned in a slow circle, heart pounding. "It looks exactly right."

"Not exactly," Bharati said. "Look closer."

Nicholas did.

The edges were too soft. The shadows are too gentle. The colors, too warm, like a memory instead of a place.

"It's how you remember it," Bharati said. "Not how it is."

Nicholas swallowed hard. "Why would it do this?"

"Because you're overwhelmed," Anna said, stepping closer. "And the mist responds to emotion. Especially yours."

Nicholas stared at the fountain, the water shimmering like liquid light. "So… I made this happen?"

"Not consciously," Bharati said. "But yes. One day, you will shape the mist with intention. With clarity. With purpose."

Chanotedah nodded. "And when that day comes, the worlds will bend for you."

Nicholas felt the warmth in his chest pulse not once, but twice, like it recognized the truth in their words.

He looked around the soft, shimmering version of his hometown square.

"It's beautiful," he whispered.

Anna slipped her hand into his. "It's yours."

The mist-formed town square shimmered gently, its edges soft like a memory still deciding how real it wanted to be. The fountain burbled with light instead of water, and the lampposts glowed with a warm amber that felt more like comfort than electricity.

The sprites reacted instantly.

They zipped around the new scene in delighted spirals, chiming like tiny bells. A few darted through the fountain's glowing spray, scattering droplets of light that evaporated before they hit the ground. Others perched on the lampposts, their wings flickering in colors that matched the mist—rose, blue, soft white.

Three sprites hovered near Nicholas's shoulder again, pulsing in that same slow, synchronized rhythm.

"They like the change," Bharati said with a smile. "They enjoy new shapes."

Nicholas swallowed. "I didn't mean to make it."

"You didn't have to," Anna said. "The mist listens to what you feel."

Before Nicholas could respond, a burst of laughter echoed across the square.

A group of young students, ten or eleven years old, came sprinting around the corner of a mist-formed bookstore, their sneakers skidding across the soft, cloud-like ground. They wore jeans, shorts, bright T-shirts, and the occasional baseball cap turned backward or sideways. The normalcy of their clothes clashed beautifully with the shimmering world around them, as if someone had dropped a group of Earth kids into a dream.

They chased a glowing orb the size of a soccer ball, shouting over one another as it bobbed and weaved through the air like it had a mischievous mind of its own. Gold dust trailed behind it in lazy spirals, drifting through the mist like sparks from a fire.

"Get it!" one of the kids yelled, nearly tripping over his own feet.

"I almost had it!" another insisted.

"You almost fell on your face," someone countered, laughing.

They skidded to a stop when they saw Nicholas and the others. The orb hovered obediently above them, dimming slightly as if sensing the shift in mood. The kids stared openly, their expressions a mix of awe and curiosity.

A girl with bright eyes and a messy bun jabbed her friend in the ribs and pointed straight at Nicholas. "Is that him?"

Her friend elbowed her back. "Don't stare."

"You're staring too."

"I'm staring respectfully."

Nicholas felt heat rise in his cheeks. He had been stared at before—at school, in hallways, in the cafeteria—but never like this. These kids weren't mocking him or whispering behind their hands. They were looking at him the way people looked at comets or rare animals or stories they had grown up hearing but never expected to see. "Uh… hi," he said, lifting a hand awkwardly.

The kids didn't move. They just kept staring, wide-eyed, like he might start glowing or levitating at any moment.

Bharati stepped forward, her voice warm but firm. "Back to training, little ones. We will introduce you properly soon."

The students nodded, though several kept sneaking glances at Nicholas as they jogged off. The glowing orb zipped after them like an excited puppy, swirling around their heads before darting ahead to lead the way.

Nicholas watched them go, his chest tightening with a strange mix of relief and dread. "They're just… normal kids," he said quietly, trying to make sense of the contrast between their T-shirts and the mist-formed buildings, between their laughter and the impossible world around them.

Anna stepped closer, her voice soft. "Normal for here."

Nicholas swallowed hard. The ground shifted gently beneath him again, the mist curling around his ankles like it was listening.

Nothing about this place felt normal to him.

And yet everyone here seemed to think he belonged.

Nicholas's breath hitched. The mist-town square suddenly felt too bright, too warm, too much like a memory he couldn't go back to. The fountain's glow blurred. The lampposts wavered. His vision tightened at the edges.

"I can't..." He pressed a hand to his chest. "I can't breathe."

Anna was at his side instantly. "Nicky. Hey. Look at me."

But the warmth in his chest surged, too strong, too fast like the triangle's pull had followed him here. His heartbeat stuttered, and the mist around him trembled in the same rhythm, trying to keep pace and failing. His knees buckled. The town square flickered like a glitching projection.

Chanotedah moved before anyone else.

Chanotedah moved closer, the mist parting around him with the same quiet deference it had shown before. Up close, the contrast of him was even sharper. His scruffy hair still fell into his eyes, his clothes still looked like he had slept in them, and he was still a little too short for someone who sounded like distant thunder when he spoke. But the steadiness in him, the way he held himself, the way the mist seemed to listen when he breathed—made him feel older than anyone Nicholas had ever met.

He knelt beside Nicholas, placing a hand on the soft, cloud-like ground rather than touching him directly. The gesture was gentle, respectful, as if he understood how close Nicholas was to unraveling. "Breathe with the mist," he said, his voice low and steady, carrying that strange resonance that didn't match his teenage frame. "Not against it."

Nicholas's breath hitched. "I don't... I don't know how."

"You don't need to know," Chanotedah said, watching him with eyes that held far more years than his face suggested. "Just follow."

The mist responded to his words, curling upward in slow, rhythmic pulses, inviting Nicholas to match its movement. Chanotedah's presence anchored the moment, grounding Nicholas in a way that felt instinctive, like the world itself had chosen him as a guide.

Nicholas tried to breathe with the mist, uncertain and shaky, but Chanotedah nodded as if he were doing exactly what he needed to. The warmth in Nicholas's chest eased, syncing with the soft rise and fall of the air around them.

For the first time since arriving in Nirvana, Nicholas felt the panic loosen its grip.

And Chanotedah, scruffy and rumpled and impossibly ancient behind his tired eyes, stayed right beside him, steady as stone.

Anna knelt on Nicholas's other side, her hand hovering near his shoulder, steady but careful not to overwhelm him. "You're okay. You're okay. We've got you." Her voice was soft, but the worry beneath it was unmistakable.

Nicholas squeezed his eyes shut, breath catching. "I don't feel okay."

"You will," Chanotedah said, though the words carried a faint tremor beneath their calm surface. He stood, brushing his palms against his rumpled jeans as if grounding himself, too. Up close, the thinness of his confidence showed in the way his shoulders tightened for a moment before he forced them to relax. "But not out here."

He offered his hand, not pushing, not commanding, just holding it out with a quiet hopefulness that didn't quite match the ancient steadiness in his eyes. Nicholas hesitated, then took it. Chanotedah's grip was warm and surprisingly gentle, and for a moment Nicholas felt the mist pulse around them in a soft ripple, as if acknowledging the connection.

Anna rose with him, slipping her arm around his back to steady him. Nicholas leaned into her without meaning to, the ground still shifting beneath his feet like a living mattress. Chanotedah stepped back half a pace, watching Nicholas with a mixture of relief and something else, something like uncertainty, as if he wasn't entirely sure he deserved the trust being placed in him.

"We'll take him to quarters," Anna said, her voice firming with purpose.

Bharati nodded, her expression full of quiet understanding. "I'll inform the Council. They can wait."

Chanotedah exhaled softly, imperceptibly, as if grateful for the reprieve. The mist curled around his ankles in a slow, thoughtful pattern, and he glanced down at it with a flicker of unease before smoothing his expression again. Nicholas caught the moment, brief as it was, and something inside him shifted. Chanotedah wasn't the unshakable guide he pretended to be. He was trying—trying to be steady, trying to be brave, trying to be what Nicholas needed. But there was a fragility beneath it, a thin layer of fear he couldn't quite hide.

Nicholas didn't know why, but that made him trust Chanotedah more.

As they began walking, the mist parted ahead of them in soft, swirling paths, guiding their steps toward the heart of Nirvana. Nicholas felt the warmth in his chest pulse again, steadier now, syncing with the rhythm of the world around him. Anna stayed close, her presence a constant anchor. Chanotedah walked on his other side, hands tucked into his pockets, shoulders slightly hunched, as if bracing himself for something he couldn't name.

For the first time since crossing the seam, Nicholas didn't feel like he was falling.

He felt like he was being led.

And Chanotedah, scruffy, uncertain, ancient behind his tired eyes, felt like someone who understood exactly how terrifying that could be.

Anna stayed close, her presence warm and steady, guiding him with the same quiet certainty she had always carried, even before he knew what she truly was. Nicholas didn't look back at the mist-town square. He didn't have to. The moment he released it from his thoughts, the place dissolved behind them, its soft colors folding into the air until only a faint scent of warm cookies lingered. Even that faded a moment later, slipping away like a memory deciding to wait for him somewhere else.

The path ahead shimmered with pale pink mist that curled around their ankles in gentle spirals, responding to every shift in Nicholas's breath. Anna's arm remained firm around his back, steadying him each time the ground softened or swayed beneath his feet. He leaned into her without thinking, the way he always had when the world felt too big or too strange, long before either of them understood why that instinct came so easily.

Chanotedah walked on his other side, quiet and watchful, but it was Anna's presence that anchored him. She didn't speak, didn't rush him, didn't try to explain the impossible world unfolding around them. She simply stayed with him, matching his pace, her warmth cutting through the uncertainty gathering in his chest. The mist brightened whenever she steadied him, as if it recognized the bond between them and approved.

Nicholas drew in a slow breath, feeling the world shift with him, feeling Anna's hand tighten just enough to remind him he wasn't alone. Whatever waited ahead, Council chambers, answers, dangers he didn't yet understand felt a little less overwhelming with her beside him.

Together, they walked deeper into Nirvana, the mist parting for them like a curtain drawn back for someone expected.

And for the first time since everything began, Nicholas felt the faint, fragile sense that he might belong here. Not because Nirvana wanted him, but because Anna did.

CHAPTER 7

Nicholas woke to a generous pour of morning light that painted his ceiling in warm strokes. For a blissful heartbeat, everything was exactly as it should be. Books sat in comfortable heaps on his desk; a scatter of LEGO pieces glinted on the rug like tiny jewels caught in sunbeams; in the corner, the half-built robot crouched wires like tendons, an open panel like a sternum awaiting a heart. He stretched and yawned, letting his arms float up until his fingertips brushed the curtain's hem. The fabric breathed against his skin, whispering a soft sigh, and he smiled without thinking. Home had a sound, and this was it.

He drew the curtains back, and the window exploded in gold. Outside, the world seemed to hold its breath. Nicholas rubbed a thumb across the glass and felt an odd coolness, not the usual morning chill but something gently sweet, like the inside of a freezer where someone had stored cotton candy.

"That was really some dream I had this time," he muttered, padding toward the bathroom on autopilot. "And everything seemed so real." He scratched his head and laughed under his breath at himself; at thirteen, he was supposed to be too old to get rattled by dreams. Yet the memory still pressed against him like a crowd: Anna's laughter, Dad's hurried voice, Mom's hand on his shoulder, the stranger named Chase buying ice cream as if it were medicine, Miss Carter becoming someone else entirely, Bharati and pastel wisps drifting like fog from a fairy tale.

He shut the bathroom door, and the small room welcomed him with the familiar mint-sharp sting of toothpaste and the damp note of last night's steam. Nicholas cupped water in his hands, splashed his face, and listened to the house breathe, floorboards expanding, the distant tick of something clocklike, a hush as if the walls were waiting for a cue. He pressed a towel against his cheeks until the cotton drank the water away.

On the other side of the door, the mattress dipped.

"How are you feeling, Nicky?" Anna's voice floated through like sunlight peeking under the sill.

Nicholas grinned; he loved that nickname only when Anna said it: "Nicky" carried a smile.

He opened the door, the towel still in his hands. "Oh, Anna, I'm glad you're here. I had the strangest dream, and it was so realistic. You were in it, and Mom and Dad, and this man named Chase; he was nice, bought a lot of ice cream." He smirked at the memory, drying his face. "And Miss Carter from the principal's office, too."

A smell rolled in from nowhere: eggs, bright and buttery, bacon, the crackling promise of salt and smoke. Nicholas paused mid-wipe. The aroma had weight, like a warm hand on the back of his neck. He sniffed again, surprised by a delicate note of spearmint threading through the breakfast like a ribbon.

"Did Mom just bring breakfast up to me?" he asked, fighting a grin and suddenly starving.

"Yeah, there's breakfast out here, Nicky." Anna covered her mouth as she giggled, the laughter twitching at the corners of her eyes. She flicked a look toward the foot of the bed and gave a near-imperceptible motion for quiet. "What about the rest of your dream?"

Nicholas fumbled for words, memory turning corners inside his head faster than he could follow. "Well, the stranger, Chase, talked to my folks, and Dad gave him the Bronco to get us to safety, and we went to this place that looked like it was made from cotton candy. That was where Miss Carter was, except she wasn't Miss Carter, she

was Bharati. Then there was this short guy with a scruffy face who smelled a little like raw…"

He stepped out of the bathroom, towel trailing from his hand, and the sentence simply evaporated.

Chanotedah sat at the foot of the bed, elbows on his knees, chin resting in his palms, listening as if the room itself had leaned closer to hear Nicholas speak. He looked exactly as he had in Nirvana, scruffy hair sticking out in every direction, patchy beard shading his jaw, clothes rumpled like he had slept in them or sprinted through a windstorm. He was unmistakably a teenager, maybe sixteen or seventeen, but his eyes held a depth that did not belong to someone who had barely lived long enough to drive. They were bright and mischievous and kind, but behind all that shimmered something older, something tired, something that watched the world with the caution of someone who had already seen too much.

The spearmint scent sharpened in the air, clean and cool, almost medicinal, yet oddly soothing. It wrapped around Nicholas like a memory he had not earned.

Nicholas shrieked. Not a dignified yelp or a startled gasp, but a full, high-pitched shriek that bounced off the walls and made Chanotedah blink in surprise. The towel thumped to the floor.

"I am sorry," Nicholas stammered, cheeks burning. "I did not expect… I mean, you are… this is… I thought it was a dream."

"I am sorry, I did not catch that," Chanotedah said, his voice a rough gravel that somehow found humor along the way. He tipped his head toward Nicholas, eyes glinting. "He smelled a little like raw what again?"

He leaned forward, pretending to listen harder. "Must be that patchy beard blocking my ears."

Nicholas sputtered, mortified, and overwhelmed all at once.

"You are real," he whispered, as if saying it too loudly might break the moment. "You are actually here. In my room."

Chanotedah's grin faltered for a heartbeat, just long enough for Nicholas to see the thinness of it, the flicker of apprehension beneath the humor. He straightened a little too quickly, as if trying to look more confident than he felt. "Yeah," he said, softer now. "Looks like it."

Nicholas's pulse hammered in his ears. The mist, the fairies, the cotton candy world, Miss Carter's robes, the way the ground had breathed beneath his feet, all of it crashed back into him at once. None of it had been a dream. None of it had been imagined.

And Chanotedah, scruffy and rumpled and ancient behind his tired eyes, was sitting on his bed like it was the most normal thing in the world.

Nicholas swallowed hard, the room tilting slightly as reality rearranged itself around him. "So, this is really happening."

Chanotedah nodded, his expression softening again, the bravado slipping just enough to show the boy beneath the myth. "Yeah," he said quietly. "It really is."

Nicholas blinked at both of them, his thoughts tripping over one another in a frantic scramble. "I do not understand how this looks so right," he said, gesturing vaguely at the books on his shelf, the half-built robot on his desk, the curtains he had picked out with his mother. "It feels like my room. It smells like my room. It even has the dent in the carpet from my chair. How is that possible? Is it the same way the town square was created?"

Chanotedah shrugged with casual confidence that did not quite reach his eyes. He lifted the breakfast tray and set it on the desk beside Nicholas's schoolbooks. "Something like that, Junior. Nirvana can shape itself when it needs to. Bharati wanted you somewhere familiar so you would not panic the moment you woke up." He flashed a grin that carried the faint scent of spearmint, a ghost of fresh leaves that drifted through the air. "You fell asleep while we were getting your things out of Chase's truck, so we brought you here. Now you need to eat, because Bharati wants to see you as soon as possible."

Nicholas stared at him, the truth settling slowly into place. "So, none of it was a dream," he said, his voice barely above a whisper.

Anna and Chanotedah both nodded with the same quiet certainty.

The floor beneath Nicholas felt less certain. The room looked perfect, but the perfection itself felt wrong, like a photograph pretending to be a memory. He turned in a slow circle, taking in every detail. "This is not really my room," he said, the realization landing with a strange weight.

Anna hopped off the bed and began a slow circuit of the space, trailing her fingers along the desk, the shelf, the window frame. "No, it is not," she said. "We had it conjured to make you more comfortable until you get used to Nirvana. I think I did a rather good job recreating it."

Nicholas watched her move, the familiarity of her presence grounding him more than the room ever could. She paused beside him, her expression softening. "You are safe here," she said. "But we cannot stay long. The Council is waiting."

Chanotedah shifted his weight, the thinness of his bravado showing for a moment in the way he avoided Nicholas's eyes. "Yeah," he said quietly. "We really need to go."

Nicholas swallowed, the last pieces of denial slipping away. The room was not real. The world outside it was. And the people standing with him were the only solid things he could trust.

Nicholas's laugh came out thin and hollow, more breath than sound. "You mean this is just my imagination, and it does not exist?"

Anna shook her head, her expression softening. "No. It is not your imagination. What you're seeing exists, but not in the way you're used to. Nirvana responds to thought. We can shape the matter around us into almost anything simply by imagining what we need."

Nicholas stared at the room again, really stared, and the familiarity began to feel unsettling. The posters on the wall were exactly where he had left them. The LEGO tower on his shelf leaned at the same impossible angle. Even the dent in the carpet from his desk chair was in the right place. Every detail was right, and that was exactly what frightened him. It felt less like his room than a memory wearing a costume.

The headache he thought he had outrun returned with a slow, lumbering persistence. He slumped into the desk chair and pressed his palms to his eyes. "I think my headache is coming back."

Anna's eyebrows lifted in concern. "It is not that bad, is it?"

Nicholas nodded without looking up. The room pressed against the back of his skull with a soft, cotton candy weight, as if the walls themselves were breathing too close to him.

Chanotedah leaned forward and tapped the plate with a finger. "May I remind you both that Bharati is waiting for us, and I have not even begun to explain Nirvana. I suggest you stop whining about your headache, eat the breakfast I brought, and get ready to learn where you are." He nudged the chair closer to the desk with a gentle insistence.

Nicholas picked up a strip of bacon and took a tentative bite. The salt cracked open against his tongue, and the fat melted like a promise. It was impossible not to keep going. He ate with a brisk, grateful fury, shoveling eggs and bacon until the plate was clean. Only then did the room feel steady enough to stand in.

He wiped his mouth with the back of his hand and let out a slow breath. "Alright. I think I am about as ready as I am ever going to be to learn about…" He turned toward the window, expecting the dependable patchwork of his backyard, the oak tree with the ladder to the treehouse, the swing's slow pendulum. Instead, the view was a swirl of pastel, thin wisps of matter drifting and reforming like breath caught in sunlight. "Well… all of this."

The sight pulled something loose inside him. The room was familiar, but the world outside it was not. The two realities pressed against each other like mismatched puzzle pieces.

Nicholas swallowed hard. "So… we should go see Miss Carter."

Anna stepped beside him, her hand brushing his arm in a quiet correction. "Bharati," she said gently. "Her name is Bharati."

Nicholas nodded; the truth settled deeper. Whatever this place was, it wasn't his room, and whatever waited beyond the pastel mist was no longer something he could dismiss as a dream.

He moved to the bedroom door and opened it. Where Nicholas expected a hallway lined with family photos, the one where his kindergarten portrait sat crooked, there was only more pastel. The wisps breathed, every color so soft it felt like the world was thinking in whispers.

"This is Nirvana," Chanotedah said as the three stepped out. The air tasted faintly sweet, like powdered sugar stirred into warm tea, and carried the cool note of spearmint drifting from the boy himself. The world around them shimmered with soft color, as if the mist were painting reality in slow, thoughtful strokes. "Home to time jumpers, scroungers, protectors, and the High Council. Imagine a spring stretched out. To a Normal, that is a timeline. Past behind, future ahead. Nirvana sits in the center of the spring, where the coils touch. Everything folds inward here."

They walked, and the ground beneath their feet felt like a memory trying to become a road. It shifted with each step, not unstable but responsive, as if deciding what shape it wanted to take. Nicholas kept glancing at Chanotedah, as if the explanations were hung around the boy's patchy beard like signposts. He did not understand everything yet, and that scared him, but the rhythm of Chanotedah's voice steadied him like a hand on his back.

"The matter that makes up our home is memory," Chanotedah continued. "Not your memories. Not mine. These are memories expelled from the Normals' timeline. Every forgotten moment, every discarded dream, every half-remembered scent or sound. They drift here, and

Nirvana shapes them into what we need. Buildings, paths, sky and even the air you are breathing. It is all made from what the world above has let go."

Nicholas stared at the pastel horizon, where wisps of matter drifted and reformed like breath caught in sunlight. "So, this place is made of… memories people forgot?"

"Memories, impressions, echoes," Chanotedah said. "The things that slip through cracks in the mind. Nirvana gathers them. From here, time does not have a beginning or an end. A jumper can access any point in time at any location they choose, because they are standing in the place where all moments brush against each other."

Nicholas tried to imagine that, but the thought bent in his head like a spoon under too much pressure.

Chanotedah went on. "We do not have time here in the way you are used to. To measure time, you need a constant, something that does not care about your feelings. For most beings, the constant is the rotation of their planet. That makes a day. The revolution around a star makes a year. Anything smaller than that is a number someone invented early in their species' existence. Useful, yes. But arbitrary."

Nicholas squinted at him. "The way you are talking… There are other planets with people on them. Is that what you are saying?"

Chanotedah nodded, letting the spearmint scent ride the tilt of his head. "Yes. Many. But the High Council does not allow species from different planets to intermingle until the Normals from those planets make contact on their own. For humans, that will not happen for a while in the timeline you came from."

Nicholas's breath caught. The mist around his ankles pulsed in a slow, curious rhythm, as if listening to his thoughts. "So, Nirvana is connected to all of them?"

"All timelines. All worlds. All species that experience time," Chanotedah said. "Everywhere that memory exists, Nirvana has a thread."

The surface beneath Nicholas's feet softened with each step, responding to his presence with an almost living warmth. The idea that he was standing in the center of everything made his chest tighten, but Anna's hand brushed his arm, steadying him.

Chanotedah watched him with a flicker of sympathy, the thin bravado in his posture slipping for a moment. "It is a lot," he said quietly. "I know."

Nicholas nodded, unable to speak. The mist curled around his feet like a welcome.

And Nirvana, vast and impossible, waited for him to understand it.

Nicholas pressed his lips together. "Is that really something I should know? Aren't you afraid I'll tell someone?"

The answer landed with a soft, cruel certainty. "There isn't anyone for you to tell," Chanotedah said. "You're really not a part of that world anymore, Junior."

Nicholas stopped walking. The pastel air gathered around him, a quiet current that wanted to carry him forward and refused to push. A park bench rose from the wisps with a soft wooden sigh, its slats forming under him as if it had always been there, waiting for weight. He sat down without meaning to, eyes fixed on a spot he couldn't name.

Anna's breath caught. "Nicky—look what you did!" She settled beside him, careful and wide-eyed. "It took me forever to learn how to manipulate the wisps into things. You just… did it." Her voice was a thrill wrapped in tenderness. "You should be really excited."

Nicholas did not smile. He stared through the bench, through the shifting pastel world, into the hollow left behind by the words not part of that world. His voice, when it finally surfaced, was thin and low. "Did you hear what he said? I am not really a part of that world anymore. My family, our school, our friends. I am not part of that anymore."

Anna had seen him drift before, back at school, his eyes going distant and dreamy when the clock ticked too slowly. This was different. The distance now was a cliff, and fear tugged him toward the edge with a force she could almost feel in her own chest. She reached for his hand, quiet and firm, her fingers warm against his cold ones, a small anchor in a world made of mist and memory.

Chanotedah hopped onto the bench between them with a fluid ease, trying to wedge himself into the space before Nicholas could fall any further. His grin was bright, almost too bright, the kind that tried to heal by distraction rather than certainty. "Hey, Junior. I wish I could understand exactly what you are feeling right now. I never had a family. The closest I had was this girl and her brother, whom I stayed with once. Long story for another time." He chuckled, and the sound warmed the air like a small sun rising. "I caused the brother some trouble. Do not worry. He survived my charm."

Nicholas swallowed against the raw edge in his throat. "If we can go to any time, any place, why can't I just go back into the timeline and pick up where I left off? Why can I not go home?"

Chanotedah's grin softened, then faded. He spoke more quietly now, with the careful cadence of someone opening a door that should not be slammed. "Even though that may be true, it is more complicated than that. When you return to a timeline, you cannot live there. We can interact with Normals, but after the interaction, they do not really remember us. We become a figment of their imagination, like a scene in a movie they watched once but cannot place."

Nicholas stared at him, confusion and hope wrestling in his eyes. "You mean to tell me that even if I could go back to my parents, they would not remember who I am? After twelve years of living with them? They would have no idea?" He looked from Chanotedah to Anna, searching for something solid to hold on to. "That is impossible. That is crazy. Do you not think that is crazy?"

Anna squeezed his hand, her voice soft but steady. "It is not crazy. It is how Nirvana works. It protects the timelines by making sure we cannot change them by staying."

Chanotedah nodded, though the motion carried a flicker of unease, as if he wished he could offer a gentler truth. "Normals remember the feeling of us, sometimes. A warmth. A shadow. A moment that mattered for reasons they cannot explain. But they do not remember us as people. Not in the way you want."

Nicholas's breath hitched. The world around him blurred, the pastel mist shifting like a watercolor left in the rain. "So, I am supposed to just accept that I am gone from them? That they will wake up and not even know I existed?"

Anna leaned closer, her presence steady and warm. "They will feel the space you left. They will feel the love. They will feel the ache. They just will not know why. And that is not your fault."

Nicholas closed his eyes, the ache in his chest tightening until it felt like the world itself was pressing against him. The bench beneath him, made from nothing more than memory and mist, held his weight with quiet patience.

Chanotedah watched him with a thin, fragile bravery, the kind that cracked at the edges. "I know it hurts," he said softly. "But you are here now. And you are not alone."

Nicholas opened his eyes, tears gathering but not falling. The fear remained, but Anna's hand in his and Chanotedah beside him kept him grounded.

Nirvana waited, vast and impossible. And Nicholas, trembling but held, took his first breath toward understanding it.

Chanotedah slid off the bench and gave Nicholas a gentle shoulder bump, more a nudge back into himself than a shove forward. "I can see this is not sinking in very well for you." He glanced at Anna, then back at Nicholas with a seriousness that softened the edges of his grin. "Let us go see Bharati. She will be able to clarify this better than I have."

The mist stirred at their feet as if it had been waiting for that decision. It gathered in slow spirals, drawing itself into a path that shimmered with pale color, a road made from memory and breath. Nicholas rose reluctantly, the bench dissolving beneath him the moment he no longer needed it. The wood softened into wisps, then into nothing at all, as if the world were reclaiming the shape it had lent him.

Anna stayed close, her hand brushing his arm in a quiet promise that he was not walking into this alone. The air around her brightened, responding to her steadiness, and Nicholas felt the warmth of it settle against his skin like sunlight filtered through water. He followed her step by step, each movement pulling him deeper into a place that felt both impossibly new and strangely familiar.

The landscape shifted as they walked. Buildings rose and fell like thoughts forming and dissolving. Trees unfurled from drifting wisps, their branches made of half-remembered dreams. The sky rippled with soft color, as if painted by someone who had never seen a horizon but understood longing. Every part of Nirvana felt alive, listening, waiting for him to understand what it was.

Nicholas's heart thudded in his chest. The more the world revealed itself, the more he felt the ache of the one he had left behind. His family. His room. His life. The realization pressed against him with a weight that made his breath catch.

Ahead of them, the path widened into a broad expanse of shimmering ground. Structures rose from the mist in tall, graceful arcs, their shapes shifting between stone and light, memory and matter. They looked ancient and new at the same time, like temples built from forgotten stories.

Chanotedah slowed, his bravado thinning as the air grew heavier with purpose. "This is the Council's domain," he said quietly. "They are expecting you."

Nicholas swallowed hard. The pastel light reflected in his eyes, turning his fear into something luminous. He felt Anna's hand slip into his again, steady and sure.

The mist parted before them, revealing a pebbled path shaped from swirling memory. It pulsed with a soft glow, inviting and intimidating all at once.

Nicholas took a breath that tasted of spearmint and sugar and something older than both.

"Alright," he said, voice trembling but determined. "Let us go see Miss Carter."

Anna's fingers tightened around his. "Bharati," she corrected gently, her smile warm enough to steady him.

Nicholas nodded.

Together, they stepped toward the Council, and the world of Nirvana shifted to meet them.

CHAPTER 8

Nicholas watched the forest dissolve behind them, the trees loosening into threads of color that drifted upward like smoke. The path ahead remained solid only as long as he looked at it. The moment his gaze shifted, the edges softened, as if the world preferred to exist only where attention fell. It made his stomach twist. Nothing stayed still long enough to trust.

"How do you know where you are going?" he asked, turning in a slow circle. The forest flickered at the edges of his vision, half real and half suggestion. "There are no roads or signs, nothing to signal direction, and everything looks the same." He pointed, then realized the gesture meant nothing. His finger could not find its way in a place that refused to recognize up and down the way he did.

"Direction falls into the same category as time," Chanotedah said. He walked forward with the easy confidence of someone who had learned to trust a compass that had no needle. "It does not exist here. Not really." He glanced at Nicholas's face, at the tightness around his eyes and the way his jaw locked, and added with a theatrical flourish, "But if it will make you happy…"

The world answered him.

The forest around them deepened, as if someone had turned the page to a richer illustration. Oaks and maples rose in stately arches, their branches weaving a green canopy overhead. Sunlight filtered through the leaves in soft, golden sheets. Birdsong threaded through the air, coming from everywhere and nowhere at once. Wildflowers gathered in bright clusters along a pebbled path that formed beneath their feet with the satisfying crunch of real stone. The air grew richer, carrying the scent of damp earth and fresh leaves, and the spearmint note from Chanotedah drifted through it like punctuation.

Nicholas spun in place, eyes wide. "How did you do that?" The question trembled in his hands, too large to hold.

"The same way you conjured a park bench," Chanotedah said, his grin slanting. "I willed the wisps. Just on a bigger scale." He lifted a hand, and a shaft of sunlight angled toward them as if obeying.

Nicholas looked back. As they walked, the forest behind them relaxed its grip and slipped away. Trees thinned into suggestion, bark shedding into color, leaves loosening into pale threads until the cotton candy wisps reclaimed the ground. It was like watching a chalk drawing erased, not to destroy it but to keep the board ready for whatever came next.

Anna stepped closer to Nicholas, her presence warm and steady. "This is the approach to the Council," she said. "They do not like to be hidden, but they do not like to be found easily either."

Nicholas's breath caught. The structures ahead pulsed with a quiet gravity, drawing him forward even as fear tightened in his chest. The world felt larger here, older, as if every forgotten moment from every timeline had gathered to watch him arrive.

Chanotedah slowed, his confidence thinning at the edges. "They are expecting you," he said, voice softer now. "And they do not enjoy waiting."

Nicholas swallowed, the pastel light reflecting in his eyes. The forest behind them dissolved completely, leaving only the shimmering path and the rising shapes of the Council's domain.

"Alright," he said, steadying himself. "Let us go."

"That is too cool," Nicholas laughed, relief bubbling up through the fear like air rising through deep water. Anna breathed out, quiet and grateful. The lively spark she knew in him had returned for a moment, and hope slid back into her bones.

They rounded a bend, and the forest parted to reveal a small stone cottage tucked among the trees, ivy curling along its walls and pale smoke drifting from the chimney. It looked almost quaint until they drew closer and its edges seemed to widen beyond their proper dimensions. Amber light glowed through the windows, and tiny engraved symbols flashed across the roof tiles when the sun struck them.

Somewhere inside, a bell waited.

"Here we are," Chanotedah said, padding up two wooden steps that carried the history of countless feet. "The High Council's chambers." He reached for a braided rope beside the door and tugged it gently.

The bell chimed. It was not a single note but a layered chord that shimmered through the air, a sound that felt like time agreed with itself. The forest hushed, as if listening.

The door edged open.

Nicholas forgot how to breathe for half a second. The cottage exterior had promised something small and cozy, but the space beyond the threshold unfolded into a hall that stretched far beyond the limits of its walls. The pastel wisps that made up Nirvana's matter organized themselves into shapes that made sense only when you looked at them directly. Arched ceilings rose high above, fringed with delicate filigree that shifted like frost patterns on glass. Walkways suspended in the air curved gracefully between platforms, yet each step felt solid underfoot, as if the world had decided to honor gravity only where it mattered.

Murals lined the walls, but they did not stay still. They shifted when Nicholas was not looking full on, each image of a story unrolling from a different corner of time. A river that flowed backward. A city built on the back of a sleeping creature. A star collapsing into a flower. The scent inside was a mixture of old books, polished wood, a hint of citrus, and the fresh spark of spearmint that followed Chanotedah like a signature.

"Stick close," Anna murmured. Her hand brushed Nicholas's shoulder for a heartbeat. He did not take it, but the touch steadied him as if she had passed him a rope.

They moved through a long corridor where the walls held carvings of springs coiling into infinity. In niches along the passage, artifacts rested behind thin veils of shimmering air. A mask shaped for a face that was not human. A clock with hands in the wrong places, ticking in a rhythm that felt like footsteps. A stone bowl filled with water that reflected the future differently depending on where you stood. Nicholas paused at the clock. Its ticking echoed in his bones. He turned away, shivering.

The corridor opened into a chamber that felt both grand and intimate, like a theater that insisted the play was about you. The ceiling rose into a dome of shifting light, and windows along the far wall showed views of nothing and everything at once. One window held a field of tall grass bending in a wind that did not exist. Another showed an ocean under a sky poured from a deeper blue than Nicholas had ever seen. A third revealed a starless void that pulsed with quiet life.

In the center of the chamber stood a circular table carved from dark wood that seemed older than the room itself. Around it, chairs waited, each one shaped slightly differently, as if crafted for the person who would sit in it.

Anna stepped closer. Chanotedah straightened, his bravado thinning at the edges.

"The Council is here," he said quietly.

Nicholas swallowed, the sound loud in the vast room.

And the chamber, vast and impossible, waited for him to step forward.

"Bharati will explain what we have not," Chanotedah said. His casual confidence dimmed just a little at the edges, as if the air itself reminded him to tread carefully. Nicholas felt the shift immediately. They were stepping into someone else's gravity.

Before they reached the table, a figure emerged from a side door with a presence so calm that the room seemed to widen for her. Bharati was neither tall nor short, neither loud nor quiet. Her eyes held a midnight depth that suggested stars hidden behind them, waiting for the right moment to appear.

"Nicholas," she said, greeting him like a traveler who had finally arrived after taking the scenic route. "Anna. Chanotedah." She inclined her head to each in turn.

Nicholas swallowed. "Hi," he said, and wished his voice did not sound so young in a place that felt older than memory.

"You came through a great deal to be here," Bharati said, motioning for them to sit. "You have questions. You should. Sit, and we will treat them with respect."

They took their seats. Anna settled beside Nicholas, her presence warm and steady. Chanotedah leaned back with practiced ease, though the alertness in his posture betrayed the truth: he was ready to spring, ready to defend, ready to run. Bharati rested her hands lightly on the table, and the dark wood rippled beneath her touch as if her fingers had stirred a pond.

"Nirvana," she began, "is not a place apart from time. It is a place made by time, from what time leaves behind when it is lived. The energy expelled from the Normals' timeline accumulates here. It is like the warm air left in a gym after a game, or the hum of a crowd after a performance ends. We gather that energy and shape it. That is why your room can appear. That is why the forest can. It is all honest. It exists. But it is honest in Nirvana's way, not in the way of the timeline you are used to."

As she spoke, the murals along the chamber walls shifted. One showed a city dissolving into mist, its towers unraveling into threads of color. Another revealed a child shaping a river with a single thought, the water bending around their hands like silk. A third depicted a creature Nicholas could not name, its body made of starlight and memory, stepping between worlds as easily as stepping across a threshold.

Nicholas leaned forward, drawn in despite the fear tightening his chest. "And me? Where does that leave me?"

Bharati's gaze softened without losing its midnight depth. "It leaves you at the beginning of your work." She glanced toward the place where the conjured bench had once stood, as if she could still see it resting in the pastel mist. "You pulled matter into meaning without thinking. That is not common, Nicholas. The prophecy has always spoken of someone who would do such things as if breathing. It is not simply power. It is ease."

Nicholas felt the weight of it settle on his shoulders. The room seemed to lean closer, listening.

Anna's hand brushed his arm, grounding him. Chanotedah's spearmint scent sharpened, a quiet sign of nerves he tried to hide.

Bharati folded her hands, and the table rippled again beneath her touch. "You are here because Nirvana has been waiting for you. The Council has been waiting for you. And now that you have arrived, the work begins."

The chamber brightened, as if the world itself agreed.

And Nicholas, caught between fear and wonder, realized he had stepped into a story that had been unfolding long before he ever knew it existed.

Nicholas shook his head. "Prophecy?" The word felt too large for his mouth, too heavy for the air around him. It sat between them like a stone dropped into still water, sending ripples through the chamber.

Anna's hand found his again. She did not squeeze. She simply existed beside him with the determined softness of someone who refused to let him drift alone. "He conjured the bench without trying," she said quietly. "He did it because he needed somewhere to sit after you…" She hesitated, glancing at Chanotedah.

"After I told him the truth," Chanotedah finished. He did not flinch. For a moment, Nicholas saw past the patchy beard and the mischief, down to a kindness he had not expected. "That he is not a part of that world anymore."

Bharati nodded, her midnight gaze steady. "The truth hurts. It should. Pain is a good compass when it points you away from lies. We do not steal you from your world, Nicholas. Your world changes around you when you begin to do what you were born to do. Normals cannot hold you in the way they once did. Their minds and hearts will tug toward you, and then, when you step away, they will say, 'I remember something,' and the memory will be true but unplaceable. It is not punishment. It is how the spring keeps its coil from snapping."

Nicholas closed his eyes. The bench he had made flashed through his mind, the ease of it, the way it had arrived without argument. He had not meant to shape anything. He had simply needed a place to sit before the world tipped sideways. The thought that he could do that without trying made his stomach twist. He did not want to be a ghost to his parents. He did not want to become a memory trapped under glass.

"Can I go back at all?" he asked. "Even for a little while?"

"Yes," Bharati said. "You can step into their days like a beam of sunlight through a window. They will feel warm. They will know. But when the light moves, they will return to their day and say, 'Wasn't it bright?' Some will cry. Some will smile. Some will go make tea. That is how love protects them. The work you have been chosen for requires you to move. Their lives require them to keep living."

Nicholas opened his eyes. Tears gathered but refused to fall. He nodded once, small and careful. He would not drag his parents through a confusion they did not deserve.

The chamber sensed his struggle. The murals along the walls shifted again, their colors deepening. One showed a figure standing at the center of a great coil of time, threads of memory stretching toward them like rivers seeking the sea. Another revealed a family at a dinner table, their faces warm with laughter, but the edges of the scene blurred, as if the memory were already drifting toward Nirvana. A third showed a child stepping through a doorway of light, leaving footprints that glowed for a moment before fading.

Nicholas stared at the images, his breath catching. The room felt alive, listening, responding to the ache inside him.

Anna leaned closer, her voice soft. "You are not losing them," she said. "You are changing. And they will feel that change even if they cannot name it."

Chanotedah shifted in his chair, the spearmint scent sharpening around him. His bravado had thinned to almost nothing, leaving only honesty. "It is hard," he said. "It does not stop being hard. But you are not alone in it."

Nicholas looked at the table, at Bharati's steady hands, at the shifting murals, at the windows showing impossible skies. The weight of everything pressed against him, heavy and bright.

"I do not know if I can do this," he whispered.

Bharati's gaze held him, calm and unyielding. "You already have," she said. "You shaped the mist. You stepped into Nirvana. You listened. You asked. The beginning is always the hardest part."

A wash of light moved through the chamber, soft but unmistakable, like an answer.

And Nicholas, trembling but held on both sides, felt the tension inside him coil tighter, ready to snap or transform.

The Council had not yet spoken its judgment. But the story had already begun to claim him.

Nicholas hesitated, the question still trembling inside him like a loose thread he was afraid to pull. The forest around them shifted in quiet agreement, leaves rustling with a sound that felt almost like breath. He wanted to understand. He wanted to feel steady. But every answer only seemed to tilt the world a little more.

"What if I pick the wrong thing?" he asked. "What if I think of something that doesn't make sense here? What if the wisps get confused? What if I get confused?"

Chanotedah laughed softly, but the sound carried a gentleness that surprised Nicholas. "Junior, the wisps are always confused. That is their natural state. They do not mind. They like being told what to do." He tapped his temple. "The trick is convincing yourself you know what you want, even if you do not."

Nicholas frowned. "That does not help."

"It is not supposed to," Chanotedah said, still grinning. "It is supposed to make you realize that confusion is normal here. Everyone feels it at first. Even me."

Nicholas looked down at his hands. They did not look different, but they felt different, as if something inside them had been rewired without his permission. The idea that he could shape the world around him made his stomach twist. He had not asked for that. He had not asked for any of this.

"I do not know what feels steady in my bones," he admitted. "Everything feels like it is slipping."

Anna touched his arm, light as a whisper. "Then start with something small," she said. "Something that feels like you. Not the new you. The you who existed before all of this."

Nicholas closed his eyes. He tried to find something steady, something that had not been shaken loose by prophecy or timelines or the idea that his parents might forget him. At first, nothing came. Then, slowly, a memory surfaced. The smell of bacon on Saturday mornings. The sound of his mother humming while she cooked. The warmth of sunlight through the kitchen window.

He held onto that.

The ground beneath his feet shifted. Wisps gathered, swirling in soft spirals, waiting for instruction. Nicholas felt the pull of them, gentle and curious, like a dog nudging a hand for attention.

"Good," Chanotedah said quietly. "Now ask."

Nicholas opened his eyes. The forest blurred at the edges, waiting for him to decide what it should become. His heart thudded hard enough to hurt.

"Make a path," he whispered. "Something that feels like home."

The wisps brightened. The air shimmered. A narrow trail formed beneath his feet, lined with small stones that glowed faintly, like embers cooling after a fire. The scent of bacon drifted through the trees, warm and impossible.

Nicholas stared at it; his breath caught in his throat. "I did that?"

Anna smiled, soft and proud. "You did."

Chanotedah gave a low whistle. "Not bad for someone who thinks he is slipping."

Nicholas swallowed. The path stretched ahead, steady and waiting. But the confusion inside him did not fade. It gathered weight, becoming something he could no longer push aside simply because he didn't understand it.

"I still do not understand any of this," he said.

Anna's hand found his again. "You will," she said. "And until you do, we are here."

Nicholas looked at the path he had made, then at the forest, then at the sky that refused to stay one color. Everything felt too big, too strange, too fragile.

But he stepped forward anyway.

And the world shifted to meet him.

"Not bad, Junior," Chanotedah said, genuinely impressed. "You have the touch."

"He has more than the touch," Anna murmured. Her voice carried quiet certainty, as if she were naming something she had already decided to believe in.

They walked on. The path Nicholas had shaped guided them into a clearing where the sky nestled lower, resting its weight on the tops of the trees. The air felt softer here, as if the world had paused to listen. Nicholas felt an impulse rise in him; the same way someone feels the urge to hum when a room is too quiet.

"Can I try something?" he asked.

"As long as it is not a dragon," Chanotedah said quickly. "Council paperwork is a nightmare when fire is involved."

Nicholas laughed, the sound small but real, and lifted his hands. He did not know what he was asking the wisps to become until they began to obey. Wood gathered itself from the air, angles finding their truth, and a simple table arrived with a patient creak. He touched the edge. The grain felt like tiny rivers running beneath his fingertips. He could have asked for marble or glass or something grand, but the plainness steadied him. It made him feel less loud.

"Nice," Anna said. "You are thinking in forms that will serve you, not impress you. That is good."

"He is thinking in forms that will not get us yelled at," Chanotedah added, approving.

They sat for a moment at the table that had not existed a moment earlier. A breeze threaded through Chanotedah's hair and cooled the sheen on Nicholas's neck. Birds moved above them in invisible paragraphs, their calls oddly reassuring, a continuation of something normal in a place that refused to be.

"I keep waiting to wake up," Nicholas said quietly. "Even though you told me I did not dream this. It feels like a dream because my room was so perfect and my parents were so close and then…" He gestured around them. "Cotton candy and forest and prophecy." The words sounded strange together, almost funny, almost frightening.

"You can hold two truths," Anna said. "It was a dream when you thought it was. Now it is a beginning. Dreams and beginnings can sit beside each other for a while if you let them."

Chanotedah leaned forward, elbows on the conjured wood. "And when one truth gets too loud, that is why you practice. Practice gives your hands something to do while your brain resets." He flicked a glance at Nicholas's fingers. "Hands that can ask the world to be kind to them should not go unused."

Nicholas traced the table's edge. He could feel the memory of the bench behind him, a small cloud of what he had shaped without meaning to. The thought unsettled him. It also tugged at something he could not name.

"When you said prophecy," he asked, "what did you mean exactly?"

Anna looked at Chanotedah. Chanotedah looked at the trees. The trees looked to the sky, as if the question had been asked many times before and the world itself was deciding how to answer.

Eventually, Chanotedah spoke. "It's an old Council story. Someone who could move through the center of the spring without getting lost. Someone who could shape matter without fear and listen to time without being swallowed by it. Someone Nirvana would listen to because it already knew them." He hesitated. "They called that person the Equal."

Nicholas frowned. "Equal to what?"

Chanotedah's usual grin did not return. "That's where the stories stop agreeing."

Nicholas felt the weight of the words settle on him, warm and heavy, like a blanket he was not sure he wanted. Confusion pressed against his ribs. Wonder pressed against it. Fear threaded through both.

He looked at the table he had made, at the path behind them, at the sky that refused to stay still. Nothing made sense. But for the first time, the confusion did not feel like drowning. It wanted to stand on the edge of something vast, with two people beside him who refused to let him fall.

The world of Nirvana waited, patient and impossible.

And Nicholas, still trembling, still unsure, took one careful breath and let the new truth settle beside the old one.

CHAPTER 9

The Atrium breathed around them, its mist-woven dome shifting in slow, tidal currents. Images flickered across its surface like memories trying to become real. A city of glass rising from water. A desert where shadows moved without bodies. The sky is split by a river of stars. Each vision lasted only a heartbeat before dissolving into drifting color. Nicholas felt as if he were standing inside the mind of something vast, something that remembered more than any single world could hold.

The lion-shaped shadow returned for a moment, stretching across the floor in a regal arc before fading. Nicholas's pulse jumped. He could not tell if the Atrium was warning him or welcoming him.

Four archways glowed softly, each one pulsing with a different hue. Gold. Deep green. A blue so dark it bordered on black. And a pale rose that shimmered like breath on glass. They felt alive, like heartbeats waiting to be heard.

Chanotedah stretched his arms behind his head, trying to look casual in a place that refused to be casual. "Alright, Junior. Time to meet the rest of the circus."

Anna elbowed him, though her eyes stayed fixed on the archways. "They are not a circus."

"They juggle timelines," Chanotedah said. "Close enough."

Nicholas swallowed. His throat felt tight. "Are they… nice?"

Anna hesitated. Chanotedah did not. He shifted subtly in front of Nicholas; his stance angled in a way that made him look older than he was. The spearmint scent sharpened, crisp and alert. "Depends on the day."

Before Nicholas could ask anything else, the mist curled around his ankles and wrists, curious and cool. It felt like fingers made of air, assessing the shape of him. A faint ringing began in his ears, soft at first, then growing, like a distant bell tuning itself. The sound vibrated through his bones, unsettling and strangely familiar.

Bharati appeared beside them as if she had always been standing there. Her presence steadied the air, and the mist loosened its grip. "Each Council member keeps their own space," she said. "They shape it according to their work."

Nicholas nodded, though the ringing deepened, threading through his thoughts. The mist tightened again, tasting his resonance, as if trying to decide what he was made of.

"Come," Bharati said. "We will begin with the Voice."

The archway of deep green brightened, its glow rippling outward like a breath. The mist parted, revealing a corridor that had not existed a moment before. Nicholas felt the world shift under his feet, not in a way that threatened to drop him, but in a way that reminded him he was standing in a place that obeyed different rules.

He took a step forward. The ringing in his ears softened, then harmonized with something deeper, something that felt like the Atrium itself humming in approval.

Anna stayed close. Chanotedah stayed closer.

Nicholas's confusion did not fade. It grew, but it grew into something with shape. Something he could almost hold.

And the Council waited for him, ancient and expectant, in the heart of a world that had already begun to recognize him.

Soft echoes drifted through the chamber like dust motes suspended in sunlight. Laughter from a moment Nicholas had forgotten brushed his ear, warm and fleeting. A whisper he had never spoken trembled in the air beside him, as if the room were sampling the shape of his unvoiced thoughts. The space felt alive, not in the way a forest breathes or a city hums, but in the way memory itself seems to linger after everyone has gone home. Every emotion ever felt in Nirvana seemed to have left a fingerprint here.

The floor was not solid. It rippled faintly underfoot, taut and responsive, like stepping on the surface of a drum stretched tight. Each step sent a soft vibration outward, and the chamber answered with a subtle shift of light. Nicholas felt as if he were walking across the skin of something ancient and listening.

A man stood in the center, eyes closed, head tilted as though he were hearing a distant choir. His dark hair, streaked with silver, lifted slightly in a breeze Nicholas could not feel. The air around him shimmered with a quiet resonance, as if he were the still point in a room full of echoes. When he opened his eyes, the chamber stilled. The mist paused mid-drift, the floor tightened beneath Nicholas's feet, and even the echoes leaned in.

"You are loud," Chittaswarup said.

Nicholas blinked. "I… what?"

"Your thoughts," he clarified, stepping closer. His voice resonated as a tuning fork struck gently, the sound vibrating through the air in soft concentric waves. "They echo. Strongly."

The ringing in Nicholas's ears spiked. He inhaled sharply and realized it was not sound at all, but a hundred of his own thoughts colliding in the echo-sensitive air. Every fear, every question, every flicker of wonder bounced back at him in faint, overlapping whispers.

Nicholas flushed. Embarrassment hit him like a spark, and the mist around his shoulders pulsed a soft, glowing blue, as if translating his emotion into color.

"Sorry," he muttered.

"Do not apologize." Chittaswarup's smile was small but warm, the kind that made the air settle. "Volume is not a flaw. It is a direction."

He lifted a hand. The air around Nicholas vibrated, not painfully, but like a soft hum brushing against his ribs. The sensation threaded through him, gentle and curious, as if the chamber were tuning itself to his presence. As Nicholas walked deeper into the room, the mist continued to pulse, shifting from pink to blue to silver, leaning subtly toward him, drawn by something he did not understand.

Anna watched him with quiet awe. Chanotedah watched him with a flicker of pride he tried to hide. Bharati watched him with the calm certainty of someone who had expected this.

Nicholas felt the weight of their attention, the weight of the chamber, the weight of his own thoughts echoing back at him. Confusion tightened inside him, but it no longer felt like drowning. It felt like standing in the center of a vast instrument, one that had been waiting for him to touch its strings.

And the Voice of the Council, listening with the patience of centuries, stepped closer.

"Let us see," Chittaswarup said, "what the spring hears when it listens to you."

Chanotedah muttered something under his breath, but Chittaswarup did not turn this time. Instead, he lifted his chin slightly, as if listening to a thread of sound only he could hear.

"It is important to be heard," Chittaswarup said, his voice carrying the calm weight of someone who had spent lifetimes listening to storms and secrets. "But sometimes it is more important to hear what the Continuum is asking."

Nicholas frowned. "The Continuum… asks things?"

Chittaswarup stepped closer, and the air shifted with him. The mist brightened, then dimmed, as if adjusting its breath to match his. "Everything that exists within time leaves a vibration. Every choice, every fear, every hope. The Continuum is the sum of those vibrations. It is not a voice in the way you understand voices. It is a pressure. A pull. A question that repeats until someone answers it."

Nicholas felt the ringing in his ears deepen, threading through his ribs. The chamber leaned closer, listening to the conversation as if it mattered more than the people standing in it.

Chittaswarup's gaze softened. "You are loud because you are new. Your thoughts have not learned to settle. Your emotions have not learned to braid themselves into the rhythm of this place. But loudness is not a flaw. It is a sign that the Continuum hears you clearly."

Nicholas swallowed. "And what am I supposed to hear?"

"That," Chittaswarup said, "is the beginning of your work. To listen without fear. To listen without assuming the meaning. To listen until the noise becomes a pattern."

He lifted a hand, and the air around Nicholas vibrated again, gentle and curious. The mist pulsed in soft colors, leaning toward him as if drawn by something it recognized.

"The Continuum is speaking to you already," Chittaswarup said. "You simply have not learned its language yet."

Nicholas's confusion tightened, but it no longer felt like a wall. It felt like a door he had not opened.

Anna stepped closer, her presence warm at his side. Chanotedah shifted behind him, the spearmint scent sharpening with a protective edge.

Chittaswarup inclined his head, the silver in his hair catching the chamber's shifting light. "Come. There is more to hear."

The room exhaled, and the echoes stirred like leaves in a soft wind.

The next archway opened into a garden that breathed.

Mist curled into vines that unfurled in slow spirals, each tendril moving with the patience of something that had never known hurry. Flowers bloomed in colors Nicholas had no names for, blues that tasted like mint on the back of his tongue, pinks that felt like warm hands pressed gently against his skin, golds that hummed faintly as if remembering a song. Trees rose and fell with the rhythm of breathing, their branches weaving themselves into new shapes as Nicholas watched, as if the garden were thinking aloud.

A woman knelt beside a pool of shimmering liquid, her fingers moving through the mist like a harpist plucking invisible strings. Each motion sent ripples through the garden. Petals shifted. Vines tightened. Colors deepened. The pool brightened in response, its surface reflecting not the ceiling above, but a sky Nicholas had never seen. Her skin glowed like bronze warmed by moonlight. Her eyes were bright copper, reflecting Nicholas back at himself in soft, shifting fragments, as if she saw not one version of him but many.

She looked up and smiled. "Nicholas Hunter. Come closer."

Nicholas stepped forward. The mist parted for him like petals bending toward sunlight, then pulsed again, shifting from pink to blue to silver as he passed. The colors felt like reactions, not decoration, as if the garden were tasting his presence and deciding what to make of him.

"I am Asiza," she said. "I shape the raw matter of Nirvana. I hear that you have already done this without training."

Nicholas flushed. The mist flickered light blue around him, betraying him before he could hide the feeling.

"I did not mean to."

"That is why it matters." She cupped her hands. Mist gathered instantly, swirling into a small sphere that pulsed like a heartbeat. "Try."

Nicholas reached out. The sphere responded before he touched it, stretching, folding, reshaping itself around the shape of his intention. It was like the mist leaned toward his thoughts, eager to become whatever he needed.

It became a tiny wooden robot.

Anna gasped. "Your project from home."

Nicholas's throat tightened. A sensory flash hit him with the force of a memory he had not braced for. His mother's laundry detergent. The creak of the treehouse ladder. His father's laugh echoed from the kitchen. The mist shimmered with the memory, colors rippling outward like a quiet applause.

Asiza nodded. "You shape from memory. From longing. That is powerful."

The garden dimmed slightly, as if agreeing. Leaves folded inward. Flowers bowed their heads. Even the pool stilled, its surface smoothing into a mirror that reflected Nicholas's face with a softness he did not feel inside.

Nicholas held the tiny robot in his hands. It felt warm, as if it remembered being made by him once before. Confusion tightened in his chest. Awe pressed against it. Grief threaded through both.

He did not understand this place. He did not understand himself in it. But the mist leaned toward him again, gentle and curious, as if the world was willing to wait while he learned.

"And dangerous," she added softly.

"Dangerous?" Nicholas echoed.

Asiza touched the surface of the pool. The reflection rippled outward, not like water disturbed by a fingertip, but like a memory being rewritten. The image shifted. His room appeared first, warm and familiar. Then his parents, caught mid-laugh in a moment he had not realized he missed until he saw it. Then the bench he had conjured, rising from pastel mist as if it had always been waiting for him.

"Longing can build," she said. "But it can also trap. You must learn the difference."

The garden responded to her words. Vines tightened. Flowers dimmed. Even the air seemed to draw inward, as if the entire space understood the warning better than Nicholas did.

A flicker of panic crossed Anna's face. The mist around her turned gold and wrapped her shoulders like a protective shawl. She stepped closer to Nicholas without thinking, as if she feared the garden might swallow him whole.

Chanotedah tugged Nicholas's sleeve. "Come on. Before she starts talking in riddles again."

Asiza flicked a strand of mist at him. It struck his forehead with a soft pop.

"Ow."

"That was not a riddle," she said.

Nicholas lingered. The tiny wooden robot sat warm in his palm, pulsing faintly with the memory that had shaped it. The ache of home tugged at him again, sharper this time, as if the memory wanted to pull him backward instead of letting him move forward. The garden sensed it. The colors around him dimmed, the vines leaning in with a quiet, unsettling curiosity.

He took a slow breath. The air tasted of mint and something older, something like the moment before a storm breaks. His chest tightened. He was not sure if he was afraid of losing home or afraid of wanting it too much.

Asiza watched him with copper eyes that reflected every version of him at once. "Be careful with what you miss," she said. "It listens."

Nicholas's pulse jumped. The mist at his feet stirred, as if agreeing.

He closed his fingers around the robot, holding it gently but firmly, and stepped back from the pool. The garden exhaled, the colors brightening again as if releasing him.

He followed the others, but the unease stayed with him, quiet and persistent, like a question he was not ready to answer.

And behind him, the garden watched.

The third archway opened into a training ground carved from motion. Mist formed walls that shifted like living stone, their surfaces rippling with the memory of battles that had never quite happened. Targets appeared and vanished in the corner of Nicholas's vision. Obstacles rose from the ground, held their shape for a breath, then dissolved back into drifting color. The air smelled faintly of iron and storm, the charged scent of a sky deciding whether to break open.

A figure moved through the space with terrifying precision. Every step was a strike. Every breath was a calculation. Every motion dissolved a threat before it fully formed. The mist reacted to her like a living thing, tightening when she advanced, loosening when she paused, as if it recognized her authority and adjusted itself accordingly.

When she turned, the mist recoiled slightly, as if respecting her.

Antonia.

Her hair was shaved close along the sides, but the center rose in a long, disciplined mohawk that swept back into a tight knot at the base of her skull. It was not a style chosen for flair. It was a declaration of control; every strand pulled into place with the precision of someone who treated even their appearance as a weapon. She stood nearly five-foot ten, her posture so exact it added another inch of authority. Her skin had a warm, leathered resilience to it, the kind earned by someone who had lived in harsh light long enough for it to leave its mark. It caught the glow of the training ground and turned it into something fierce. Her cheekbones were sharp, her jaw set with the quiet certainty of someone carved by discipline rather than ease. Her eyes were sharp and assessing, the kind that missed nothing and forgave even less. When she looked at Nicholas, it felt as though she had already calculated every danger in the room, including him.

"You brought the Equal here without escort?" she said. Her voice was clipped, her cadence half a beat off, as if she spoke in a rhythm the rest of the world had not learned.

Chanotedah groaned. "Here we go."

As Antonia strode forward, the ground firmed beneath her feet. The mist solidified in deference, becoming stone where she stepped. The air thickened, charged with a quiet electricity that made Nicholas's skin prickle. His heartbeat synced with the rhythm of the room, fast, then faster, as if the training ground itself had decided to test him.

Antonia stopped a few paces away. She did not soften. She did not smile. She looked at him the way a seasoned soldier looks at a recruit who might be a liability or a miracle, and she had not yet decided which.

Her gaze flicked to Anna, then to Chanotedah, then back to Nicholas. "He is not ready for this space," she said. "And this space is not ready for him."

Nicholas swallowed. The mist at his feet stirred, uncertain.

Antonia's eyes narrowed. "Control your resonance," she said. "Or it will control you."

She lifted one hand, fingers slicing through the air with the precision of a blade. The mist obeyed instantly. It coiled upward, tightening into a long, straight column that hardened as it rose. In the space of a breath, a stave formed in her grip, its surface etched with faint, shifting lines that looked like the memory of lightning.

Without breaking eye contact, she drove the stave into the stone floor.

The impact rang through the training ground. The mist walls shuddered. Targets flickered out of existence. Even the air seemed to recoil, as if the room itself recognized the command embedded in the sound.

Nicholas flinched. The mist around his ankles rippled in a startled wave.

Antonia did not soften. She leaned slightly on the stave, posture exact, gaze sharp enough to cut through the haze gathering in Nicholas's mind. "This place listens to you," she said. "Even when you do not mean to speak. That is dangerous. For you. For everyone."

The stave hummed faintly, a low vibration that traveled through the floor and into Nicholas's bones. It felt like a warning. It felt like a promise.

Chanotedah shifted behind him, the spearmint scent sharpening. Anna stepped closer, her presence steady but tense.

Antonia's voice stayed clipped, controlled. "If you cannot steady yourself, the ground will steady you. The mist will steady you. I will steady you."

She pulled the stave free with a clean, practiced motion. The mist at its tip curled like smoke, then it stilled.

Nicholas's heartbeat thudded in his ears. The room felt too bright, too sharp, too aware of him. He tried to breathe, but the air tasted like storm metal and expectation.

Antonia watched him, unreadable. "Again," she said. "This time, do not let the room answer before you do."

And the training ground waited, holding its breath with her.

The words landed like a command, not a warning. The training ground responded, the walls tightening their shape, the air sharpening with expectation.

Nicholas felt the pressure of it, the weight of her attention, the sense that she could dismantle him with a single sentence if she chose. She was jagged with edges and unyielding lines; a person carved from necessity rather than comfort.

And yet, beneath the steel, there was something else. A flicker of recognition. A faint, buried note of someone who had seen too much and survived it. Someone who understood danger because she had lived inside it.

Nicholas did not know that. But the room did. And it held its breath.

Antonia did not answer immediately. Instead, she pivoted on the ball of her foot in a clean, controlled spin, the kind that revealed both training and instinct. The mist reacted at once, pulling back from her rotation as if wary of being cut by the precision of her movement. When she stopped, the stave in her hand hummed with the leftover momentum, and her attention locked onto Chanotedah and Anna with the force of a command.

"If Rhet senses him again," she said, her voice sharp as a snapped branch, "the consequences will not wait for your optimism."

Anna's gold resonance flared. It rose from her shoulders like heat from a forge, brightening with each word Antonia spoke. "He will not," Anna said, steady but burning.

Antonia's gaze flicked to her. The shift was small, but the air tightened. "You cannot promise that."

The gold mist sharpened. It wrapped closer to Anna, no longer a shawl but a mantle. Nicholas felt it before he saw it, a warm pressure brushing against his own resonance.

He stepped back. The mist around him tightened, pulsing silver-blue in a nervous rhythm.

"I am… sorry?"

Antonia did not look at him. Her focus stayed on Anna and Chanotedah, as if they were the ones who needed correction. "Do not teach him to apologize for fear," she said. "Fear is not weakness. It is information."

Anna's gold rose higher. "He is not afraid of you."

The training ground responded. The mist walls stiffened. The air thickened. The floor beneath Nicholas's feet grew more solid, as if bracing for impact.

Chanotedah stepped forward, placing himself between Nicholas and the rising tension. "Antonia," he said, voice low. "Dial it back."

She ignored him. Her eyes stayed on Anna, assessing, measuring, deciding. "You shield him too quickly."

"And you push him too hard," Anna said. The gold mist climbed higher, curling like protective wings. Nicholas's silver-blue answered instinctively, reaching toward hers. The two colors touched, then braided together in a thin, shimmering strand that hovered between them.

Antonia's gaze dropped to the braid. For the first time, something flickered across her face. Not softness. Not approval. Recognition. The kind that carried weight.

Nicholas's stomach dropped.

Antonia straightened, the stave steady in her hand. "He needs the truth," she said. "All of it."

Chanotedah grabbed Nicholas's arm, pulling him back before the mist could tighten further. "And he will get it," he said. "Later. Preferably when he is not about to faint."

The braided mist trembled, then slowly unraveled, drifting back into gold and silver, blue. The training ground exhaled, the walls loosening their shape.

Antonia watched the colors separately, her expression unreadable. The stave dimmed in her hand.

Nicholas felt the echo of the braid in his chest, a strange warmth that did not belong to fear alone.

And Antonia, sharp as a blade and twice as unforgiving, finally looked at him again.

Antonia crossed her arms. "He looks like he is about to faint now."

Nicholas was about to faint.

"Next!" Chanotedah said loudly.

The final archway opened into a shoreline that breathed sunlight.

Warm sand stretched out beneath the sky, the color of calm water. A teak wood shack rested near the edge of the trees, its boards weathered to a soft silver, the door hanging open as if waiting for someone to wander in. Loons called across a wide lake, their voices long and echoing. Dragonflies drifted over the surface in lazy arcs, their wings catching the light like tiny pieces of glass.

Nicholas stepped forward, and the scent hit him first. Chocolate and strawberries. Sweet, warm, familiar in a way he could not place. The mist parted around his ankles, turning soft and pale, as if the entire space had lowered its voice.

A blond woman rose from a low hammock strung between two posts of the shack. Her hair was long, sun-kissed, wavy and frizzy in a way that suggested she had never tried to tame it. Most of it was pulled into a loose ponytail that had clearly been tied without a mirror. She wore a turquoise tank top and linen pants rolled to her calves. Her feet were bare, toes sunk into the sand like she belonged to it.

When she moved, the air shifted. Nicholas smelled the beach his parents used to take him to. Salt. Sun. That sweet scent he could never name.

She smiled, soft and bright. "Hello, Nicholas," she said, her voice warm as a tide rolling in. "I am Melusine."

Something inside him shifted. Subtle. A single note plucked in the center of his chest, searching for harmony. The mist trembled. His heart skipped. The light along the water flickered in perfect sync.

Anna inhaled sharply beside him. Nicholas felt her gold resonance stir, then tug toward his own. A thin thread of something unspoken pulled between them, warm and strange.

Melusine stepped closer, her presence gentle but sure. "You carry a storm inside you," she said. "Most new jumpers do. But yours is loud."

Nicholas flushed. The mist around him shivered, silver-blue and uncertain.

"Sorry."

“No need to apologize.” She crouched to pick up a smooth stone, tossing it lightly from hand to hand. “Storms are not bad. They just need a place to land.”

She lifted her palm. The mist stirred, gathering like a breath held too long. Dragonflies paused mid-flight. The lake stilled. Even the loons quieted, as if waiting for her to finish the thought.

Nicholas felt the tug again. A soft harmonic pull. Anna felt it too. Their colors brushed, then drifted apart before either of them could understand what had happened.

Melusine watched them with a knowing tilt of her head, her smile widening just a little. Not strict. Not solemn. More like an older sister who had seen this moment before and was trying not to rush it.

“Come on,” she said, stepping back toward the water. “Let us see what your storm wants to say.”

And the beach, warm and bright and impossibly familiar, leaned in to listen.

“Close your eyes,” she said.

Nicholas hesitated, then obeyed. The sand warmed his feet. The lake breathed in slow, steady ripples. Somewhere across the water, a loon called, its voice long and low.

“Listen,” Melusine whispered. “Not with your ears. With the quiet part of you. The part that knows before you think.”

Nicholas tried. At first, he heard nothing but his own heartbeat, too fast and too loud, thudding against the inside of his ribs. The scent of chocolate and strawberries drifted past him, soft and grounding.

Then something shifted.

A soft hum. A gentle pulse. The mist around him breathed with him, matched him, waiting for him.

Melusine’s voice floated through the calm. “Good. You found it.”

Nicholas opened his eyes. The lake shimmered. The dragonflies hovered in a slow, suspended dance. “Found what?”

“The stillness beneath the noise,” she said.

The mist settled. The shoreline quieted. A soft glow formed around Nicholas as the storm inside him folded into a single, steady breath. The sand beneath his feet felt firmer, as if the beach itself approved.

“It will keep you steady when the mist wants to follow your fear instead of your intention.”

Chanotedah leaned in and whispered, “She is the emotional compass of the Council. Do not let the beach vibes fool you. She is scary good at reading people.”

Melusine smiled without looking at him. “I heard that.”

Chanotedah winced. Nicholas almost laughed. The sound fluttered into the air and dissolved like a spark.

Melusine's gaze returned to him, warm and steady. "You will learn to listen, Nicholas. To the mist. To yourself. To the spaces between."

Nicholas nodded, though he was not sure he understood. Something tugged inside him again, soft and harmonic, like a note searching for its chord. Anna shifted beside him, her gold resonance brushing his silver-blue for a moment before drifting apart. She felt it too. Neither of them had words for it.

"That is alright," Melusine said gently. "Understanding comes later. Listening comes first."

She stepped back toward the water, her linen pants brushing the sand, her bare feet sinking into the warm grains. The turquoise tank top she wore caught the sunlight and rippled like a wave retreating from shore.

"Go on," she said. "The others are waiting."

Nicholas felt the faint hum in his chest again as he turned to leave. Soft. Curious. Unfinished. A single note waiting for its chord.

And somewhere in the mist, a second note answered. Faint. Harmonic. The beginning of something larger.

Chapter 9.5 Interlude

The fracture came without warning.

One moment, the air in the abandoned rail yard was still. Cold metal. Rusted tracks. The faint hum of a timeline that had long since forgotten it existed. Shadows stretched long and thin across the gravel, bending toward Rhet as if pulled by an unseen tide. Even the rails vibrated in a faint, uneven rhythm, like a heartbeat trying to remember its pattern.

Rhet stood at the center of it all, his coat drifting around him like smoke, his jagged-glass eye catching the dying light in sharp, fractured glints. The air thinned near him. The ground beneath him felt brittle, stretched too tight, as if the timeline had been pulled to its limit and was waiting for someone to snap it.

His hoppers circled the perimeter, restless shadows in human shape. They were never fully still. Their bodies twitched and flickered, vibrating with the unstable energy that kept them tethered to him. Their movements synced in strange, glitching pulses, a hive-mind rhythm that shifted with their mood. They watched him the way wolves watch a storm, wary and reverent and hungry.

Rhet lifted his head.

Something in the Continuum shifted.

A tremor rolled through the air, subtle at first, then sharper. A pressure behind his ribs. A tightening in the world around him. A note struck in the center of the spring, so faint that any other being would have missed it. But Rhet felt it. He felt it before the hoppers did, before the rails shivered, before the shadows recoiled.

The ripple hit him like a blow.

Rhet buckled. His knees slammed into the gravel, hands clawing at the rusted tracks as the world warped around him. The air thickened, bending inward, as if the spring itself had inhaled sharply. The sky flickered. The shadows twisted. A faint blue-silver shimmer flashed across the horizon, bright and impossible, then vanished as quickly as it came.

Nicholas's resonance.

Rhet dragged in a ragged breath. The fracture inside him answered the call, sharp and hungry.

The hoppers froze. Their heads snapped toward the sky in perfect unison, bodies trembling with the aftershock of the signal. The rail yard fell silent, the kind of silence that feels like the world holding its breath.

Rhet lifted his face from the gravel. His jagged eye glowed with a fractured light, shards of color flickering in its depths.

"He is awake," he whispered.

The fracture answered with a low, resonant hum, and the world around him shivered.

The hoppers recoiled at once, chittering in alarm. Their bodies glitched in unison, silhouettes stuttering like broken film caught between frames. The air around them crackled with static, the kind that prickles along the spine before a storm breaks.

"Master?" one hissed. Its voice scraped like metal dragged across stone, layered with the whispers of the others. "What is that?"

Rhet did not answer. He could not.

The resonance tore through him again. Not pain. Something deeper. A recognition that did not belong to memory, yet felt older than anything he had lived. A presence rising in the center of the spring, bright and steady and unbearably familiar. The Equal. Awakened.

Rhet's breath hitched. His jagged eye flickered, shards of fractured light scattering across the gravel. For a heartbeat, another face layered itself over the present. An Equal from centuries past. The one who had nearly undone him. The one he had failed to break.

"No," he whispered, voice raw. "Not yet. Not now."

The hoppers crept closer, their forms glitching at the edges. One reached toward him, hesitant, devotion and fear warring in its fractured silhouette. Its limbs twitched, trying to hold a shape that would not stay still.

Rhet snarled. The sound was low and feral, pulled from a place inside him that had never healed. The hopper jerked back, limbs folding in on themselves like a collapsing shadow. The others skittered away, their outlines flickering in frantic pulses.

The resonance surged again.

This time it was not a tremor. It was a wave.

It rolled through the yard with the force of a collapsing timeline. The rusted rails bent. The air warped. The hoppers shrieked in distortion, their bodies scattering like torn reflections. The sky flickered between dusk and midnight, unable to decide which moment it belonged to. Microfractures spidered through the air, glowing with brief, violent light before sealing shut.

Rhet forced himself upright. Nicholas's resonance still echoed across the sky, faint but unmistakable.

The Equal lived.

Nicholas's resonance had just confirmed it.

He had felt it once before, centuries ago, when the last Equal had risen. When the spring had steadied. When his plans had nearly unraveled. When the prophecy had whispered its warning through the coils of time. But this was different. Stronger. Younger. Untrained. Uncontrolled. A dangerous combination.

Rhet's lips curled into a slow, trembling smile.

"So," he murmured, voice cracking like ice under pressure. "The child has met the Council."

The hoppers stilled. Their heads tilted in eerie unison, bodies flickering as if caught between shapes. One whispered "Equal..." before dissolving into a burst of static that drifted away like ash.

Rhet rose fully, his coat settled around him like a shadow reclaiming its shape. The jagged eye gleamed with fractured light, refracting the last remnants of Nicholas's resonance across the gravel in thin, trembling lines.

"He does not know what he is," Rhet said. "He does not know what he can do."

The hoppers hissed in agreement, their voices overlapping in a chorus of distortion that made the air ripple.

"And the Council..." Rhet's smile widened, sharp and hungry. "They think they can shape him. Control him. Bind him."

He stepped forward, boots crunching on gravel. The shadows around him twisted into unnatural forms, bending toward his voice as if listening for instruction.

"They forget," he whispered, "that the spring does not choose lightly."

The air crackled. The last remnants of the resonance faded into a low, trembling hum. A faint echo vibrated through the Continuum, distant but unmistakable. Nicholas's second note. Soft. Unsteady. Searching.

"Find him," he said softly.

The hoppers scattered instantly. Their bodies unraveled into streaks of shadow that slipped between the cracks of the timeline, leaving behind static footprints that evaporated in the air. The rail yard fell quiet again, settling back into its abandoned stillness. But inside Rhet, the tremor lingered. A warning. A promise. A beginning.

He closed his eyes, letting the last pulse of the resonance settle into his bones.

"Equal," he whispered, almost reverent. "Let us see what you become."

The world around him held its breath.

And the fracture inside him smiled.

Chapter 10

Nicholas woke from his nap feeling as though he had slept for a century. His body was heavy, his mind fogged, but the warmth spilling through the window coaxed him gently back into himself. Sunlight pooled across the floorboards in soft gold, yet today the light carried a faint tremor, a subtle shiver that made the shadows quiver at the edges.

He took a slow breath. The air tasted like home.

A hint of his mother's laundry soap drifted through the room, warm and clean, braided with the soft sweetness of freshly baked chocolate chip cookies. The combination hit him square in the chest. Behind it all, the ringing in his ears hummed quietly, ever present now, like a distant tuning fork vibrating in the back of his skull.

It felt real. Comforting. Safe. But he knew better. Everything in this room, the sunlight, the breeze, the smell of home, was an illusion shaped from the mist. A memory of home, not home itself.

He sat up slowly, rubbing his eyes. The silence pressed in around him, thick and unfamiliar. He never thought he would miss his mother yelling up the stairs that he was late for school. Now the absence of her voice felt like a hollow carved into his chest.

Then a phantom echo drifted through the room.

"Nicholas! Breakfast!"

His mother's voice. Soft. Warm. Impossible.

A pulse of light blue rippled through the room, rolling across the walls like a breath of color. The mist shivered in response.

Nicholas swallowed hard. "Mom…"

He wondered where Anna was. And Chanotedah. He never imagined he would get used to old scruff face hanging around, but the little guy had grown on him.

A knock sounded at the door. Not Anna's light tap. Not Chanotedah's impatient rattle.

"Come in," Nicholas called, tugging a T-shirt over his head.

The door cracked open. Chase stepped inside.

Nicholas blinked. He had not seen Chase since the night he arrived in Nirvana, half-conscious and terrified, clinging to the last threads of his old life. Chase had been the first steady thing in that moment, a quiet presence in the chaos. Seeing him now felt like a memory resurfacing.

"Hey, Nicholas," Chase said. "How are you doing?"

His voice was calm, but something beneath it vibrated with a quiet tension. As he crossed the room, the mist shifted, settling in a way Nicholas had not seen before. Calming. Aligning. A phantom tick-tick-tick echoed faintly through the room, the unmistakable rhythm of the mantle clock from Nicholas's house. The scent of peppermints drifted in with Chase, subtle but unmistakable.

Nicholas's chest tightened. The ringing in his ears softened, as if adjusting to Chase's presence.

Chase sat at the desk near the foot of the bed, posture careful, almost apologetic. "I heard I missed some fireworks after your meeting," he said. "I am sorry all of this was dumped on you. We did not do a particularly good job preparing you."

Nicholas studied him. There was something strange about the way the room responded to Chase. The mist leaned toward him, not in fear or obedience, but in something Nicholas could only interpret as recognition.

A faint harmonic tug pulled at Nicholas's chest, the same one he had felt in Melusine's presence. Softer here. Quieter. But real.

Chase looked up, and for a moment their eyes met. Something passed between them, a flicker of familiarity that did not belong to memory. A resonance brushing resonance. A thread pulled taut, then released.

Nicholas looked away first, heart thudding.

He did not understand it. Chase did not seem to either.

And it waited.

Nicholas huffed. "Yeah, well, none of it makes sense. Maybe it never will. Why did you disappear? You promised my parents you would protect me, then you were gone."

Chase nodded, accepting the sting without flinching. "We needed to learn what Rhet was planning. I thought I could head him off."

"And…?"

"As near as I can tell," Chase said, leaning forward, "you scared him in the clock shop. You were not supposed to be there, and we did not know he would be either. But your gift is accelerating faster than Bharati, or I expected. It took us all by surprise."

Nicholas swallowed. "So, what now?"

"Now," Chase said gently, "we work together. We figure out what Rhet wants, how he plans to stop time, and until then, you train. You learn control. I know you would rather be playing baseball or fishing, but you can do this."

There was something in Chase's voice, a mix of humility and regret and quiet understanding, which eased the tightness in Nicholas's chest. Chase was the only one who talked about time in minutes and years instead of coils and springs and echoes. It made Nicholas feel less alone, as if someone still remembered the world he came from.

The mist around Chase settled into a soft alignment, like gears clicking into place.

"Chase… Can I ask you something?"

"Anything."

"When did you find out you were a jumper?"

Chase smiled, but it was a sad smile, softened by memory. "About your age. Feels like a lifetime ago. I was an apprentice in a clockmaker's shop in Boston. Before the war."

Nicholas's eyes widened. "You mean… colonial America? You saw battles? History?"

"It was not as romantic as it sounds," Chase said. "There was no understanding of ADHD. And anyone who claimed to see the future was tried as a witch. The clockmaker kept me close. Taught me to keep quiet. Then one day, I had a vision so strong it slowed time in the shop. Just the shop."

He paused, the memory settling over him like dust from a long-collapsed building. His voice softened. "He was the first person who ever believed I was not broken. Back then, people did not have words for what I could do. They called it witchcraft. Madness. Possession. But he saw something else. He said I had a mind that ran ahead of time."

Nicholas felt the words settle into him. Not just the story, but the tone beneath it. A quiet ache. A familiarity he could not explain. The ringing in his ears softened again, adjusting to Chase's cadence as if it recognized it.

The mist leaned toward both of them now, drawn by something neither boy understood. This time the sensation in Nicholas's chest deepened, warmer and more immediate than before, like an invisible thread drawing taut between them.

Chase's attention shifted toward Nicholas. The instant their gazes crossed, something stirred between them. Not memory. Not recognition. Something older, threaded through the spring.

As Chase spoke, the mist behind him shimmered faintly, forming the outline of gears and cogs and brass tools. The shapes drifted in and out of focus, as if the memory itself had weight. The scent of oil and metal threaded through the room, warm and familiar, like a workshop that had been lived in for years.

"That is when he gave me a special watch," Chase continued. "Showed me how to use it. Brought me here. I learned everything you will learn. And since then, I have spent my life in timelines finding kids like you."

Nicholas's chest tightened. Something in the air shifted, a soft pull in the center of his ribs that felt like recognition without memory.

"He sounds kind," Nicholas said quietly.

"He was," Chase replied. His voice softened, carrying a grief that had settled into him long ago. "Kinder than I deserved. When he died, I promised myself I would do for others what he did for me. Find the ones who did not fit. The ones who saw too much. The ones who felt time tugging at them like a loose thread."

He gave Nicholas a small, sad smile. "Kids exactly like you."

Nicholas frowned. "But the Council is young. How could they have trained you? And how are you older if time does not affect you here?"

Chase chuckled softly. "Time does not affect you in Nirvana. But I have lived in timelines, sometimes a year, sometimes ten. Every minute out there ages me. When I return, I stop aging until I leave again."

Nicholas nodded slowly. It was the first explanation that made sense. The mist around them pulsed in quiet agreement, as if pleased that something had finally clicked into place.

Chase cleared his throat. "Anyway. I did not disappear because I did not care. I disappeared because I cared too much. I wanted to stop Rhet before he ever got near you."

Nicholas nodded again, but this time the motion carried weight. "Thank you… for telling me."

Chase smiled. "You deserved to know."

The mist shifted once more, drifting toward Chase in a slow, deliberate curl. It wrapped around him like a memory recognizing its source, then extended toward Nicholas, forming a faint bridge of pale blue light between them. Nicholas felt the tug again, subtle and warm, like a thread tying itself to something he could not name.

Chase felt it too. His breath caught for a moment, barely noticeable

Nicholas looked down at his hands, unsure why his chest felt tight and steady at the same time. Chase watched him with a quiet understanding that did not belong to strangers or mentors or even friends. It was older than that. Deeper. Something older than Nicholas understood connected them.

Neither of them spoke.

The mist filled the silence, humming softly around a truth neither of them was ready to name.

And it waited.

And that was when the door swung open.

A pixie stood in the doorway holding a tray piled high with food. The mist behind her brightened instantly into soft pinks and yellows.

Nicholas jumped. "What… who are you? Where's Chanotedah?"

"My name is Rosette," she said brightly. She was barely four feet tall, wearing a white dress decorated with colorful ribbons that fluttered as she moved. Her wavy brown hair was pinned back with a gold comb shaped like a tiny sun. She looked like someone's kid sister playing dress-up, except the air around her shimmered with a faint, glittering aura. "Chanotedah asked us to bring your meals today. He said something about a meeting with the High Council."

Before Nicholas could respond, Anna appeared behind her, eyes wide with disbelief. "Rosette. What are you doing here? You know you are not supposed to be around Nicholas. What did you do with Chanotedah?"

Rosette winced, her wings flickering into view for a moment before settling again. "I am sorry, Miss Anna. We heard the new jumper was super cute, and I wanted to see for myself. I put a spell on Chanotedah and delivered the Viator's lunch to him. I did not think it would hurt anything."

Anna's jaw dropped. "You put a spell on Chanotedah?"

Rosette perked up. "Only a little. He is napping. Very peaceful. Drooling, actually. It was adorable."

Nicholas stared. The mist around Rosette pulsed with tiny bursts of color, each one shaped like a flower petal or a spark of light. Pixie magic. It felt different from the Council's resonance, lighter and more chaotic, as if it had been woven from laughter and mischief instead of discipline.

Anna pointed to the door. "Out. Now."

Rosette trudged toward the exit, wings tucked, shoulders slumped. Then she spun with a grin so bright it made the mist ripple. "He is super cute. Totally worth it."

Her wings burst open in a flash of iridescent color, and she zipped down the hallway, leaving behind a trail of glittering mist that immediately tried to rearrange itself into heart shapes. The hearts popped like soap bubbles, more violently near Anna, whose oriole wings flickered beneath her skin in irritation.

Nicholas's face flushed crimson. "Did she just…?"

"Yes," Anna said, rubbing her temples. "And no, we are not talking about it."

Chase coughed into his fist to hide a laugh, but the mist betrayed him. It shimmered with a soft peppermint glow, the same scent that always followed him, and Nicholas felt a faint tug in his chest again, subtle and warm.

Anna shot Chase a look. "Do not encourage her."

"I would never," Chase said, though his eyes sparkled with barely contained amusement.

The mist settled again, but not completely. A few stubborn sparkles drifted near the ceiling, refusing to dissipate, as if Rosette's magic had left fingerprints on the air.

Nicholas exhaled slowly, trying to steady himself. "Are all pixies like that?"

Anna groaned. "Worse. Rosette is one of the responsible ones."

Chase nodded. "Pixies are drawn to strong resonance. They can sense it before anyone else. They are harmless, mostly, but they love chaos. And they love new jumpers."

Nicholas swallowed. "Great."

The mist pulsed once, soft and amused.

And somewhere deep in the Continuum, something else pulsed back.

But something stranger, and larger, was beginning.

Chase stepped forward again, clearly trying to smooth the tension still lingering in the room. Anna's shoulders were pulled tight, her feathers visibly ruffled beneath her skin, and the mist still sparkled with the remnants of Rosette's mischief. Chase's presence steadied it. The sparkles dimmed. The air settled.

"Nicholas," he said gently, "I cannot stay much longer. But there is something I need to give you."

He reached into the inner pocket of his coat and pulled out a small wooden box. The grain was dark and polished, edges worn smooth by years of being carried. Chase held it with a kind of reverence, as though the box itself carried a history only he could feel.

"I made this for you when we first identified you as a Viator," he said. "I have carried it with me ever since, waiting for the day I could give it to you."

He placed the box in Nicholas's hands.

The moment Nicholas touched it, the mist shifted. The Regulatori pulsed beneath his fingers. Nicholas opened the box with the bright, unguarded excitement of a kid on Christmas morning.

Nestled in velvet lay a gold pocket watch. Elegant. Weighty. Gleaming softly in the conjured sunlight. He lifted it carefully.

The Regulatori pulsed once, silver-platinum light blooming beneath his fingers. The beveled glass shimmered, revealing a swirl of silver mist inside that pulsed to Nicholas's heartbeat, a half-beat off, like a second rhythm waiting to align.

His excitement faltered into confusion. "Chase… there is nothing on it."

Chase smiled. "It is not a normal watch. It is a Regulatori. A tool. A powerful one. The clockmaker who took me in gave me mine when I first came to Nirvana. I've made one for every Viator I've brought here since. But yours… yours is special."

Nicholas did not know what to say. The mist around him thickened, warm and expectant, as if waiting for his reaction. Instead of speaking, he crossed the room and wrapped his arms around Chase in a tight, earnest hug.

Chase froze for a heartbeat, surprised. Then he returned the embrace with a quiet steadiness that felt older than either of them. The mist gathered around them, swirling softly. A faint blue-gold shimmer rippled through the air, stabilizing the room for a moment.

"Thank you," Nicholas whispered. "I am sure I will use it a lot."

Chase's hand rested briefly on the back of Nicholas's shoulder. "You will."

A soft harmonic thread lingered between them, unnoticed.

It always did.

A tear gathered in the corner of Chase's eye. It had been a long time since anyone had held onto him like that. Longer still since he had let himself feel it.

After a breath, he gently pulled away.

"I need to get back to my shop," he said, clearing his throat. "See if I can find anything more about Rhet." He started toward the door, then paused and looked back. "I will be back soon. Listen to the Council. Practice. You can do this."

"Okay, Chase."

As Chase slipped out, the light outside the window dimmed, as though clouds drifted across a sun that did not truly exist. The room felt different without him, quieter in a way Nicholas could not explain. The mist settled, but not fully. It hovered near the door, as if reluctant to let him go.

Anna stepped closer, looping an arm around Nicholas's shoulders. "Nicky… cheer up. Chase will be back. It is going to be all right."

Nicholas looked down at the Regulatori in his hand. A small smile tugged at his lips, but it carried an edge this time. A spark of something sharper. Something restless.

Something like readiness stirred inside him. And something else too, tucked beneath it. A flicker of irritation. A quiet, simmering pressure that made the air feel too tight around him.

"Okay," he said, grabbing the sandwich from the tray and taking a massive bite. "Let's get moving. If I am stuck with this gift, I might as well learn how to use it before someone else tries to kill me."

Anna blinked. "That is… not the attitude I expected."

Nicholas shrugged, crumbs falling from his mouth as he marched toward the door. "Yeah, well. Turns out almost dying is a great motivator."

Anna let out a breath she did not realize she had been holding. This was not the turnaround she expected, but it was better. Much better. Even if it came with a new sharpness in his voice, a new tension in the way he held himself.

She watched him go, wondering what Chase had said to him. Wondering why the mist still hummed faintly in the space Chase had left behind. Wondering why Nicholas's resonance felt different now, brighter and heavier at the same time.

Something had shifted.

Anna led Nicholas out of the room and into the corridor of mist, which shifted around them like a living hallway. Today it felt calmer, pale blues and soft greens drifting in slow curls, but Nicholas sensed something underneath it, a faint tremor like a held breath waiting for release.

The corridor pulsed with Nicholas's heartbeat. On every half-beat, gray streaks flashed across the walls. He couldn't shake the feeling that the mist was listening more closely than before.

Nicholas clutched the Regulatori, feeling its weight settle into his palm as though it belonged there. The metal was cool beneath his fingers.

Anna noticed him turning it over. "It is beautiful," she murmured, her voice softened by something like awe.

"Chase said it is special," Nicholas replied. "But he did not say why."

"He would not," Anna said. "Regulatori choose how much they reveal. They are temperamental."

Nicholas raised an eyebrow. "It is a watch."

Anna smirked and gave him a tiny shove. "You keep thinking that."

He rolled his eyes, but the sarcasm was a thin cover for the tension humming beneath his skin. The corridor felt too close, the air too charged.

They walked deeper into the mist corridor, colors shifting around them like drifting watercolor. Nicholas kept glancing at the Regulatori, half expecting instructions or some hidden message. It remained silent.

"Anna," he said finally, "what did Chase mean when he said my gift is accelerating? Why is that happening?"

Anna hesitated. Not the casual kind, but the kind that meant she was choosing her words with surgical precision. Her wings flickered faintly beneath her skin, a soft gold shimmer that pulsed in time with the corridor.

"Because you are not like other jumpers."

"That is not an answer."

"I know." She exhaled, shoulders dropping. "Most jumpers develop slowly. They see flashes, echoes, maybe a ripple or two. But you… You shaped the mist without training. You created a path. A room. A field. And earlier today, you nearly turned half of Nirvana into a volcanic wasteland."

Nicholas winced. "Sorry."

"It is not about being sorry," Anna said. "It is about understanding what that means."

She stopped walking and turned toward him. The mist around her brightened, gold rising from her shoulders like a soft halo. Nicholas felt the tug again, that strange harmonic pull he had felt with Melusine, but stronger now. Closer. It brushed against his chest, warm and steady, and the Regulatori pulsed in response.

Anna noticed. Her eyes widened slightly, not in fear, but in recognition. The gold around her shimmered, reaching toward the silver-blue gathering around Nicholas.

"You felt that too," Nicholas said quietly.

Anna swallowed. "It is stronger today. Stronger since you accepted what you are."

Nicholas tried to laugh it off. "Great. So now I am a walking mood ring."

Anna's lips twitched. "More like a tuning fork."

"Fantastic. That sounds so much better."

But beneath the sarcasm, something in him tightened. The corridor pulsed again, the gray streaks brightening in time with his heartbeat. Anna stepped closer, her presence steadying the air around them.

"Nicky," she said softly, "whatever is happening… You are not facing it alone."

The harmonic tug pulsed again, stronger this time, threading between them like a note searching for its chord.

They stepped into a wider clearing of mist, a circular space where the ground firmed into something like marble, though it shimmered faintly as if remembering it was mist. A few other jumpers drifted through, their outlines blurring at the edges like reflections in rippling water. Their movements were soft, cautious, almost reverent.

As Nicholas passed, their forms flickered with awe, some with fear. The mist leaned subtly toward him, drawn by the resonance clinging to him like a second skin. A few jumpers paused mid-stride, their colors shifting in subtle ripples. One bowed his head without realizing he had done it. Another stepped back, eyes wide, as if standing too close might burn.

Nicholas watched them, fascinated and unsettled. "Do they know who I am?"

Anna nodded. "Everyone knows. The Equal is not exactly a small title."

Nicholas swallowed. "Do they expect something from me?"

"Some do," Anna admitted. "Some are scared. Some are hopeful. Some think you will fix everything. Some think you will break everything."

Nicholas stopped walking. "And what do you think?"

Anna turned to him, her expression softening in a way that made the mist around them glow a little warmer. "I think you are still Nicholas. And that is enough."

A low hum vibrated through the air, faint but unmistakable. The mist flickered, colors shifting from blue to violet to a sickly gray before stabilizing again. The ground beneath them trembled, just slightly, like a breath caught in the throat of the world.

Anna stiffened. "There it is again."

Nicholas looked around. "What was that?"

"A fracture," she said. "A small one. They have been happening all morning."

"Because of Rhet?"

"Because of something he is doing," Anna corrected. "He is pushing against the boundaries of Nirvana. Testing them. Trying to find a way in."

A chill crawled up Nicholas's spine. "Can he?"

"Not yet," Anna said. "But the Council is worried. And when the Council worries, everyone worries."

Nicholas looked down at the Regulatori again. It pulsed, silver-platinum light flashing once. The mist around it tightened, as if bracing.

A jagged streak of gray tore through the air above them, then vanished. The sound it left behind was a faint ringing, like a crack forming in glass.

Nicholas's pulse quickened. "That was not small."

"No," Anna whispered. "It was not."

They exchanged a look, fear and determination and something unspoken passing between them. The harmonic tug pulsed again, threading between their resonances, binding them for a moment before drifting apart.

Nicholas tightened his grip on the Regulatori. "Okay," he said quietly. "I want to learn. I want to help. Show me where to start."

Anna's smile was proud, relieved, and a little sad. "Come on. Bharati is waiting."

They stepped forward together, the mist parting before them like a curtain. The corridor brightened, then dimmed, as if adjusting to their combined resonance.

And somewhere far beyond the shifting colors, something watched. Something patient. Something hungry. Waiting for its moment to strike.

CHAPTER 11

The path to the Council chambers curved through a stretch of open mist that slowly resolved into a wide training field. As the shapes solidified, a faint shimmer rippled through the air—the mist pulsing in a soft light-blue glow. A subtle tremor ran beneath Nicholas's feet, and a thin gray streak flickered through the mist like a hairline crack before vanishing.

Laughter, shouts, and the thud of feet echoed across the space. Nicholas slowed, drawn toward the sound like a moth to a porch light.

A dozen students, all roughly his age, darted across the field in a fast-paced game that looked like dodgeball... if dodgeball had been invented by ancient gods with a flair for chaos.

Instead of rubber balls, the players hurled gleaming spheres the size of softballs. Silver ones streaked through the air like comets. Gold ones pulsed with a faint inner glow. Nicholas winced just imagining the impact.

One of the silver spheres struck a player square in the chest.

A burst of colored smoke exploded around them—and when it cleared, the player was gone.

Vanished.

Nicholas's jaw dropped. "What are they doing?"

"That, junior," Chanotedah said, barely glancing over, "is Viatori training. Evanidus and Suppressio spheres. Preparation for battle situations."

Nicholas took a step toward the field, mesmerized. A phantom echo of laughter, not from the field, but from his old school, brushed past him. The mist around his legs warmed, leaning toward him, and a soft pulse of light blue radiated outward as longing tightened in his chest.

Anna caught the back of his shirt and tugged him firmly back onto the path. As she did, gold mist flared from her hand, weaving with the light-blue mist that clung to Nicholas. A protective pulse radiated from her warm and steady, pushing back the tremor in the air.

"Nicky, we don't have time. You have your own training to start."

He didn't move. His eyes stayed locked on the field.

Around him were kids his age: laughing, shouting, competing, alive. Not council members. Not guardians. Not people who already knew everything he didn't.

Peers. People who might understand what he was going through. People who might get him.

"Just a few minutes," he said quietly. "Please. Look at them, Anna. Don't you miss… all of that? Recess? Playing outside? The noise? The stupid arguments?"

Anna's expression softened. Her gold aura pulled subtly toward Nicholas, wrapping him in a thin protective cover; warm, steady, instinctive.

She looked at Chanotedah, who shrugged helplessly. They both knew pushing Nicholas right now could backfire badly.

Chanotedah sighed. The sharp scent of spearmint cut through the air. His hands clenched at his sides, and the mist swirled around his fingers in tight spirals, a silent tell that he was more worried than he let on.

"I'll run ahead and tell Melusine there will be a… necessary delay."

Nicholas and Anna sat on the grass. Nicholas leaned forward, arms wrapped around his knees, eyes glued to the game. Anna watched him instead, the focus, the longing, the flicker of something like hope.

She hadn't seen him look this engaged since they arrived.

"So," Nicholas said suddenly, startling her, "explain the game."

Anna blinked, then gathered her thoughts. "It's not exactly a game. It's training. The silver spheres are Evanidus spheres. If a Viator thinks they're about to be trapped, they can throw one at their feet. It teleports them somewhere they picture. They can also use it to protect a partner or displace an opponent."

"These aren't toys," Anna added quietly. "They're shaped from intention, and they're dangerous if you don't know what you're doing."

Nicholas nodded slowly, absorbing every word.

"The gold ones," she continued, "are Suppressio spheres. They freeze an opponent in place for a few seconds. But they only work well if you're close."

Nicholas frowned. "So… they're training for a fight? A battle? I thought we are time travelers, not warriors."

Anna hesitated. She wished desperately that Bharati or Chase were here to answer this one.

"Sometimes," she said carefully, "a Viator has to be both."

Before Nicholas could respond, the match ended. The players jogged toward them, laughing and shoving each other, their colors flickering in bright, competitive bursts. Nicholas watched them with wide-eyed awe, like a kid seeing professional athletes up close.

Two of them led the group.

Antonia was exactly as he remembered her from the Council chamber. Tall, athletic, dark-haired, wearing a black-and-red uniform that made her look like she had stepped out of a championship match. Her dark brown eyes were sharp and assessing, the kind that missed nothing. She carried herself like someone who had already survived too much and refused to be surprised again.

Beside her walked Lazer, shorter and stockier, blond buzz cut, rectangular glasses perched on his nose. He looked like a bulldog who had learned to read ancient runes for fun and enjoyed correcting people about them.

They stopped in front of Nicholas and Anna. Antonia gave Anna a curt nod, then turned her attention to Nicholas. Her gaze narrowed slightly, not in hostility, but in recognition. As if she were checking to see whether he was still the same boy she had met earlier, or whether something inside him had shifted.

Nicholas stood, trying to look confident. "Hi. That was… really impressive."

Antonia studied him for a long moment. "You look steadier than you did this morning."

Nicholas blinked. "I feel steadier."

"Good." Her tone was clipped, but not unkind. "You will need that."

Chanotedah reappeared at Nicholas's side, brushing dust off his coat as if he had been there the whole time. Antonia's gaze flicked to him, then to Anna, then back to Nicholas. The look sharpened, but there was no cruelty in it. Only calculation. And something else beneath it, something she did not seem to expect.

"I will be keeping a close eye on you," she said. "The Council assigned you a trainer, but your development is… unusual. If anything changes, I want to know."

Nicholas nodded, unsure whether to feel reassured or terrified.

Antonia stepped past him, brushing his shoulder lightly. The contact was brief, almost accidental, but the mist reacted instantly. A burst of red-gold flared from her skin, colliding with the light blue that hovered around Nicholas. The two colors twisted together, forming a thin, shimmering braid before snapping apart.

Nicholas sucked in a breath. The Regulatori in his pocket pulsed sharply, once, then again, syncing with his suddenly accelerated heartbeat.

Antonia paused mid-stride. For a moment, her expression flickered, as if she had felt the same jolt. She did not turn around, but her voice carried back to him, low and steady.

"Stay focused, Nicholas. The mist listens to you more than you realize."

Lazer adjusted his glasses, eyeing Nicholas with a mixture of curiosity and concern. "She is right. And she does not say that lightly."

Nicholas swallowed.

Something had shifted, subtle but undeniable, threading itself through the air like a new current. Antonia felt it first, a sharp pull beneath her ribs that made her pause mid-stride. Nicholas felt it too, a sudden tightening in his chest as the Regulatori pulsed in answer. The mist shivered through the clearing while the strange pull between Nicholas and Antonia remained.

Nicholas felt it. Anna felt it too. Her head snapped toward him, eyes widening for a heartbeat before she smoothed her expression into something neutral. "Did you…?"

Nicholas swallowed. "Yeah."

Anna exhaled slowly, though the breath trembled at the edges. "Ignore it. Probably just the mist reacting to everything."

But she did not sound convinced. And Antonia did not look back.

Lazer gave Nicholas a sympathetic smile as he followed after her. "Do not take it personally. She is intense."

Nicholas watched them go, unsettled in a way he could not name. The mist around him shifted in thin, restless curls, as if echoing the unease building beneath his ribs.

"They were sent back?" he asked quietly. "So, I can go back to my parents after training?"

Chanotedah and Anna exchanged a look, the kind that said please do not make me be the one to crush him. The mist dimmed around them, softening into muted blues.

Anna spoke gently. "Nicky… the Council decides when and where a Viator is placed. Going back to your exact timeline… to your parents… it is unlikely."

Nicholas's jaw tightened. He turned abruptly and headed toward the commissary, the mist parting around him in sharp, irritated swirls.

"Whoa, junior," Chanotedah said, stepping in front of him. "We have to meet Melusine."

"I just want to talk to them," Nicholas insisted. "They are like me. They were taken from their homes. They will understand."

Chanotedah hesitated, torn between orders and empathy. Then he stepped aside. Anna shot him a glare sharp enough to cut stone, but she followed Nicholas inside.

The commissary doors slid open with a soft hiss, and Nicholas stopped short.

The room was enormous, shaped from mist that had been coaxed into long tables, floating lanterns, and drifting ribbons of color that pulsed with the energy of dozens of jumpers. As students approached each stall, the mist reformed the stands in real time, shifting colors, shapes, and menus to match their intentions. A girl thinking of soup passed by, and the stall before her melted into a steaming broth bar. A boy craving something sweet walked up, and the mist twisted itself into a pastry counter dusted with powdered sugar.

Nicholas inhaled sharply as a familiar scent drifted toward him. Burgers from the corner café, which he and his dad visited every Saturday. His chest tightened. The mist around him brightened in response to the memory, then softened into a warm blue.

Before he could take a step, Antonia came into view.

A thin layer of light-blue mist rose around Nicholas before he consciously summoned it, forming a subtle protective barrier between them.

"What is that…" he whispered.

Anna tugged his arm. "Come on. I am getting lasagna. Do you want a burrito? They are your favorite."

Nicholas opened his mouth to answer, but Antonia was already striding toward them, her black-and-red uniform still carrying the heat of the match she had just finished. She stopped in front of him with the same sharp presence she always carried, but her expression was calmer now, more focused than confrontational.

"Relax, Hunter," she said. "Everyone looks overwhelmed their first week."

Nicholas blinked. Was that almost kind?

"I wanted to ask you something," he said quickly. "About Nirvana. And time jumping."

Antonia's expression shifted, not closing off completely, but tightening with the weight of responsibility. "You will learn what you need to learn. The Council will make sure of that."

Nicholas frowned. "But you said earlier you'd be keeping an eye on me."

"I will," she said. "And Nicholas? Don't assume something is harmless simply because it feels familiar."

The mist around her darkened for a moment, a faint static ripple brushing the air. Nicholas felt a sudden tug deep in his chest, sharp and instinctive, as if something inside him bristled at the shift in her tone.

Antonia placed a hand on his shoulder, firmer this time, but not unfriendly. The mist dimmed again, static whispering at the edges. Nicholas felt that same tug in his chest, sharper now, as if something inside him recognized her touch and recoiled.

She turned and walked away, her black resonance trailing behind.

Nicholas called after her, "Where can I find you? When?"

"I will be around," she said without turning. "Ask Anna."

The mist curled around his ankles, warm and unsettled, as if it too had opinions about Antonia.

And somewhere deeper in the Continuum, something tugged again. Stronger this time. Waiting.

As they walked toward the Council chambers, Nicholas's thoughts churned. Antonia knew something. Something the Council was not saying. Something Anna was not saying. For the first time, Nicholas found himself wondering who in Nirvana he could actually trust.

They reached the marble steps leading to the Council chambers, and that was when it happened.

A soft vibration plucked itself deep inside Nicholas's soul, clear and bright, impossible to ignore. A faint reply followed, warmer and softer, like a second string answering the first. He turned instinctively toward Anna, certain the echo had come from her.

Anna stopped too.

"You felt that?" she whispered.

Nicholas nodded. "What was it?"

Anna hesitated. Her wings, invisible to most but not to him, fluttered once beneath her skin. The gold shimmer they cast was faint but unmistakable. "I… do not know. But it was not the mist."

The note faded, leaving only a faint echo behind, like a memory trying to cling to the air.

Anna shook her head and forced a smile. "Come on. Melusine is waiting."

But Nicholas noticed the way she kept glancing at him as they walked, as if she were trying to solve a puzzle she did not want to admit existed. The harmonic tug between them had grown stronger, threading through the mist like a quiet chord neither of them knew how to name.

Melusine waited for them outside the Council chambers, leaning casually against one of the marble columns. The mist brightened the moment she came into view, softening into gentle lavender hues that followed her like a tide. Her sandy-blonde hair was pulled back into a loose ponytail, revealing a constellation of freckles scattered across the bridge of her nose and the tops of her cheeks. Her skin was a deep bronze, sun-warmed and glowing, as if she had stepped straight out of a shoreline dream.

She had traded her turquoise gown for a pair of light blue, baggy cargo shorts that looked like she had borrowed them from an older brother rather than chosen them herself. The fabric hung loosely on her hips, pockets bulging with who-knows-what. A soft lavender tank top completed the outfit, the color catching the light in a way that made her look both impossibly young and impossibly ancient.

As she shifted her weight, Nicholas caught sight of something he had never seen before. A small dolphin tattoo curved along the side of her thigh, just visible where the cargo shorts rode up. It was inked in shimmering silver, the lines delicate and fluid, as if the creature might leap off her skin at any moment. He realized he never could have noticed it when she wore her linen pants.

The mist curled around her ankles, swirling in soft spirals that mirrored the motion of waves. Melusine's presence always did that. She carried the ocean with her, even here in Nirvana's marble halls.

She smiled when she saw them, warm and steady. "There you two are. I was starting to think the mist swallowed you."

Nicholas felt the tension in his chest ease, just a little. Melusine had that effect. She was calm in a place that never stopped shifting. A fixed point in a world made of echoes.

And yet, even as she stepped forward, the faint echo of that harmonic note still lingered between him and Anna, threading through the air like a question waiting to be answered.

"Nicholas," she said warmly, her voice carrying a calm that settled the air itself. "How are you holding up?"

"I'm… fine," he said, though the word felt flimsy even to him. "Still not sure what's going on."

His fingers curled around the gold pocket watch Chase had given him. He lifted it slightly. "Chase gave me this. I figured maybe you could tell me what it does?"

Melusine took the Regulatori with a reverence that made Nicholas straighten. Her bronze skin caught the light, warm and sun-kissed, and the freckles across her nose brightened as she studied the watch. "Chase does make beautiful work," she murmured, turning it over in her hands. "But this is not my domain. You will learn how it works, truly works, from Elfego. He teaches the mechanics of time."

She handed it back to him, then stepped away from the chamber doors.

"Come," she said. "We are going for a walk."

The mist around them shifted. Not swirling, not drifting, but deciding. In a blink, the marble floors and towering columns dissolved into a white sand beach. Waves crashed fifty feet away, gulls cried overhead, and the air smelled like the lake Nicholas's parents took him to after summer storms.

Nicholas inhaled sharply. "Whoa."

Far down the shoreline stood a driftwood shack with mismatched chairs out front. Melusine led them toward it, her feet sinking into the warm sand. The ocean-blue mist followed her like a tide, curling around her ankles in soft spirals.

"To understand where we are going," she said, "you must first understand where we have been. Most intelligent races ignore their own history. That is why hoppers can manipulate timelines so easily. The people affected do not realize anything has changed."

The waves rolled in, steady and rhythmic, as if echoing her words. The mist brightened around her, responding to her presence the way water responds to the moon.

Nicholas followed, sand warm beneath his feet, the Regulatori cool in his hand.

Something about this place felt older than Nirvana. Older than the Council. Older than anything he had been told.

And Melusine walked as though she remembered every moment of it.

Nicholas frowned. "But… how would they know? If the change happened before they were born, wouldn't it just feel like normal history to them?"

Melusine smiled, the kind of smile that suggested she had been waiting for that question. "A particularly good question. And the answer begins with Baalto."

Nicholas blinked. "Who is Baalto?"

Melusine laughed softly, the sound warm and bright like sunlight on water. "Honesty is a good start."

They reached the driftwood shack. She stepped inside, grabbed four beach towels from a weathered shelf, and handed one to each of them. Nicholas spread his out on a sun-bleached chair, the fabric warm from the conjured light. Melusine sat, then lifted her hands and rotated them as if shaping an invisible sphere.

The mist obeyed instantly.

A massive globe of swirling vapor formed above them, images flickering inside it. A muscular man in a leather loincloth appeared, spear in hand, standing in a prehistoric landscape of volcanic rock and towering ferns. His skin was dark and weathered, his hair braided with bone and sinew. The air around him shimmered with the faintest distortion, like heat rising from stone.

"Baalto," Melusine said. "Was the first time jumper on Earth. He stumbled into time travel thousands of years before any of your ancient civilizations."

Nicholas stared at the image. "So, he… what? Just started jumping around?"

"We do not know how it began," Melusine said. "Perhaps dreams, like many Viatori. Perhaps, he found a tear in the Continuum. But he began visiting other eras. At first, only within his own lifetime. Eventually, he learned to move freely across the timelines."

The globe shifted, showing Baalto stepping through a shimmering rift into a snow-covered valley, then into a desert, then into a primitive village lit by firelight.

"And he left… traces?" Nicholas asked.

"Exactly. Not physical ones. More like radiation." She glanced at him. "You know how radioactive material can affect people who have never touched it?"

Nicholas nodded.

"Baalto's presence altered chromosomes. Subtle changes. Over generations, those changes created hundreds, perhaps thousands, of potential jumpers. And it made the entire human race susceptible to disruptions in time."

Nicholas stared at her. "So… everyone could be a jumper? Then why am I here?"

Melusine stood and paced, her bare feet sinking into the warm sand. Her bronze skin caught the shifting light, freckles brightening across her nose as clouds gathered overhead, dimming the sun. The dolphin tattoo on her thigh glimmered faintly, as if reacting to the change in atmosphere.

The mist around them tightened, listening.

"Nicholas," she said softly, "you are here because Baalto did not just change humanity."

She paused, eyes meeting his.

"He changed the Continuum itself."

Another wave folded onto the shore, its rhythm strangely synchronized with the silence that followed her words.

Anna pointed upward. "Melusine. The sky."

Melusine looked up, startled, then laughed. The clouds dissolved instantly, leaving the sun bright and warm again. "Sorry. Thinking too hard."

She settled beside Nicholas, placing a gentle hand on his knee. Her touch was grounding, steady, the kind that made the mist quiet down to listen.

"Have you ever heard someone say they experienced déjà vu? Or a memory so vivid they could smell it?"

Nicholas nodded. "Yeah."

"That is what I mean. Those people felt a compression in the timeline, caused by a jumper or a hopper. Their conscious mind did not understand it, but their subconscious recorded it."

Nicholas leaned forward, elbows on his knees, eyes fixed on her. He was no longer overwhelmed or confused. He was captivated. Every word she spoke seemed to pull him deeper into the story, deeper into the truth of the world he had been thrown into.

Above them, Baalto's image hovered in the swirling globe of mist, watching with ancient patience.

Melusine sighed, brushing a strand of sandy-blonde hair from her face. "All right. I will continue."

The globe shifted, showing Baalto older now, standing beside a woman with kind eyes and a steady posture.

"Baalto returned to his own time without realizing he had altered the future. He married Davina. They had three sons: Arotza, Gergori, and Sergius. All three inherited his gift."

The images moved like living murals. 'The brothers grew, traveled, learned. Primitive villages rose and fell around them. Seasons changed in seconds." Melusine explained.

"When they came of age, they each married. Arotza to Clotho, Gergori to Lacheis, Sergius to Atropos."

Nicholas sat up straighter. "Wait. Those names. I know those names."

"You should," Melusine said, her voice softening. "You will understand why soon."

The globe shifted again, showing farms, battlefields, and early cities. Gergori plowed fields with techniques far beyond his era. Sergius stood on a ridge, directing troops with knowledge no one else possessed. Arotza walked through a shimmering rift into Nirvana, his expression filled with awe.

"Arotza came here," Melusine said. "He built the first colony for travelers."

Nicholas watched, entranced. The mist reflected the images across the sand, turning the beach into a living tapestry of ancient history.

"But the wives," Melusine continued, "were not content. They had seen the future. They wanted wealth. Influence. They stole wisps from Nirvana and shaped them into an eye, a powerful artifact that let them see the fates of others and slowed their aging."

Nicholas shivered. "So, they became fortune tellers."

"Yes. And they lived for generations. Until a Viator destroyed the eye."

Nicholas exhaled, overwhelmed but unable to look away. "This is… a lot."

Melusine nodded. "And it gets worse."

The globe darkened. The air cooled. A child appeared in the mist, pale and intense, eyes too old for his face.

"Atropos bore two sons. Abbadon and Aurelion. Because of her time with the mist, both were born with extraordinary power. Most Viatori can shape mist into objects. Some can manipulate energy. Abbadon and Aurelion could change anything they touched."

Nicholas swallowed hard. His pulse quickened. The Regulatori in his hand pulsed with it, as if responding to the story.

He leaned closer, eyes locked on the swirling images. "What happened to them?"

The mist tightened, as if bracing for the answer.

"When they were eight, they found their way to Nirvana. Arotza recognized Abbadon, and he recognized the darkness in him. He cast Abbadon into a void outside time. He invited Aurelion to join him in determining the destiny of timelines."

Nicholas whispered, "But Abbadon came back."

"Yes. He found a way to slip between his exile and the timeline. He recruited travelers who rejected Arotza's rules. He built a society with one purpose: to tear down what Arotza created and rule whatever remained."

Nicholas stood abruptly, sand shifting beneath his feet. Only then did he realize Anna and Chanotedah were gone. He had not even noticed them leave.

"Is that who Rhet works for?" he asked.

Melusine's expression tightened. "We don't know the connection. Abbadon's influence survived him—through followers, factions, even hoppers. Rhet may have inherited part of that legacy, or simply learned how to use it. We can't assume he serves anyone but himself."

Nicholas frowned. "So, he could be trying to finish what Abbadon started."

Nicholas paced a few steps, the Regulatori closed in his hand. "Can't you send a spy into the void? Find out what they're doing?"

Melusine blushed, freckles brightening across her nose. "We do not know where the void is. Or how they enter the timeline. They compress time violently and move through the blur."

Nicholas's eyes widened. "So that's when normal people feel déjà vu."

"Yes. We travel gently. They travel like a storm."

The mist above them rippled, echoing her words with a low, distant tremor. Nicholas felt it in his chest, a faint vibration that matched the pulse of the Regulatori. The story was no longer just history. It was a warning. A map. A shadow stretching toward him from a past he had never known.

And Melusine watched him with quiet understanding, as if she already knew the part he would play in what came next.

Melusine stood suddenly. Her cargo shorts and lavender tank top shimmered, dissolving into a sleek ocean-blue swimsuit that matched the mist curling at her ankles. The shift was effortless, like the Continuum had simply decided she should be dressed for the water.

"I am drained," she said with a grin. "Come on. Let's go swimming."

She sprinted toward the ocean, calling over her shoulder, "Are you coming or what?"

Nicholas hesitated at the edge of the surf, the cold foam curling around his toes. The sand was warm, the air smelled like summer storms. For a moment, the weight of Nirvana, the Council, the fractures, the whispers about his power, all faded beneath the crash of the waves.

He took one step deeper.

The mist reacted instantly.

A cool ripple swept over him, brushing his skin like a breeze. His jeans softened, blurred, and dissolved into shimmering particles. His T-shirt followed, unraveling into threads of light. In their place, a fitted navy swimsuit formed around him, the fabric settling against his skin as naturally as breath.

Nicholas gasped. "What… did I just—?"

Anna laughed behind him, the sound warm and relieved. "Your first Continuum shift. It means you are syncing with Nirvana. It will happen more often now."

Nicholas stared down at himself, stunned. The swimsuit felt like something he had always owned, something the mist had pulled from a memory he did not know he had.

Melusine splashed water at him from the shallows, laughing like someone who had never carried the burden of entire timelines. Nicholas laughed back, the sound surprised even himself. He ran into the surf, letting the cold water crash against his legs.

For the first time since arriving in Nirvana, he felt like a boy again. No destiny. No danger. Just sunlight, saltwater, and the illusion of safety.

Far behind them, unnoticed, the mist shivered. A faint ripple moved through it, subtle but deliberate, like something distant had stirred. The beach brightened, then dimmed, as if the Continuum were holding its breath.

But Nicholas did not see it.

He dove into the waves after Melusine, letting the ocean swallow every fear he had been holding onto. The water lifted him, carried him, and washed the tension from his shoulders.

Tomorrow, the questions will return. Tomorrow, the truth will find him. But for now, he let the water carry him.

And the Continuum watched.

Chapter 11.5 Interlude

The fracture hit like a hammer.

A shimmer of gray light split the air, pulsing once in silver-blue, once in gold, once in soft lavender. Three colors vibrating out of sync, reaching each other but never touching. The ground beneath Rhet trembled as if the coils of the spring had tightened all at once, compressing the world into a single, unbearable moment.

Rhet staggered midstride, boots skidding across the cracked concrete of the abandoned overpass. Shadows bent toward him, drawn like iron filings to a magnet. The air thinned, refusing to breathe near him. His jagged-glass eye flickered violently, warning him a heartbeat too late.

The sky above him flickered through day, night, dusk, and dawn, as if the timeline could not decide what moment it belonged to. For a split second, the spiral of the spring shimmered faintly across the clouds, then vanished into the haze.

His hoppers froze. Every one of them.

Their glitching silhouettes snapped into stillness, heads tilting in eerie unison toward him. A hive-mind whisper rippled through them, static layered with something like fear. The void inside them recognized the shift before Rhet did.

Rhet pressed his hand to his chest. The first note struck. A sharp, piercing resonance that vibrated through his ribs and into the marrow of his bones. silver-blue light flashed across the overpass. The ground quivered. Rhet gasped, dropping to one knee as the world around him warped inward.

"Master?" one hopper rasped, its voice stuttering like a corrupted file.

The second note hit.

Lower. Deeper. Gold light pulsed outward, warm and protective, and it burned him. The overpass shuddered. Rusted beams groaned. A car half buried in weeds lifted an inch off the ground before slamming back down. The void inside Rhet recoiled, snarling against the intrusion.

His breath hitched. His jagged eye fractured internally, shards of light scattering across the asphalt. A memory, the last Equal, flashed through him like a blade. The void had swallowed that moment long ago, but the resonance dragged it back into the open.

"No," he whispered. "Not again."

The hoppers twitched, their forms glitching at the edges. One took a step toward him, drawn by instinct or fear or both.

Rhet snarled, the sound raw and animal. The hopper recoiled instantly, limbs folding in on themselves like a collapsing shadow. The void inside Rhet surged, hungry and restless, sensing the fracture's power and reaching for it.

Then the third note struck.

Not loud. Not soft. Simply inevitable.

A perfect, crystalline tone that hummed through the Continuum with terrifying clarity. Lavender light rippled through the air like a wave, soft but unstoppable. The resonance vibrated through the overpass, through the rusted metal, through the weeds, through the air itself. Through him. The void inside him screamed in answer, a sound only he could hear.

Rhet's own scream tore from his throat, ripping through the timeline like a blade. The sky above them cracked, a thin jagged seam of white light splitting the horizon before sealing itself shut. It looked disturbingly like the seam Nicholas had opened in the clearing, but this one carried the scent of the void, cold and metallic, as if something ancient had pressed its face against the fabric of time and breathed.

Something had awakened. Something that recognized him. Something that wanted him back.

And the void, his void, answered.

The hoppers skittered backward in panic. Rhet remained on his hands, the three resonances lingering inside him like a brand.

Three notes. Separate. Distinct. But reaching for each other. Reaching for a chord.

Rhet's fingers dug into the asphalt. When he finally spoke, his voice trembled.

"They are aligning."

The hoppers stilled. Rhet rose slowly, unsteadily, like a man standing after being struck by lightning. His coat hung in tatters, the edges burned and curled from the resonance. He brushed the dust from his sleeves with the slow, deliberate movements of a gunslinger checking his gear after a firefight. His jagged eye glowed with fractured light, shards of violet and silver flickering deep within the glass.

"They do not even know," he whispered. "The boy has no idea what he is being given."

A flicker of something crossed his face. Not envy. Not fear. Something sharper. The void inside him stirred, whispering in a voice that was not quite Abbadon's but carried the same cold amusement.

Good.

Rhet laughed, a broken, breathless sound that scraped the air raw. "Good."

He lifted his face to the sky, letting the last echo of the three notes vibrate through him. The resonance hummed against the void, two forces circling each other like predators.

"Let them find each other," he murmured. "Let the boy gather his little team."

His smile sharpened, slow and dangerous.

"It will make breaking them so much sweeter."

"Find the boy," he said softly. "Find the girl. And find the one who hides. I want to know who the third is."

A faint pulse of lavender shimmered far in the distance, barely visible through the haze. The hoppers did not notice it. But Rhet did. His jagged eye flickered, narrowing with predatory precision.

"Hidden," he whispered. "Of course she is."

The hoppers vanished into the cracks of the timeline. Rhet remained alone on the overpass, the world still trembling around him.

He closed his eyes. And for the first time in centuries, he felt fear. Not of the boy. Not of the team forming around him. Not even of the spring.

He feared the fight the spring was preparing for him.

And he feared how ready it was becoming.

CHAPTER 12

Nicholas enjoyed swimming in the ocean with Melusine. In fact, it was the first time he had enjoyed anything since arriving in Nirvana. The waves lifted and carried him, the salt spray cooling his face, and for a fleeting moment, he felt like a normal boy again. No destiny. No Council. No fractures in time. Just sunlight, laughter, and the warmth of someone who felt like the older sister he had always imagined.

A faint shimmer of lavender mist followed Melusine wherever she moved, soft and calming, like the echo of a lullaby. Every time she laughed, Nicholas felt a subtle vibration in his chest, warm and steady, almost musical. He did not understand it, but he leaned toward it instinctively, the way someone leans toward a familiar melody without realizing they know the tune.

Anna appeared beside him so suddenly that he nearly inhaled seawater.

"Where did you disappear during the lesson?" he sputtered, giving her a halfhearted shove. "One minute you're there, the next you and gruff face are gone."

Anna smirked. Her wings flickered beneath her skin, a brief shimmer of gold light. "You are not the only one who must learn things here. Just because I have been watching you since you were this tall"—she held her hand at three and a half feet..."does not mean I know everything."

Nicholas blinked. "Oh. I didn't… I mean, I just didn't know."

Her gold aura tugged subtly toward him, wrapping around him in a thin, protective veil. The mist around them pulsed silver-blue in response, answering her instinct without either of them noticing. The ocean breeze carried the faintest hint of lavender from where Melusine floated nearby, and for a moment the three colors brushed against each other in the air, soft and fleeting, like chords warming up before a song.

Anna giggled at how flustered he became. "So? How was your lesson?"

"It was fine. A lot of history. Is this going to be like school, where we take a test and forget everything afterward?"

Anna stopped so abruptly that he nearly ran into her. She grabbed his arm and spun him to face her. A faint gray shimmer flickered at the edge of the sky, gone before he could register it.

"Nicholas Michael Hunter," she said, voice low and fierce, "listen to me. This is not school. You need to remember everything you are taught here. Everything. There is a reason Melusine went through the early history of time jumpers. There are things in those stories you may need to survive."

The word hit him like a punch.

"Survive?" His voice cracked. "What do you mean by 'survive?"

Anna's eyes widened. "I did not mean… I was not saying you could…"

"I could die?" His voice rose, thin and sharp. "What are you talking about?"

"Nicky," she said softly, her tone shifting to something warm and protective, "being a Viator is dangerous. Rarely, very rarely, things happen in timelines. Everything you learn here is meant to protect you. I will be with you, but you must think for yourself. Do you understand?"

The gold around her brightened, brushing against the silver-blue that clung to him. Farther down the beach, Melusine turned toward them, lavender mist drifting in a slow, curious curl, as if she had felt something shift.

Nicholas did not notice the colors. But the Continuum did.

Nicholas stared at the sand. His aura flickered, dimming. "Yeah. I guess. It's just… when I was swimming with Melusine, I forgot. I forgot about all of this. I forgot someone out there might want to hurt me. She felt like the big sister I always imagined."

A soft lavender glow rippled across the water at the mention of Melusine's name, as if the ocean itself remembered her.

Anna brightened. "You went swimming with Melusine? That is great."

She bounced around him in loose circles, trying to lift his mood. Nicholas reached out to grab her, but she slipped away with a laugh that sent a warm pulse of gold through the mist.

"You said you had lessons too," he said. "What did you learn?"

"Oh, let us see…" She raised her arms above her head and brought them down sharply. The moment her palms touched her thighs, her body dissolved into a burst of orange and black feathers. An oriole darted around him twice, wings catching the sunlight in quick flashes, then landed lightly on his shoulder. When she fluttered down to the sand, her form shimmered and reformed into Anna. The mist pulsed gold, then blue, then settled into a soft, blended glow that lingered between them.

Nicholas rubbed his eyes. "That's… that's way cooler than history."

"Well, you have to do the thinking," she teased, "and I should do the guarding. Curas cannot travel through time alone. We have to be with a Viator or a Sustentet. That is why I traveled with Chase and Bharati."

"So, you turn into a bird to travel with me?"

"Yes. It is the most compact form. I already learned to shift into an oriole when you took your day trips at school."

Nicholas froze. "You were there? In my daydreams?"

Anna's expression softened. "A form of me was always with you when you drifted off in class, when you stared out the window and forgot the world for a moment. When you panicked and did not know why. I was there."

Nicholas felt the words settle into him, slow and heavy. Memories flickered through his mind the strange warmth during his worst panic attacks, the sudden calm that came from, nowhere, the flashes of gold he always assumed were tricks of the light. He had never been alone. Not once.

He swallowed. "All those times… that was you."

Anna nodded. "You were never as alone as you thought."

He did not know what to say. Instead, he reached up and plucked two apples from a tree that had not existed a moment earlier. The mist surged toward his hand too quickly, forming the apples with a speed that made Anna blink.

She laughed, delighted. "You know some Viatori cannot do that after years of training."

The mist around him pulsed silver-blue, as if agreeing.

The path opened into a clearing, and Nicholas slowed, blinking in surprise. The air shifted, warm and expectant, as though the Continuum itself had been waiting for him to understand something essential.

And for the first time, he did. Anna had always been there. Melusine was beginning to feel familiar in a way he could not explain. And something inside him, something quiet and harmonic was beginning to answer them both.

Asiza and Chanotedah were not sitting idly on the timber bench this time. They were in the middle of a game. A shimmering sphere of wisp hovered between them, darting left and right like a mischievous firefly. Chanotedah lunged for it, missed, and landed face-first in the grass. Asiza flicked her wrist, and the wisp zipped behind her back, taunting him with a playful pulse of light.

A faint gray streak flickered across the sky, unnoticed by either of them. The mist felt it, though. It tightened for a heartbeat, then relaxed again.

"You cheated," Chanotedah sputtered, spitting out a leaf.

"I used strategy," Asiza said, her voice smooth as silk. "You should try it sometime."

Nicholas laughed, and the sound made both of them turn.

Chanotedah's spearmint scent sharpened instantly. The mist swirled around his hands in tight spirals, a protective reflex he did not bother hiding. The wisp responded too, dimming slightly as if waiting for Nicholas to approach.

"Ah," Asiza said, brushing a strand of fiery hair behind her ear. "Our prodigy arrives."

Anna landed beside Nicholas in a burst of orange and black feathers. Her oriole form shimmered before folding back into her human shape. Nicholas still was not used to it, the way her wings folded into arms, the way her bright plumage dissolved into her dark curls. The gold around her pulsed once, warm and familiar, brushing lightly against the silver-blue that clung to Nicholas.

Chanotedah groaned. "Showoff."

Anna winked. "Jealous?"

Asiza stepped forward, her presence warm and commanding. "Nicholas, today we explore what you can do with the wisp."

Nicholas nodded, though his stomach fluttered. The mist leaned toward him, eager and listening. The wisp drifted closer, its surface rippling like liquid light, as if it recognized him.

"Okay. I will try."

"Good," Asiza said. "Start simple. Change the environment."

Nicholas closed his eyes.

The forest dissolved into a 1950s diner. Pastel walls gleamed under neon lights. Chrome stools lined the counter. The air smelled of waffle cones and warm sugar. Behind the counter, Chanotedah now wore a white apron and a paper hat, looking utterly betrayed by the universe.

Asiza did not miss a beat. She plucked a chocolate malt from the counter as if it had always been there. "Excellent choice," she said, taking a slow, appreciative sip.

Nicholas grinned.

"Again," she said.

He closed his eyes.

The diner vanished. A NASA launch pad roared beneath them, engines rumbling, smoke billowing. The ground vibrated under their feet. Nicholas staggered, the force of the scene too real.

Asiza lifted her hand.

The rocket vanished, replaced by a burst of floating balloons in every color imaginable. They drifted around them like weightless jewels, brushing Nicholas's shoulders with soft pops of color.

"Maybe not rockets yet," she said, tapping a balloon until it burst into harmless mist.

Nicholas laughed, breathless. "Okay. Fair."

Asiza let the balloons fade. The clearing returned, warm and bright. "Now we move to something more advanced."

The wisp drifted toward Nicholas, its surface shimmering with silver-blue light. Anna stepped closer too, her gold aura brushing his shoulder. Farther back, Melusine's lavender mist curled along the treeline, faint but present, as if she had paused mid-stride to listen.

Nicholas did not notice the colors gathering around him. But the wisp did. And the Continuum answered.

Asiza knelt and scooped a handful of wisps from the ground. It shimmered pink, then twisted into a glass globe swirling with mist.

"This is a viewer," she said. "A window into the timeline. We can see any moment, past or present, if we know where to look."

Nicholas leaned closer. "Can I try?"

"Not this one," she said. "Make your own."

He blinked. "I… don't know how."

"Yes, you do," she said softly. "You've been shaping the mist since you arrived. Try."

Nicholas swallowed, then crouched and touched the wisp. It curled around his fingers like warm smoke. He focused. The mist twitched.

Then it collapsed into a puddle at his feet.

Nicholas frowned. "Okay… that was terrible."

Anna tried not to laugh. "It was a very enthusiastic puddle."

Nicholas tried again. This time the mist rose, wobbling like a soap bubble trying to remember how to be round. It held its shape for half a second before popping with a sad little pfft.

Chanotedah clapped slowly. "Bravo. Truly, a masterpiece of… whatever that was."

Nicholas groaned. "I'm trying!"

"Don't try, you just need to think of what you want to happen," Asiza said. "You're forcing it."

Nicholas exhaled sharply and tried again. The mist rose; lopsided, flickering, trembling—then folded in on itself like a deflating balloon.

He rubbed his face. "Why is this so hard?"

"Because you're thinking about the result," Asiza said. "Not the intention. The mist doesn't respond to force. It responds to clarity."

Nicholas closed his eyes. He breathed.

The mist breathed with him. He reached out again—slower this time, gentler, not demanding, just inviting. The wisp curled upward, forming a loose coil. Then a sphere. Then glass. Then swirling mist. It wasn't perfect. It wobbled slightly. The surface rippled like water disturbed by a breeze. But it held. A faint lavender undertone shimmered through it.

Asiza's eyes softened. "There. That is a viewer you shaped, not one you wrestled into existence."

Nicholas stared at it, breathless. "I… did it."

Anna beamed. Her wings flickered again. "You did."

Chanotedah shrugged. "Eh. Seven out of ten."

Nicholas laughed, a small, shaky sound, and held the viewer closer.

"Okay," he whispered. "Show me something."

He thought of ancient Egypt—pyramids rising from the desert. The viewer responded instantly, forming a vivid image of workers hauling stone blocks under a blazing sun.

He thought of medieval Europe and saw knights training in a courtyard. The viewer shifted, showing armor glinting in torchlight.

He thought of the moon landing and saw the lunar module descending, dust pluming beneath it.

He exhaled. "This is… incredible."

"Careful," Asiza warned. "The timeline is vast. It will show you what you ask for, and sometimes what you don't."

Nicholas hesitated. Then he thought of the future. Not a specific year. Not a specific place. Just… the future. The viewer reacted violently. Colors twisted. The mist inside churned like a storm. The sphere pulsed in his hands, hot and cold at once. A faint gray crack flickered across the sky above them.

"Nicholas…" Asiza stepped forward.

But it was too late. The viewer stabilized and revealed something Nicholas was not ready to see.

A city in ruins stretched across the sphere's surface. Skyscrapers cracked open like broken bones. Smoke curled upward from streets split by jagged fractures of light, each one pulsing with the same unstable shimmer he had seen in the mist. The fractures crawled across the pavement like living veins, glowing with a sickly brilliance that made the air itself look wounded.

And standing in the center of it all was Rhet.

Nicholas's breath caught. His eyes glazed, unfocused. His fingers tightened around the viewer as if it were the only thing anchoring him to the world. He did not hear Anna calling his name. He did not feel Chanotedah's hand gripping his shoulder. He did not notice the mist recoiling from his feet, pulling back as if burned.

Because behind him, unseen by all but Asiza, the air thinned.

A faint line appeared. A seam. No wider than a thread. No brighter than a dying ember. But real. It quivered like a hairline crack in glass, pulsing in time with Nicholas's heartbeat. The mist around it flattened, as if bowing to something it did not understand.

Asiza's eyes widened. "Bharati… he is—"

The seam flickered. Stretched. Then snapped shut the instant Nicholas gasped and dropped the viewer. The sphere floated in midair, spinning slowly, the ruined city still visible. Rhet turned inside the vision as if he sensed Nicholas watching. As if he had been waiting for him.

The viewer cracked. A thin spiderweb fracture spread across its surface, and the image dissolved into drifting wisps of light.

Nicholas staggered back, shaking violently. Chanotedah's steadying hand tightened on his shoulder, but it was not enough to ground him. His breath came in short, broken pulls, his eyes unfocused and glassy.

Anna reacted before anyone else could move.

Her body shimmered, feathers bursting outward in a flash of orange and black. The oriole shot forward, wings slicing through the air with a sharp, urgent beat. She reached Nicholas in a heartbeat, landing against his chest with a soft thud. As her feet touched the ground, her form expanded again, feathers dissolving into skin and curls as she shifted back into herself.

She wrapped her arms around him in the instant she solidified.

"Nicky," she said, her voice trembling with fear she tried to hide. "I have you. You are safe."

Her gold aura flared, warm and protective, curling around him like a shield. The mist responded to her instinct, pulling close in a soft silver-blue pulse that wrapped around both of them. Nicholas clung to her, shaking so hard she had to brace her feet in the grass to keep them both upright.

Behind them, the last echo of the seam faded from the air, but the Continuum still trembled with the memory of it.

But Asiza's gaze stayed fixed on the empty air behind him, where the seam had been. Her voice was barely more than a whisper. "He opened something."

Bharati and Paloma appeared at the edge of the clearing as if drawn by the words themselves. The mist parted for them, uneasy.

"What did you say?" Bharati demanded.

Asiza pointed to the space behind Nicholas. "A seam. Only for a moment. But it was there."

Chittaswarup stepped forward, the ground humming under his feet in recognition. "I felt the tremor. A pull in the Continuum."

Bharati's expression darkened. "A novice cannot open a seam."

"He did not open it," Asiza said. "It opened through him."

Anna tightened her hold on Nicholas. "What does that mean?"

Chittaswarup answered, his voice was low and heavy. "It means the Equal is beginning to wake."

Nicholas did not hear them. He was still shaking, still seeing the ruins, still feeling Rhet's gaze burning through him like a brand.

"He saw me," Nicholas whispered. "Rhet saw me. He looked right at me."

Anna cupped his face, her gold aura wrapping around him like a shield. "You are safe. You are with us."

"No," Nicholas whispered. "I am not. He is coming. I felt it."

Chanotedah knelt beside him, placing a steadying hand on his shoulder. "Junior, whatever you saw, you are not facing it alone."

Asiza stepped closer, her expression a mixture of awe and fear. "Nicholas, no novice should be able to reach that far into the Continuum. What you touched was not just a future. It was a possible collapse."

Nicholas's breath hitched. "I did not mean to. I did not want to see any of that."

The mist around him pulsed silver-blue, trembling with the same fear he felt. The air held its breath. The Continuum listened.

And somewhere far away, something answered.

Anna brushed his hair back, her fingers gentle and sure. "Look at me." He did.

"You are not alone," she said, her voice steady even as her gold aura trembled with emotion. "Not now. Not ever. I am your Cura. I am with you until the end of time and longer if I must be."

Nicholas felt the truth of it settle into him, warm and familiar, like the echo of every moment she had steadied him in his childhood without him knowing. The panic attacks. The drifting daydreams. The strange calm that always came from nowhere. It had been her. It had always been her.

Chanotedah stepped closer, his royal blue aura tightening around his shoulders like a coiled ribbon of light. The color deepened with concern, rich and protective. "And I am here too. Even if you keep turning me into an ice cream man."

A tiny, broken laugh escaped Nicholas. The first crack of light through the fear.

Anna smiled, relief softening her features. "There he is."

Nicholas wiped his eyes with the back of his hand. "I am scared."

"We know," Anna said. "And that is why we are here."

Asiza knelt so she was eye level with him. Her fiery hair glowed in the clearing's light, and the wisp hovering near her shoulder pulsed in quiet sympathy. "Nicholas, what you saw means the timeline is shifting faster than we realized. The Council will need to know. But first, breathe."

Nicholas inhaled shakily. The mist around them pulsed, responding to his heartbeat with a soft silver-blue glow.

Anna noticed. "Nicky, the mist listens to you. Even when you are scared."

Chanotedah added, "Especially when you are scared." His royal blue aura flared, steady and grounding, wrapping around Nicholas like a second anchor.

Nicholas looked between them, his guardian, his friend, his teacher. Their colors brushed against him, gold and royal blue and a dull orange, weaving around the silver-blue that clung to his skin. For the first time since the vision, he felt the faintest thread of grounding.

"Okay," he whispered. "Okay."

Anna squeezed his hand, her thumb brushing the back of it in a slow, steady rhythm. "We will face whatever comes next together."

The sky above them darkened for a heartbeat, as if something vast had passed between Nirvana and the world beyond. Nicholas felt it. A pull. A pressure. A presence. Rhet.

Asiza straightened, her expression sharpening. "Your training begins in earnest now."

The mist behind them stirred.

Lavender light drifted through the trees, soft at first, then brightening as Melusine stepped into the clearing. Her bronze skin glowed in the shifting light, freckles bright across her nose, and her sandy hair clung damply to her shoulders as if she had run straight from the shoreline. The dolphin tattoo on her thigh shimmered faintly with each step.

"I felt the shift," she said, her voice low and steady. "The Continuum trembled."

Her lavender mist curled toward Nicholas, brushing against Anna's gold and Chanotedah's royal blue, the colors touching for a moment before drifting apart again. A soft, harmonic vibration rippled through the clearing, so faint Nicholas barely noticed it.

What he did notice was Melusine herself.

As she stepped fully into the light, the dolphin tattoo on her thigh shimmered. Nicholas blinked. For a heartbeat, he could have sworn the dolphin had changed orientation, as if it had turned to face him. The shimmer faded the moment he focused on it, leaving him unsure whether it had moved at all or whether the mist had played a trick on his eyes.

But the feeling lingered. A quiet recognition. A pull he could not name. Nicholas swallowed hard. Because somewhere in the fractured future he had glimpsed, Rhet was waiting. And the timeline was already shifting toward him.

And now, for the first time, he was not facing it alone.

Chapter 13

The mist still trembled. Even after the vision had faded, even after Anna's arms had steadied him and Chanotedah's royal blue aura had grounded him, Nicholas felt the echo of Rhet's gaze like a cold fingerprint pressed against his spine. A faint silver-blue pulse rippled through the air around him, answering the panic still lodged in his chest. Overhead, a thin gray streak flickered through the mist, a fracture echo sliding across the sky, and riding along its edge was a faint green shimmer that moved like a warning signal from somewhere far beyond Nirvana.

Everyone thought he was calming down. Nicholas thought so, too. But the moment that green shimmer rippled across the fracture echo, something inside him tightened. The air felt too thin, too sharp, too full of a pressure he could not name. His pulse spiked. The mist recoiled. The ground shifted beneath his feet as if the realm itself sensed the shift inside him.

He did not run because he feared Rhet. He ran because the vision had awakened something in him that he did not understand, something that felt too big and too dangerous to let anyone else see.

The forest blurred around him, shifting too fast, as if Nirvana were scrambling to keep up with his panic. Trees bent toward him, their branches reaching like worried hands. The ground pulsed beneath each step, moss to sand to grass to stone, the realm reacting to his fear in frantic, disjointed bursts. The mist tore behind him in ragged streaks, thinning like something was chasing him through it.

He did not care. He just needed to get away. Away from the cracked viewer. Away from the ruined city. Away from the knowledge that Rhet had seen him, truly seen him, away from the terrifying truth that the seam had opened through him.

His lungs burned. His legs buckled. He collapsed in a grove of towering pines, their trunks rising like ancient pillars into a canopy so high it vanished into shadow. The air here was still, heavy, sacred, a place that felt older than Nirvana itself. The mist curled around his ankles, trembling, then settling as if holding its breath.

Nicholas pressed his back against one of the massive trees, chest heaving, vision swimming. His thoughts spiraled. My parents do not remember me. I was not in my own memories. Rhet is coming. Something inside me opened a seam. I am not ready. I will never be ready.

A soft flutter broke through the storm in his head. An oriole, bright orange and black, landed on a low branch beside him. Its green eyes watched him with a calm, steady intelligence. A faint gold shimmer pulsed around it, answering the silver-blue panic radiating from Nicholas.

"Anna…?" he whispered.

But the bird did not shift. Instead, it hopped closer, tilting its head in a way that felt almost curious. Nicholas exhaled shakily, the breath catching in his throat. "Not Anna."

The oriole shimmered. Feathers dissolved into mist, drifting upward in a soft spiral that caught the faint green shimmer still riding the fracture echo overhead. The mist reformed, gathering into the shape of a woman whose presence warmed the grove like sunlight breaking through winter clouds.

Paloma stepped forward, her flowing gown brushing the pine needles with the softness of a whispered prayer. The air warmed around her, pine needles lifting in a gentle spiral as if drawn to her presence. A faint rose glow radiated from her skin, calming the grove itself, smoothing the ragged edges of Nicholas's fear.

She knelt beside him, picking up a sprig of evergreen and twirling it gently between her fingers. "I felt your fear," she said softly. "It rippled through Nirvana like a tremor. I thought you might need someone who understands what it means to be overwhelmed by the truth."

Nicholas did not answer. He could not. His throat felt tight, his chest hollow. His hands shook so violently, he pressed them against his knees just to keep them still. The mist around him pulsed silver-blue, flickering with each tremor of his breath.

Paloma sat beside him, her presence warm and impossibly calming, like a lullaby woven into human form. A soft Triad vibration hummed beneath her voice, subtle but unmistakable, the kind of resonance that soothed without asking permission.

"I am going to assume," she said gently, "that your lesson with Asiza did not go the way you hoped."

Nicholas let out a broken laugh, thin and unsteady. "That is one way to put it."

"Would you like to talk about it?"

He did not want to. But the words came anyway, pulled loose by the quiet safety of her presence.

"I realized… people I have known my whole life do not even know I exist. My parents. My friends. Everyone. I looked into the viewer and saw a day I remember perfectly, the first day of second grade, and I was not there. Anna was not there. It was like… like the universe erased me."

A faint gray flicker pulsed at the edge of the grove, reacting to his pain. The green shimmer along the fracture echo brightened for a heartbeat, then faded again.

Paloma listened without interrupting, her eyes soft and full of understanding. A gentle rose glow radiated from her hands, steadying the air around him, smoothing the tremors in the mist.

"And then," Nicholas whispered, "I saw the future. Or… a future. But the worst part was Rhet. He knew I was there. Somehow, he knew I was watching."

A cold shiver rippled through the grove, a distant resonance brushing the realm like a warning. Paloma's breath hitched. She reached out and took his hand, her fingers warm and steady against his trembling ones.

"I know it feels impossible," she said. "I know it feels cruel. But you are not erased, Nicholas. Not where it matters."

He shook his head, eyes stinging. "My parents…"

"Your parents," she said gently, "carry you in their hearts. Even if they cannot name the feeling, they feel the strength you gave them. You are not gone from them. You are transformed."

Nicholas swallowed hard. "It does not feel like that."

"I know." Paloma squeezed his hand, her fingers warm and steady. "But you are not alone in this. And you are not forgotten."

Nicholas leaned into her, the way a child leans into a mother when the world becomes too heavy. Paloma wrapped her arms around him, holding him until his breathing steadied. Her rose glow softened the shadows beneath the pines, warming the grove with a quiet, maternal calm. The mist around them warmed as well, pulsing in soft lavender and gold, the colors weaving together in slow, soothing waves.

A faint vibration rippled through the grove, soft and almost imperceptible, like the pluck of a distant string. Paloma felt it immediately. Her breath caught, her posture tightening for a heartbeat. Nicholas did not notice the shift, but the mist did. It shimmered once, a quick silver-blue flicker, then stilled again as if listening for something more.

Paloma said nothing. But her eyes lingered on Nicholas a moment longer than before, studying him with a depth that held both wonder and worry.

"Paloma?" Nicholas whispered into her shoulder. "Can I… come to you when I miss my mom?"

Her embrace tightened, warm and protective. "Always."

They stayed like that for a long moment, long enough for the mist to settle, long enough for Nicholas's heartbeat to slow into something steady. A faint silver-blue pulse radiated from him, answered by a soft gold shimmer from Anna's distant presence and a dusty rose echo from Paloma. The colors brushed against one another like threads testing a weave, then drifted apart again.

When they finally rose, Nicholas wiped his eyes with the back of his hand and turned toward the edge of the grove. The towering pines swayed gently overhead, their needles whispering in a language older than Nirvana itself. The mist curled around his ankles, no longer trembling, but watchful, as if waiting for his next step.

And somewhere beyond the trees, the faintest green shimmer rode the fracture echo again, a reminder that the Continuum had felt him too.

Anna, Melusine, Asiza, Chanotedah, Bharati, and Chittaswarup stood there, silent and waiting. Not intruding. Not judging. Simply present, as if the grove itself had gathered them. A faint pulse rippled through the air at the sight of them, soft and instinctive, like a chord warming before it finds its shape.

Nicholas blinked. "How long have you been standing there?"

Paloma leaned down, her voice a warm whisper against his ear. "What do you think?"

Nicholas shrugged, still wiping the last traces of tears from his eyes. "Maybe two minutes… maybe two hundred years."

The group laughed, even Chanotedah, though he tried to hide it behind a hand that glowed faintly with royal blue light.

Only Bharati did not laugh. She exhaled slowly, relief softening her usually stern features. Because Nicholas had not broken. He had bent. He had shaken. He had run. But he had not broken.

The grove around them shifted as Nicholas steadied himself. Not dramatically, not with the theatrical flourish of a wisp change, but subtly, like a living thing adjusting its posture. The pine branches lowered, forming a canopy that felt protective rather than oppressive. The air warmed by a few degrees. Even the ground pulsed faintly beneath his feet, as if checking his heartbeat and finding it stronger than before.

A second vibration answered the first, warmer and brighter, threading through the branches like a hidden melody. It brushed the edges of the grove with a soft shimmer, almost curious.

Anna stiffened beside him, wings flickering beneath her skin like trapped light. A gold flare pulsed from her chest, bright enough to catch the needles overhead.

She glanced around sharply. "Nicky… did you feel that?"

He shook his head, though the mist curled around his ankles as if it had felt something on his behalf. Paloma noticed. She always noticed. Her rose-hued glow deepened, her eyes softening with a maternal understanding that reached him before her words did.

Her gaze lifted toward the branches, watching the trees bow toward Nicholas with a reverence usually reserved for the Council. A faint coral shimmer brightened in her irises. "The realm responds to you," she murmured. "More strongly than I expected."

Chittaswarup heard her. His gaze sharpened, the earth beneath him humming in recognition. "It is beginning."

Bharati's expression darkened. "Too soon." A faint gray tremor rippled through the air behind her, echoing her concern.

Chittaswarup's voice softened, almost thoughtful. "Not just him. Something else stirred with him. A second note."

Paloma's gaze flicked toward Anna, the movement small but full of meaning.

Anna looked away, gold mist curling protectively around Nicholas, her wings pressing tight beneath her skin as if bracing for something she could not yet name.

Nicholas did not understand any of it. The grove hummed once, then fell still.

Paloma stepped closer to Nicholas, her hand resting lightly on his back. Her touch was warm, steady, and full of the quiet strength of someone who had carried many frightened children through many storms. The grove seemed to lean toward her as well, as if recognizing the mothering presence she brought into the world.

"You are safe," she murmured, her voice a soft anchor in the shifting air. "And you are not facing this alone."

For one heartbeat, silver-blue, gold, and lavender threaded through the mist like three notes testing the shape of a chord that had not yet learned its name.

Anna stepped closer, instinctively placing herself between Nicholas and the Council. Her hand found his shoulder, steady and warm.

Chanotedah, for once, did not crack a joke. His royal blue aura tightened around him like a coiled ribbon of light. His eyes were fixed on Nicholas with an intensity that made the boy's skin prickle. The scent of spearmint sharpened in the air, crisp and unmistakable.

"You felt him, did you not?" Chanotedah asked quietly. "Rhet."

Nicholas nodded, his throat tight. "It was like he reached through the viewer and grabbed me."

"He did not grab you," Asiza said, though her voice trembled. "But he saw you. And that is dangerous enough."

The mist around them pulsed once, then again, like a heartbeat trying to steady itself.

Chittaswarup lifted his head, sensing something beyond the grove. "The fractures are stirring."

Bharati's jaw tightened. "He is testing the boundaries."

Nicholas swallowed. "Rhet?"

"No," Bharati said. "Something older. Something that moves when the timeline is threatened."

Nicholas did not know what that meant, but the way the mist recoiled told him it was nothing good.

Paloma placed a hand on his shoulder. Her rose glow steadied the air, smoothing the tremors in the mist. "Nicholas, listen to me. What you saw was not destiny. It was a possibility. A warning. And warnings are meant to be heeded, not feared."

Nicholas looked up at her, eyes shining. "I do not want to be afraid anymore."

"Then choose not to be," she said softly. "Choose to be prepared."

He took a shaky breath. A faint silver-blue pulse radiated from his chest, answering her calm. "Teach me."

The grove exhaled, a soft rush of wind through the branches, as if the realm itself approved.

Bharati stepped forward, her presence commanding. "Your training begins now. But before we take you to the Atrium, you must understand who stands with you."

She gestured to the Council, and the grove brightened as if listening.

"Chittaswarup," she said. "Keeper of Continuum. He senses shifts in the timeline before they manifest."

Chittaswarup bowed his head slightly. The ground beneath him hummed in response, a deep, resonant vibration that made the pine needles quiver.

"Asiza," Bharati continued. "MistWeaver. She shapes the wisp with extraordinary precision."

Asiza lifted her hand, and a ribbon of wisps curled around her fingers like a tame serpent, shimmering in soft silver light.

"Paloma," Bharati said. "Heart Binder. She calms the mind, steadies the spirit, and anchors those who would otherwise be lost to fear."

Paloma's presence warmed the air, softening the edges of Nicholas's panic. A faint lavender pulse radiated outward, brushing the grove with a maternal calm that felt older than Nirvana itself.

"And Chanotedah," Bharati added, pausing with a faint smirk. "Well… he is Chanotedah."

Chanotedah spread his hands in a grand, exaggerated gesture. "You are welcome."

Nicholas almost smiled.

"And I," Bharati said, "am the Fracture Seer. I read breaks in the timeline and where they may lead."

Nicholas stared at her, hope and fear tangled in his chest. "Can you stop the future I saw?"

Bharati hesitated. A long, heavy silence settled over the grove. Even the mist held still.

"We are not supposed to be able to," she said finally. "But you might.

The grove shifted again, branches lowering, air warming, the realm itself leaning toward him as if waiting for his next breath. The mist surged upward, rising like a tide around their ankles. The grove dissolved in layers, color first, then sound, then shape, until only the hum of the Atrium remained.

Stone walls formed around them like a memory rebuilding itself. Nicholas gasped. The Atrium of Echoes. It was enormous, a circular hall with walls that rose impossibly high, etched with symbols that shifted when he tried to focus on them. The air vibrated with whispers, faint and distant, like echoes of voices long gone. The chamber felt alive, ancient, and aware of every heartbeat within it. "Are those people?" Nicholas whispered.

"Yes," Asiza said. "every Viator who has trained here leaves an imprint. Their echoes remain to guide those who come after."

Nicholas stepped forward, and the floor rippled beneath his feet, not like water but like memory. A silhouette formed in the mist. A young woman with braided hair. Then a man with a staff. Then a child no older than Nicholas, eyes bright with determination. Their forms flickered, half real and half remembered.

"Who are they?" Nicholas asked.

"Those who came before you," Paloma said. "And those who failed."

Nicholas's breath caught. "Failed?"

Bharati stepped beside him. "Training here is not about strength. It is about balance. Control. Understanding the weight of what you carry."
Nicholas swallowed. "And what do I carry?"

Chittaswarup answered. "Potential."

The word echoed through the chamber, bouncing off the walls like a living thing. Nicholas felt it settle into his bones, heavy and electric.

Asiza stepped forward, her eyes glowing faintly. "The mist reacts to you more strongly than any novice we have seen. That means your training must be accelerated."

Chanotedah added, "And it means Rhet will come for you sooner than we hoped."

Nicholas's heart pounded. "Why me?"

Paloma touched his cheek, her glow softening the air around him. "Because the timeline seems to recognize you."

A shadow swept through the chamber without any visible source. The echoes fell silent. Even the mist hesitated.

Nicholas shivered. "Did you feel that?"

Bharati nodded, her expression grim. "Rhet is watching."

Nicholas clenched his fists. "Then teach me how to stop him."

The mist surged around Nicholas as the symbols on the walls brightened.

Asiza raised her hands. "Then let us begin."

Far beyond Nirvana, where time fractured like glass, a presence stirred.

Rhet opened his eyes. And the Continuum trembled.

Chapter 13.5 Interlude

The fractured world stirred. Not with wind. Not with movement. But with memory. The air itself seemed to remember something it had not felt in an age, and the act of remembering it made it tremble. A faint silver-blue pulse rippled through the broken sky, the echo of the first note, followed by a thin gold shimmer threading through the cracks like sunlight slipping through storm clouds. Beneath both, too soft to notice, a lavender undertone trembled like a heartbeat waiting to be born.

Rhet felt the resonance before he understood it. Silver-blue crossed the broken sky, gold threading close behind. Beneath them trembled a third note, faint and unfinished.

Every hopper froze and turned toward the horizon.

Rhet lifted his face.

The first note had nearly brought him to his knees. Sharp, piercing, violent, like a blade driven straight through his ribs. This one was different. It did not strike him like a weapon. It unfolded inside him, slow and deliberate, like a memory he had forgotten he possessed. Warm. Bright. Protective. A resonance that felt maddeningly familiar, as if it had once belonged to him before the spring shattered and tore him apart.

A flash of gold light seared across his vision.

A child's shoe. A cracked street sign. A sliver of a forest canopy. A piece of a clock tower. A broken mirror reflecting nothing. A feather, bright orange and black. A child's drawing of a house beneath a smiling sun. A golden shimmer that pulsed like a heartbeat.

And in two shards, faint and flickering, reflections of an oriole and a diner.

They spun faster.

Rhet's jagged glass eye flickered. Something inside him recoiled while something else reached toward the resonance with a hunger he did not understand.

"No," he whispered. "Not again."

The third vibration strengthened. Rhet's jagged eye flashed violet—a color he did not recognize and instantly despised.

The fracture world convulsed. White cracks split the sky, the ground rippled, and the hoppers dropped as the resonance tore through them.

The three notes strained toward a chord the fracture world had not heard since the spring was whole.

"Master," one rasped, its voice stuttering like corrupted audio. "The spring… it shifts."

Rhet pressed a hand to his chest. Recognition hurt worse than the resonance.

"They have found each other," he whispered.

"Who?" one asked, its voice breaking into static.

Rhet's smile was small and dangerous, a thin curl of satisfaction that did not reach his eyes. "The boy," he murmured. "And the bird."

A vision flickered across the broken sky: Nicholas in the grove. Anna beside him, wings beneath her skin. Mel holding him close, lavender aura bright around her. A Council trying to hide its fear.

"Two notes," he whispered. "Two threads."

His jagged eye glowed with a feverish brilliance.

"But the third…"

He tilted his head, listening to the silence between the notes. The void inside him strained toward it, hungry and restless.

"…the third has not yet awakened."

A faint lavender flicker shimmered in the distance, too soft to pinpoint, but enough to make his eye twitch in pain. The hoppers recoiled, glitching violently as the color brushed the edges of their forms.

"Master," one said, its voice trembling, "the resonance grows. It will tear the spring apart."

Rhet laughed, a soft, breathless sound that held no humor. "No," he said. "It will tear me apart."

A memory flashed across his mind. A boy with a gentle face. A hand reaching toward him. A warmth he had once known and crushed. Vulnerability flickered across his expression, raw and unguarded, before he forced it down, burying it beneath cold resolve. He lifted his face to the broken sky, letting the fractured light cut across his features.

"And I welcome it."

Rhet closed his eyes and saw Nicholas—not clearly, but enough. A boy who had opened a seam without meaning to. A boy becoming something Rhet had spent centuries trying to destroy.

Rhet's smile sharpened, thin and cold.

"Find him," he whispered.

The hoppers rose, glitching violently, their forms stuttering like corrupted reflections.

"Find the boy. Find the bird. And watch the third."

At the word third, lavender shimmered at the edge of the fracture world. The hoppers recoiled.

Rhet remained alone, one hand over his heart.

An incomplete three-note chord trembled through the fracture world.

Rhet opened his eyes. And for the first time since the spring had shattered, he felt something he had forgotten how to feel.

Fear. Not of them. But what the chord would become.

Chapter 14

The Atrium hummed when Nicholas entered. Not loudly. Not dramatically. But with a low, resonant vibration that settled beneath his ribs, as if the chamber itself were acknowledging him, or warning him. A faint silver-blue pulse rippled through the floor beneath his feet. A thin gray crack shimmered high on the far wall, vanishing when he blinked. And beneath it all, a faint lavender resonance stirred at the edge of perception, quiet but persistent.

The mist curled around his ankles, warm and cool at once, brushing against him like curious fingers. It leaned toward him; not aggressively, but expectantly, as if listening for something. When Anna stepped beside him, a faint gold flicker threaded through the mist. When Melusine joined them, a soft lavender shimmer settled over the air like a calming veil.

The air shimmered with faint silhouettes, echoes of Viatori from ages long gone, shifting like reflections in rippling water.

Nicholas swallowed. "Sorry, I'm late."

His voice echoed strangely, bouncing off the stone walls and returning to him layered with whispers. "He comes. He rises. He remembers." The whispers carried a faint ache, like a warning wrapped in grief.

Nicholas flinched. "They're talking again."

Anna brushed his arm, her aura pulsing softly. "Ignore the warnings. Listen to the guidance."

Melusine added, her presence smoothing the air, "And don't let them freak you out."

Nicholas nodded, though his stomach fluttered.

Asiza stepped forward, her expression calm but focused. "We begin with grounding. Reach for the mist."

Nicholas extended his hand. The mist surged toward him, too fast, almost eager. He flinched, jerking back. The mist recoiled, swirling in confusion.

Melusine bit back a smile. "Try again. Slower."

Nicholas tried again. This time, the mist approached cautiously, brushing his fingertips before wrapping around his hand in a loose coil. A faint silver-blue pulse shimmered through it.

"Good," Asiza said. "Now shape it."

Nicholas pictured a sphere. The mist twitched. Then sagged. Then formed something vaguely round…ish.

Anna tilted her head. "It looks like a lopsided potato."

Nicholas groaned. "I was going for a ball."

Melusine grinned, warming the air. "It's a very earnest potato."

Nicholas tried again. The potato became a slightly less lopsided potato.

Asiza nodded. "Better. Again."

Nicholas exhaled, focusing harder.

The mist tightened, smoothed, brightened and for a heartbeat, it almost looked like a sphere.

Then it popped like a soap bubble.

Nicholas flinched. "Sorry!"

"Don't apologize," Asiza said. "You're doing well."

Bharati murmured, "Better than well."

Nicholas tried a ribbon next. It came out more like a tangled rope. He tried a flame. It sputtered, flickered, and died. He tried a bird. It looked like a melting snowman with wings.

Anna snorted. "Okay, that one's adorable."

Nicholas covered his face. "This is humiliating."

Melusine crouched beside him, her essence settling around his shoulders. "Nicholas… you're doing better than most novices do after weeks. You're just not in sync yet."

"Sync?"

"With the mist," she said. "It's not a tool. It's a partner."

Nicholas took a breath and remembered what the mist had already taught him. Don't force it. Invite it.

He opened himself to the resonance and waited.

The mist responded.

Nicholas nodded, bracing himself. He pictured a shield.

The mist gathered, uneven and trembling, flickering like a candle in a draft, but it formed a barrier in front of him. Not tall. Not strong. But real. It pulsed silver-blue, uneven but unmistakably his.

Anna's eyes widened. "Nicky… you did it."

Nicholas stared at the shimmering, unstable shield. "It is crooked."

Melusine laughed, lilac mist curling upward. "So are most beginnings."

But Asiza's expression changed. Her eyes narrowed, studying the shield with a focus that made the air tighten. "That should not be possible yet."

Before Nicholas could ask what she meant, Bharati's gaze snapped toward the far wall. The symbols etched into the stone flickered, then dimmed.

"The fractures…"

A sharp crack split the air. Nicholas froze. A thin line of blinding white light tore open in the center of the Atrium, small and unstable, pulsing like a heartbeat out of rhythm. The crack mirrored the seam he had opened in the grove, thin and trembling and hungry. The echoes fell silent. The chamber itself seemed to inhale.

Then the whispers began. Soft at first, then rising in a chorus that brushed the edges of Nicholas's mind.

Beware.

The word vibrated through the stone, through the mist, through his bones. Nicholas felt it, a pull that began as a whisper and grew into a force that bent the air around him. It tugged at him like gravity, like memory, like something calling his name from the other side of the Continuum.

A faint echo of Rhet's voice brushed the back of his mind. Not words. Not sound. A presence. Cold. Familiar. Reaching.

Nicholas staggered forward.

Anna grabbed him, her gold aura flaring bright enough to cast shadows across the walls. "Nicky, stop."

"I… cannot," Nicholas gasped. "It is pulling me."

The fracture brightened and the Atrium trembled. Symbols twisted across the walls while the echoes recoiled.

Chittaswarup stepped forward, his voice low and grim. "The fractures are responding to him."

Bharati's eyes widened, fear breaking through her composure. "No. They are responding through him."

The crack widened by a fraction, just enough for a sliver of impossible light to spill into the chamber. The air thickened, heavy with the scent of ozone and something older, something that tasted like the beginning of time.

Lavender mist curled protectively around Nicholas, but Melusine stepped back as the fracture pulsed again.

Asiza whispered, "This is not a seam. This is a call."

Nicholas felt the truth of it. The pull was no longer subtle. It was a hand closing around his ribs, a voice pressing against his thoughts, a memory he had never lived reaching for him.

Anna tightened her grip, wings flickering beneath her skin. "Nicky, stay with me."

The fractures had awakened. And somehow, they were responding to him.

Melusine darted to his other side, lavender mist wrapping around him in a steady, protective glow. "Breathe with me. Fight it." Her voice was calm, but the mist around her trembled in warning.

The pull intensified. Nicholas's feet slid across the floor as if the Atrium itself were tilting toward the light.

Bharati's voice cut through the rising panic. "Asiza. Now."

Asiza dropped to her knees and pressed both palms to the floor. The mist surged outward in a shockwave, forming a shimmering lattice of pink and gold threads that raced toward the fracture. A faint silver-blue pulse threaded through it, Nicholas's resonance bleeding into the spell without his permission.

"Stabilizing," Asiza said, her voice tight with effort.

The lattice struck the fracture and buckled instantly, warping like metal under unbearable heat. The crack shuddered wider. Impossible light flooded across the floor, and the pressure in the Atrium surged hard enough to make Nicholas stagger.

"It is resisting," Asiza said, her breath catching.

Bharati stepped beside her, raising her hands. Fracture light reflected in her irises, turning them into twin shards of broken glass. "Then we force it closed."

She thrust her hands forward. A ring of bright pink energy erupted around the fracture, tightening with a slow, crushing inevitability. The floor trembled. The walls flickered with silhouettes of past Viatori recoiling in alarm. The echoes whispered in frantic unison, their voices rising like a warning carried across centuries.

The pull seized him. Not from across the chamber this time, but from somewhere inside his own chest. For one terrifying instant, Nicholas couldn't tell where his thoughts ended and whatever waited beyond the fracture began.

"Bharati," Asiza said, her voice strained. "It is feeding on him."

"I know. Hold the lattice."

Asiza gritted her teeth and poured more mist into the shimmering web. It brightened, buckled, and nearly failed as Nicholas slid another foot forward.

Anna dug her heels into the floor, her gold aura blazing with fierce determination. "Hold on."

Melusine wrapped both arms around him, her lavender aura tightening like a protective tide. "Nicholas, breathe with me."

A violent pulse rolled the floor beneath them. The echoes fell silent.

The fracture was no longer reacting to the room. It was reacting to him.

And the shift rippled outward through the Continuum.

The stakes had changed. Whatever slept inside the fractures was no longer dormant, and Nicholas had somehow become its point of focus.

But the fracture's pull was relentless. It tightened around Nicholas like a tide that had chosen its shore. The Atrium trembled, its ancient stones humming with a warning older than any Viatori alive.

The fracture flared, a blinding burst of white that sent a shockwave through the chamber. The shimmering lattice shattered in an instant. Asiza was thrown backward, sliding across the floor as the mist recoiled from her hands. Bharati staggered, catching herself against the trembling stone.

The fracture widened, its edges crackling with unstable light that bent the air around it. Nicholas stumbled forward, no longer held by anything but the pull itself. The force grew stronger, irresistible, as if the Continuum had reached through the crack and wrapped invisible fingers around him.

Anna and Melusine cried out together, their voices sharp with fear. Nicholas reached out blindly, searching for Anna's hand, for Melusine's arm, for anything that could anchor him. But the mist twisted around him, spiraling upward in a vortex that lifted the hair from his forehead and pulled at the edges of his aura.

Bharati lunged, reaching for him. "Nicholas, do not move."

Asiza, still on her knees, thrust her hand toward him, trying to anchor him with a strand of mist. The thread stretched, trembling, then snapped as the fracture opened beneath him. Light swallowed him whole.

Nicholas fell.

He did not hit the ground. He did not hit anything. He fell through light, blinding and white and endless, until the light thinned into mist, and the mist thinned into nothing, and the nothing became a place that was not a place at all. Silence closed around him like a held breath.

Then the world exhaled.

He landed on his knees in a shallow pool of shimmering water. The surface rippled outward in concentric rings, each ring reflecting a different sky. Dawn. Dusk. Storm. Stars. The skies shifted too quickly to belong to any single world. A faint lavender shimmer drifted across the horizon. A soft silver-blue glow pulsed beneath his feet. A thin gold flicker danced at the edge of the water like a memory trying to form.

Nicholas gasped. The air tasted like metal and memory. The ground beneath him was not ground at all. It was a mosaic of fractured timelines, shards of moments suspended in a thin layer of mist. Beneath his feet, he saw pieces of things that did not belong together.

A child's chalk drawing. A broken bicycle wheel. A streetlight flickering in the rain. A feather. A handprint. A tear.

The fracture world.

But not the one Rhet lived in. This one was quieter. Older. Listening.

Nicholas pushed himself upright, trembling. "Hello…"

His voice echoed strangely, not outward but inward, as if the world were repeating his words from inside his own chest. He took a step. The water rippled. The sky cracked. A voice whispered from everywhere and nowhere at once.

He rises.

Nicholas spun, heart pounding. "Who is there?"

The mist swirled, forming shapes that dissolved before they could become real. Faces flickered in the water, some he recognized, some he did not, some he hoped he never would. He took another step. The fracture pulsed beneath him. A second voice whispered, soft and certain.

Two notes. Two threads.

Nicholas's breath hitched. "Anna…"

The mist brightened, warm and golden, the same color that had answered him in the grove. For a moment, he felt her presence, steady and familiar. But then the warmth vanished. Replaced by cold.

A shadow fell across the water.

Nicholas turned.

Rhet stood on the far side of the pool. Not glitching. Not distorted. But still in a way that made the world hold its breath. His round-brimmed hat cast a deep shadow over half his face. The other half gleamed with the jagged light of his fractured eye. His coat drifted behind him like smoke, edges fraying and reforming with every shift of the broken sky.

But it was his hands that froze Nicholas in place. Rhet's fingers tapped lightly against his hips. Tap. Tap. Tap. Right where holsters should have been. Right where phantom six-shooters waited in a world that no longer existed.

He did not walk toward Nicholas. He glided, boots whispering across the water without disturbing a single ripple. A gunslinger. A ghost. A fracture made flesh.

Rhet smiled beneath the shadow of his hat, and the fracture world tightened around them, listening.

"Hello, cousin."

The word struck Nicholas harder than the pull of the fracture. It landed in his chest like a truth he had never asked for and never wanted. He stumbled back, breath catching. "Stay away from me."

Rhet stepped forward, boots sinking into the water without making a sound. The surface stilled beneath him, as if the fracture world itself refused to ripple in his presence. "You opened a seam. You called about the fracture. You called me."

"I did not call you."

"Oh, but you did." Rhet tilted his head, studying him with an unsettling familiarity. "Fear is a beacon. And you shine so very brightly."

Nicholas clenched his fists. "I am not afraid of you."

Rhet laughed, soft and almost gentle, the kind of laugh that made the air tighten. "You should be."

The water around Rhet darkened, turning black and still. The skies above him flickered through a dozen broken timelines, each one showing a different ruin. Rhet lifted his hand. The water beneath Nicholas's feet froze, locking him in place.

"You saw a future," Rhet said. "One of many. One where I stand in the ashes of a world you failed to save."

Nicholas's breath caught. "I did not fail."

"You did." Rhet stepped closer, the fractured light in his eye brightening. "Or you will."

Nicholas shook his head. "No. I will not let that happen."

"You will not have a choice."

Rhet's voice rose with agitation. He lifted his hand higher. The water around Nicholas rose with it, spiraling upward, forming a vortex of shimmering shards. Each shard reflected a different version of Nicholas. A boy running. A boy crying. A boy is fighting. A boy falling. A boy breaking. And now, new reflections. A boy with gold wings. A boy with lavender eyes. A boy with a jagged glass eye like Rhet's.

Nicholas squeezed his eyes shut. "Stop."

Rhet's voice softened. "Look at them."

"No."

"Look."

Nicholas opened his eyes.

The shards spun faster. One showed him older, scarred and exhausted, standing alone in a world that no longer remembered him. Another showed him younger, terrified, reaching for someone who was not there. Another showed him standing beside Rhet, eyes cold, expression empty, the two of them bound by something ancient and terrible.

Nicholas staggered. "That is not me."

"It could be," Rhet whispered. "The fracture shows possibilities. And you… You are full of them."

Nicholas's knees buckled. The water rose higher, swirling around him like a storm that had learned his name.

Rhet stepped closer, voice low and intimate. "You do not understand what you are, what you carry. What will you become?"

Nicholas forced himself to stand. "I am not like you."

Rhet's smile sharpened. "No. You are worse."

The vortex tightened. Nicholas was lifted off his feet, suspended in the storm of fractured reflections. His heartbeat thundered in his ears. The shards spun faster, each one showing a different fate, a different version of him, a different path he could take.

Then a sound broke through the storm. Soft. Warm. Familiar. A note. The second note. Anna.

Nicholas gasped as warmth flared in his chest. The vortex faltered. The shards flickered. A gold pulse rippled across the fracture world.

Rhet's expression changed, surprise flashing across his face before fury overtook it. "No. Not her."

The note grew stronger. Then the third note joined it, softer and deeper, resonant as the tide. Melusine. A lavender shimmer rippled across the water.

Rhet staggered back. "Stop this."

The three notes aligned. The fracture world trembled. The skies cracked. The water shivered.

The completed chord rolled through the fracture world. Nicholas froze. Rhet's eyes widened. His jagged eye flickered violently in emerald.

"No," he whispered. "Not yet. Not now."

The chord pulsed again. The vortex shattered. Nicholas fell.

But he did not hit the water. He hit the light.

A beam of gold mist wrapped around his waist, yanking him upward. Another wrapped around his arm. Another around his chest, lavender and silver-blue intertwining. Voices shouted his name. Anna. Melusine. Asiza. Chanotedah. Bharati. Chittaswarup. The Council. They were pulling him back.

Rhet lunged, reaching for him. "Nicholas."

Nicholas reached back, not for Rhet, but for the light. The fracture world screamed. The mist tightened. And Nicholas was ripped out of Rhet's grasp.

Rhet's roar shook the broken sky. "You cannot escape me."

The fracture world pulsed, the skies cracking wider, the water trembling as if in fear of what had awakened. Rhet stood alone in the storm of broken timelines, his coat drifting like smoke, his jagged eye burning with fractured light.

The truth settled into him like a blade, cold and immediate.

The chord was forming. The bloodline was waking. And Nicholas, his cousin, was no longer his to claim.

Light swallowed Nicholas whole. The fracture collapsed behind him. And the last thing he heard was the faint echo of the third note, humming in the darkness like a promise.

CHAPTER 15

Nicholas woke to warmth. Not sunlight. Not blankets. But the warmth of a small, feathered body pressed against his ribs. Anna. Her oriole form lay curled against him, wings limp, feathers dulled to muted golds and oranges. Even in oriole form, she looked drained, as if someone had wrung the color out of her. A faint gold shimmer pulsed weakly from her chest, answering the soft silver-blue glow beneath Nicholas's ribs. A thin lavender undertone shimmered in the air around them, Melusine's presence lingering like a protective veil woven through the mist.

Nicholas blinked, vision swimming. And then he saw the Atrium. It did not look damaged. It looked wounded.

The floor was clouded with a thick, low-lying haze, not mist and not smoke, but something heavier, like the breath of a creature that had run too far and too fast. It clung to the ground in swirling patches, glowing faintly with exhausted light. The pillars, once sharp, crystalline, and perfect, were melting. Not collapsing. Not cracking. Melting. Slow rivulets of shimmering stone dripped down their sides like icicles on a warm winter day, each drop hitting the floor with a soft hiss before dissolving into the haze.

The ceiling sagged in places, its edges drooping like wax too close to a flame. A faint gray fracture shimmer pulsed across the highest arch, the same color Nicholas had seen in the seam he opened. The Atrium was breathing hard, each pulse of its walls a strained exhale.

Nicholas's heart clenched. "What… happened?"

A soft groan came from his other side. Melusine. She lay sprawled on the floor, hair tangled, cheek pressed against the stone, breathing as if she had run through a hurricane. When Nicholas whispered her name, her eyes fluttered open.

"Mel?" she echoed, blinking. "Since when am I Mel?"

Anna shimmered back into human form beside him, collapsing against his shoulder. Her gold aura flickered like a candle in a draft. "Since now."

Melusine huffed, trying to sit up. A faint lavender glow pulsed from her palms. "I do not know if I like it."

Nicholas steadied her. "We do."

She froze, surprised by the certainty in his voice, then softened. Instead of leaning on him, Melusine pushed herself upright, still breathless, and without hesitation slid an arm around both Nicholas and Anna. She drew them in against her sides, protective and steady, anchoring them with a quiet strength that felt older than her years. Her lavender radiance settled over them like a warm shield, smoothing the tremors in the air.

Nicholas felt the tension in his chest ease as she pulled them close, not leaning on him but holding him, bracing him, grounding him. The silver-blue beneath his ribs steadied. Anna's gold brightened by a fraction. Melusine's lavender deepened, warm and sure.

Then he looked up again. And the full devastation hit him.

The Council lay scattered around the chamber in various states of collapse. Not just tired. Spent. As if they had poured every last drop of themselves into dragging Nicholas back from the fracture. Asiza lay slumped against a pillar that sagged beneath her weight, her hands still faintly glowing with the remnants of the lattice she had tried to hold. Her muddy orange glow sputtered in uneven bursts. Chittaswarup was on one knee, the stone beneath him cracked from the force of his grounding. Chanotedah sat with his back against a half-melted column, royal blue flickering like a dying ember. Bharati lay on her side, one hand pressed to the floor as if she were still trying to read the fractures even in unconsciousness, her magenta aura dim and unstable.

Paloma was the only one still upright. She knelt a few feet away, her rose glow dim but steady, her hands pressed to the floor as if she were holding the Atrium itself together by sheer will. Her eyes lifted to Nicholas, soft and full of relief, but shadowed with something deeper. Something ancient. Something afraid.

The Atrium shuddered beneath them, a long, low tremor that rippled through the haze.

Melusine tightened her arm around Nicholas and Anna. "The realm is reacting to him."

Paloma's voice was quiet, but it carried through the wounded chamber. "No. The realm is reacting through him."

Nicholas swallowed hard. The resonance beneath his ribs pulsed once, then again, answering something he could not see.

The fractures had not just touched him. They had marked him. And the Atrium, ancient and alive, seemed to feel the difference.

Asiza slumped against a half-melted pillar, hair plastered to her forehead, hands trembling as faint sparks of mist flickered uselessly between her fingers. Her muddy orange trace sputtered in uneven bursts, each one dimmer than the last. Bharati knelt in the haze, palms pressed to the floor, whispering calculations under her breath. Sweat dripped down her temples, and her usually precise posture sagged with exhaustion. A magenta aura crackled with unstable fracture light, the color of a warning the Atrium itself could barely contain.

Chittaswarup sat cross-legged, eyes closed, chest rising and falling in slow, deliberate breaths as he tried to steady the Continuum's rhythm within himself. His shoulders shook with effort. A faint tremor of gray-white light pulsed beneath him, struggling to find coherence. Paloma leaned against a sagging wall, eyes red, hands clasped tightly as though holding the emotional threads of the room together by sheer will. Her aura flickered weakly, a light pink, dimmer than Nicholas had ever seen it.

Chanotedah stood hunched over his staff, knuckles white, jaw clenched, looking as though he had aged a decade in the last hour. His breath rattled in his chest, each inhale a battle. The sharp scent of spearmint cut through the haze, a warning signal that even he was close to collapse.

The Atrium's light flickered weakly, dimming and brightening in uneven pulses, like a heartbeat struggling to find its rhythm.

Nicholas's voice cracked. "Did… did I do this?"

A faint silver-blue tremor rippled across the floor beneath him, answering before anyone else could.

Chanotedah looked up, eyes heavy. "No, kid. He did."

Nicholas shivered. Rhet's gravity. Rhet's presence. Rhet's hunger. The fracture world still clung to him like a cold shadow.

Anna squeezed his hand, her gold aura tightening protectively. "You are safe now."

Melusine's arm tightened around both of them. "For the moment."

The Atrium groaned softly, a long, deep sound like ice cracking under strain. Nicholas felt it in his ribs. The chamber was not just reacting to the battle. It was reacting to him. The fractures had touched him, marked him, and somehow the Atrium seemed to feel the change.

The Council needed to regroup. They needed to breathe. They needed something to anchor them before the Atrium sagged any further.

Asiza pushed herself to her feet, wobbling slightly. "Everyone… sit. I am conjuring something."

Chanotedah snorted, though the sound was thin. "If it is another lecture…"

"No," Asiza said, then softened. "Something better."

She lifted her hands.

Mist gathered, sluggish at first, then brighter as she coaxed it gently, lovingly, like a mother soothing a frightened child. Colors swirled: pink, blue, mint, gold, lavender. The air filled with the scent of vanilla, sugar, and warm waffle cones. A storefront materialized in the center of the Atrium, whimsical and pastel, glowing softly like a memory of childhood joy. Asiza's Ice Cream and Confection Shop.

Above the door, a neon sign flickered into existence: TREATS. Each letter lit up in sequence. T in silver-blue. R in gold. E in lavender. A in silver-blue. T in gold. S in lavender. The colors pulsed gently, forming a soft, rhythmic pattern that echoed the Triad's resonance.

Nicholas blinked. "You… have an ice cream shop?"

Asiza wiped her brow. "I do now."

Melusine, who had been curled on the floor catching her breath, perked up instantly. "Thank the Continuum. I need sugar."

Anna nodded weakly. "Same."

Even Bharati cracked a tired smile, the fracture light in her aura dimming for a moment.

Inside, the shop was warm and bright, a stark contrast to the cold fracture world Nicholas had just escaped. Glass jars lined the counters, filled with shimmering candies that pulsed with soft light. Scoops of ice cream floated in midair, swirling with mist-infused flavors that glowed like tiny galaxies.

But beneath the sweetness, beneath the warmth, beneath the soft hum of comfort, the Atrium still trembled. The haze still clung to the floor. The pillars still sagged. And every Council member still bore the weight of what it had cost to pull Nicholas back.

The levity was real. The danger was greater. And the fractures were not finished with him.

Nicholas took a seat at the long counter. Anna slid onto the stool beside him, her shoulder brushing his. Melusine draped an arm across the backs of both stools, keeping them close, her presence settling around them like a soft protective net. The shop's warm glow contrasted sharply with the wounded Atrium beyond its walls, but the tension in the room clung to them like a second skin.

Asiza handed Nicholas a bowl of something blue and sparkling. "Eat. Your brain needs it."

Nicholas took a bite. It tasted like blueberries, starlight, and relief. But the comfort dissolved too quickly, leaving only the cold weight in his stomach. The Council gathered around him, each holding their own conjured treat, though none of them seemed to have much appetite. Their hands shook. Their eyes were hollow. Their auras flickered like dying lanterns.

Nicholas sat hunched over the counter, fingers curled around the cold bowl Asiza had placed in front of him. The blue-sparkling ice cream had already begun to melt, untouched. His breath came in shallow, uneven pulls, the kind that never quite reached the bottom of his lungs. Anna sat on his right; her shoulder pressed against his. Melusine sat on his left, hand resting lightly on his back. Both watched him with quiet, aching worry.

Chanotedah leaned forward, elbows on the counter, eyes heavy with exhaustion. "Alright, kid. Tell us. What did you see?"

Nicholas swallowed. The spoon in his hand rattled against the bowl. "I… I saw…" His voice cracked on the first word, thin and frayed. He tried again, but the second attempt trembled so hard it nearly broke. "I saw him."

The Council stilled. Even the floating scoops of ice cream paused mid-swirl, as if the shop itself were listening.

Nicholas's eyes unfocused, staring past them, not at the shop, not at the Atrium, but at something far away and still too close. "He was… he was standing there," Nicholas whispered, each syllable shaking like a loose windowpane in a storm. "Not standing. Floating. Or… gliding. Like the mist was carrying him."

His breath hitched. Melusine's hand pressed gently into his back. "You are safe," she murmured.

Nicholas nodded, but his voice did not steady. "He had this hat," he said, fingers twitching as if trying to trace the shape in the air. "Round. Pulled low. I could not see his face at first. Just the shadow."

He swallowed again, throat tight. "And his eyes…"

A tremor ran through him so sharply his whole body jerked. "His eyes were like broken glass. Sharp. Bright. Wrong."

Asiza's knuckles whitened around her spoon. Magenta flickered from Bharati with a dangerous crackle.

Nicholas's breathing quickened. "And the worlds… pieces of them. Floating around him. Like he was… like he was the center. Like everything was orbiting him. Like he was gravity."

The word gravity left his mouth in a whisper that barely held together. Anna took his hand. Nicholas squeezed back, desperate for something solid.

"He spoke to me," Nicholas said, voice trembling on every third syllable, rhythm stuttering with fear. "He… he knew my name. He knew everything. My parents. The viewer. The clock shop."

The Council exchanged a look that made Nicholas's stomach twist. Not fear of Rhet. Fear of what Rhet knowing those things meant.

Nicholas's voice dropped to a whisper. "He called me cousin."

The room went still. Even the haze outside the shop seemed to pause, listening.

Melusine's hand tightened on his back. Anna moved closer.

The Atrium groaned again, a long, low sound that vibrated through the floorboards of the shop.

Nicholas stared at the melting ice cream in front of him, hands shaking. "Why would he call me that?"

No one answered.

Because whatever Rhet knew, the Council clearly knew enough to be afraid of it.

And because Rhet had spoken the word with certainty.

His breath faltered. Nicholas's eyes filled, not with tears, but with the hollow terror of someone who had seen something he was never meant to see.

"He showed it to me," Nicholas whispered. "My home. My parents. Me. Like it was real. Like I could touch it."

His voice broke. Melusine slid her hand up to his shoulder, grounding him with a steady warmth.

Nicholas shook his head, trembling. "He said I could have it back. All of it. If I just… if I just took his hand."

The room went silent. Even the floating scoops of ice cream stilled, their soft glow dimming as if the shop itself held its breath.

Nicholas's next breath came out in a shudder. "I almost did."

Anna's grip tightened. The Council exchanged a look that carried centuries of fear.

Nicholas's voice dropped to a whisper that trembled so violently it barely formed words. "He said we were not done. He said we would finish this."

He finally looked up. His eyes were wide, glassy, haunted. "And I believe him."

Bharati's face had gone pale. "He is stronger than we feared."

Chittaswarup murmured, "The void has been feeding him."

Paloma whispered, "And he is feeding on Nicholas."

Nicholas's stomach twisted. "What does that mean?"

Chanotedah slammed his staff against the floor, the sound sharp enough to rattle the jars on the shelves. "It means we are out of time."

Bharati stood slowly, her exhaustion replaced by something heavier. Dread. Resolve. The weight of a truth she had hoped never to speak. "There is something you must understand. Something we hoped we would never have to explain."

She conjured a small orb of magenta mist, letting it hover above her palm. "This is a memory of Eunomia."

The orb expanded, projecting images into the air: a vast chamber of light, a crystalline artifact suspended at its center, and Arotza, the first Viatori, forging it from threads of mist.

Nicholas stared. "What is it?"

Bharati's voice softened. "Eunomia was among the earliest great artifacts. Arotza built it to help measure and maintain balance across the Continuum."

Asiza added, "Not a weapon. More like a regulator—a rhythm running through the timelines."

The image shifted. Eunomia shattering. Light exploding outward. Timelines fracturing. Abbadon standing at the center of the collapse.

Nicholas flinched. "Rhet's relative."

Bharati's eyes darkened. "Yes. And when Eunomia shattered, the Continuum lost its balance. The fractures began."

Nicholas swallowed. "What does this have to do with me?"

Asiza stepped closer, placing a gentle hand on his shoulder. Her pink aura flickered softly. "Because the fragment you touched at the beginning of your journey, the one that pulled you into Nirvana, was the heart of Eunomia."

The mist bowed toward him. Nicholas's breath caught.

"It reacted to you," Asiza whispered. "It has not reacted to anyone since Aurelion."

A faint Triad chord hummed in the air. The room fell silent. Nicholas felt the weight of their words settle over him like a mantle he was not ready to wear.

"I am not special," he whispered.

Anna squeezed his hand, her gold aura warming. "You are to me."

Melusine's arm tightened around both of them, lavender frequency steady. "And to the mist."

Chanotedah grunted. "And to the entire Continuum."

Fear rippled through the room.

Bharati said, "He must be contained." Asiza said, "He must be trained." Chittaswarup said, "He must be protected." Chanotedah said, "He must be trusted." Paloma said, "He must be supported."

Nicholas sat frozen as they argued around him, voices rising, exhaustion cracking their composure. The mist swirled in agitation, colors flickering in chaotic bursts. The Atrium groaned again, its wounded walls trembling.

Anna stood abruptly, stepping between Nicholas and the Council. "Stop."

Her voice was quiet. Deadly quiet. Her gold aura flared like a shield. Melusine rose beside her, lavender aura wrapping around Nicholas like a protective cloak.

"He is not a threat," Anna said. "He is a child. He is our child."

Nicholas's throat tightened. The Council fell silent. For the first time, they looked at him not as a prophecy, not as a danger, not as a hinge, but as a person.

The Atrium's lights flickered. The haze pulsed. The Triad chord trembled in the air, incomplete and waiting.

Nicholas looked at the Council, at the melting pillars, at the wounded chamber that had nearly died pulling him back. He felt the silver-blue beneath his ribs pulse once, then again, answering something ancient.

The fractures had awakened. Rhet had found him. And somehow, the Continuum was responding to him.

CHAPTER 16

The Atrium had not stopped trembling. Even after the ice cream shop dissolved. Even after the Council staggered upright, even after Nicholas was led to the quieter chamber beyond, the tremors continued in soft, uneven pulses, like the Continuum itself was breathing through clenched teeth.

Nicholas sat on a low stone bench, elbows on his knees, hands clasped so tightly his knuckles ached. Anna and Melusine flanked him, silent and watchful, their presence the only thing keeping him from unraveling. The air around him pulsed in faint, uneven waves, miniature ripples of silver-blue light skimming over his arms and legs as if his nervous system were broadcasting its panic through his skin. Each pulse sent a shiver through the mist at his feet.

The Council gathered in a loose circle a few paces away. They were not whispering. They were not hiding their fear. They were not pretending anymore.

Asiza paced in tight, surgical lines, fingers twitching with sparks of a dull orange mist she could not quite control. "He is destabilizing the Atrium. Every tremor is a feedback loop. If this continues, the chamber will fold in on itself."

Chanotedah leaned heavily on his staff, jaw clenched so hard the muscles jumped. A royal blue vibration spiked sharply. "Or the Atrium is reacting to him, which is worse. A wounded creature thrashes hardest."

Paloma pressed a hand to her chest, her rose aura flickering like a candle in a draft. "He is terrified. Anyone would be. The emotional bleed is enormous. It is flooding the room."

Chittaswarup sat cross-legged, eyes half-closed, voice calm but strained. A faint gray-white pulse radiated beneath him. "Fear is a form of resonance. It amplifies. It echoes. It seeks mirrors."

Bharati scribbled calculations in the air with trembling fingers, equations unraveling as fast as she wrote them. Her magenta aura crackled with fracture light. "The Continuum is thinning. Rhet is pushing. If Nicholas's resonance spikes again, we may trigger a sympathetic collapse."

Melusine snapped, lavender aura flaring. "Say that again, and I will show you a spike." Her tail flickered into existence for half a second, a flash of serpentine instinct, before she forced it away.

Anna shot her a warning look, but her own gold aura was already burning hot. "Enough. He can hear you."

Asiza did not stop pacing. "He should hear us. He needs to understand the danger."

Chanotedah growled, "He understands fear. Look at him."

Paloma's voice softened. "He needs comfort, not condemnation."

Bharati shook her head sharply. "Comfort will not stop Rhet."

Chittaswarup murmured, "But fear will feed him."

Melusine stepped forward, voice low and dangerous. "Then stop feeding him."

Nicholas's breath faltered.

Nicholas's breath stuttered. His hands began to shake, then his shoulders, silver-blue ripples racing along his skin as his heartbeat fell into step with the trembling floor.

He pressed his palms to the stone bench, but it trembled beneath him. He folded inward. He was thirteen. Thirteen. He had watched Rhet tear at worlds, watched the Atrium melt, watched the Council fall—and he had almost taken Rhet's hand.

His chest tightened. His throat burned. His thoughts spiraled. I should not be here. I am not ready. I am not strong enough. I want my mom. I want my dad. I want my room. I want the mantle clock ticking the way it always did. I want to go home.

The mist around his feet flared, muddy orange, then magenta, then a frantic, flickering gold. A shimmer rose around him. Moments from other whens flickered into existence, translucent and trembling like reflections on water.

To his left, his bedroom door stood half open, hallway light spilling in. To his right, his father reached for the coffee pot, humming off-key. Behind him, the mantle clock ticked in perfect sync with his pulse. In front of him, a younger Nicholas curled on the couch watching cartoons.

The images overlapped, stuttering between frames. Nicholas's breath hitched. His eyes filled. "I want to go home."

The ghost timeline pulsed, brightening, sharpening, as if answering him. The Atrium trembled in sympathy. The pillars shivered. The ceiling rippled, and the melting stone above them glowed not in Triad colors but in the aura colors and memory echoes of every Viator past and future. Muddy orange. Gold. Magenta. Silver-blue. Lavender. Rose. Royal blue. Indigo. Colors Nicholas did not even have names for, all dripping like molten history.

The floor hummed beneath his feet. The mist climbed his legs, swirling in frantic colors, orange and magenta and gold, then a deep, aching blue that felt like longing made visible.

Anna's breath caught. "Nicholas…"

Melusine's expression softened. "Oh, kid…"

The ghost timeline flickered faster, his mother's hand brushing his hair, his father laughing, the mantle clock glowing, Rhet's shadow stretching across the floor.

Nicholas squeezed his eyes shut. "I do not know what is happening. I do not know how to stop it."

Anna knelt in front of him, hands warm on his shaking knees. Her gold aura flared like a shield. "You are scared. That is all this is. Fear echoes."

Nicholas's voice broke. "I want my family."

Anna's eyes softened. "You have one."

Melusine nodded. "Right here."

The ghost timeline dimmed, just slightly, as if listening.

Melusine shifted so she was facing him fully. "It means you need tools. And we are going to teach you."

Nicholas swallowed. "I do not know how."

"That is alright," Anna whispered. "We will start small."

Melusine's voice gentled. "Close your eyes."

Nicholas obeyed.

"Good," she murmured. "Now breathe with me. Slow. In through your nose."

Nicholas inhaled, shaky and uneven. Anna inhaled with him. Melusine inhaled with him. The mist dimmed.

"Hold it," Melusine said softly. "Just for a moment."

Nicholas held. The Atrium held with him.

"Now let it out."

They exhaled together. The tremors softened. The ghost timeline thinned. The mist settled around his feet like a blanket instead of a storm. A faint harmonic vibration shimmered in the air. The mist shifted into a three-pointed pattern around them. A soft glow connected their hands and shoulders. The Atrium quieted, as if listening.

Three breaths. Three rhythms. One resonance.

Paloma whispered, "They are syncing."

Asiza murmured, "That should not be possible."

Chanotedah muttered, "Is it dangerous?"

Chittaswarup breathed, "It is necessary."

Bharati whispered, "It will attract Rhet."

But none of that mattered.

Right now, Nicholas was breathing. Right now, he was not alone. Right now, he had a family.

The mist glowed with something steadier. Something hopeful. Something beginning.

"STOP."

Bharati's voice cracked through the chamber like a whip. Nicholas jolted. The Triad glow snapped. The ghost timeline flared in a violent burst of silver-blue and gold and lavender. Equations unraveled around Bharati's hands in frantic spirals, dissolving as quickly as she formed them. Fracture light flickered in her eyes. She took a step forward, almost reaching for Nicholas, then stopped herself, fear twisting her expression into something sharp and unfamiliar.

"This is dangerous," she said, her voice shaking. "You cannot sync with him. You cannot anchor him. You cannot allow this to continue."

Nicholas flinched at every word. The silver-blue ripples along his arms and legs spasmed violently. His breath stuttered. His chest tightened. The tremor returned, harder and sharper, as if her fear had become fuel.

Melusine rose. "Bharati, stop."

"No," Bharati snapped. "If his resonance stabilizes with yours, it will amplify. It will escalate. It will be called to Rhet. It will bring him here."

Nicholas's breath broke. The Atrium groaned. Cracks raced across the nearest pillar and the ceiling sagged. Then a sound rose—not human, not singular, but a chorus.

The Viatori's Past.

Their voices rose like wind through broken glass, layered and ancient. Faces flickered in the wounded pillars—some familiar, some lost to time.

A pressure settled on Nicholas's chest, ancient grief, crushing and cold. He clamped his hands over his ears, but the cries were not in the air. They were in the stone. In the mist. In him.

Melusine's face drained of color. "Oh no. The echoes."

Anna's voice trembled. "They are hurting."

The cries swelled. A chunk of ceiling slid downward like a melting star, and Melusine lunged, pulling Nicholas back as it struck the floor and dissolved into mist.

Chanotedah shouted, "Everyone out."

The walls sagged inward. Mist poured from the cracks, and the chorus rose toward a crescendo.

Nicholas stumbled backward, breath coming in panicked gasps. "I cannot. I cannot. I cannot."

Anna reached for him. "Nicholas, stay with me."

But he tore away. The ghost timeline surged, blinding him with images of home. He ran. He sprinted through the trembling archway, down the mist-lit corridor, past the echo of the Council shouting his name. He did not stop running until the lavender sky opened above him. Until the lake came into view. Until his legs gave out.

He collapsed onto the sand, chest heaving, tears burning hot tracks down his cheeks.

Behind him, the Atrium groaned, a wounded creature collapsing under the weight of its own memories, and the cries of the Viatori's Past faded into a long, shuddering silence.

The Council stood in the ruins of the chamber, breathless and shaken, each of them staring at the place where Nicholas had been. Their auras flickered in uneven pulses. Their eyes did not meet. The fracture was no longer only in the Atrium.

It had begun forming between them.

And outside, alone beneath the lavender sky, Nicholas curled into the sand, the silver-blue beneath his ribs trembling like a frightened heartbeat, the Continuum whispering around him in a language he did not yet understand.

Nothing is stable. Nothing is safe. And nothing will ever be the same again.

CHAPTER 17

A breeze crossed the lake, stirring the reeds. Nicholas felt Anna before he heard her, a familiar steadiness at the edge of his awareness.

Nicholas did not turn. He did not need to.

Her footsteps stopped behind him.

Then she stepped into view and lowered herself onto the driftwood beside him. She did not speak. She did not reach for him. She simply sat with her knees drawn up and her arms resting loosely over them, mirroring his posture without making it obvious. A faint gold shimmer pulsed around her, and the reeds leaned toward her in response.

The sky above them shifted, lavender deepening into bruised gold, the colors swirling like someone was stirring the horizon with a slow, uncertain hand. A loon called again, its cry stretching across the water like a thread trying to stitch the world back together.

Anna watched the ripples fade before she finally said, in a voice soft enough not to disturb the fragile calm, "You ran."

Nicholas's throat tightened. "I did not mean to."

"I know."

The reeds whispered. The water breathed. The world held its breath.

Then Anna added, "I ran too."

Nicholas blinked, turning toward her. "You."

Anna's gaze stayed on the lake, her bright copper eyes reflecting the shifting sky. "The first time I saw a fracture."

Something in her voice—a tremor, a memory—made Nicholas wait.

Anna exhaled slowly, the breath leaving her like something she had been holding for years. "I was eight," she said. "Younger than you are now. I was not chosen yet, not officially. I was just a kid in a village near the edge of the Continuum. My biggest worry was whether my brother would steal my bread roll at dinner."

Nicholas tried to imagine her that way, small and ordinary and unscarred by the weight she carried now. It felt impossible.

Anna's fingers brushed the sand, tracing a line that the next breeze immediately erased. "One night, the sky split open. Not like a storm. Not like lightning. It was wrong. A tear. A fracture. And everything inside it was moving backward and forward at the same time."

Nicholas shivered. He knew that feeling too well.

Anna's voice lowered, the memory pulling her inward. "The air tasted like metal. The ground hummed. The animals went silent. Even the mist hid from it. I remember standing there with my brother's hand in mine, and for a moment I thought the world was breathing in reverse."

The lake stilled completely, as if remembering with her.

"I ran," she said. "I ran so fast I could not feel my legs. I ran until the sky closed and the world felt real again. And when I stopped, I realized I had left my brother behind."

Nicholas's breath caught.

Anna's gold aura dimmed to a soft, aching glow. "He was fine. He found me. He laughed. He told me I ran like a startled bird. But I never forgot the feeling. The fracture did not just scare me. It marked me long before the Council ever found me."

Anna finally turned to Nicholas, her voice steady but threaded with something ancient. "You are not the only one who has run from what you are. And you are not the only one the fractures have touched."

Nicholas swallowed, the silver-blue beneath his ribs pulsing once in answer.

"I froze," Anna said. "Everyone else ran. My brother grabbed my arm and pulled me, but I could not move. I could not breathe. I thought the world was ending."

Her voice softened, but the memory sharpened the air around them. The lake rippled outward in a slow, sympathetic pulse, as if the water itself remembered what it meant to be afraid.

"I was terrified, Nicholas. Terrified in a way I did not know a person could be."

Nicholas frowned, his voice barely above the whisper of the reeds. "But you were brave."

Anna's lips curved, not into a smile, but into something quieter and almost fragile. "Brave," she repeated, tasting the word as if it belonged to someone else. "Nicholas… I was eight."

A breeze lifted a strand of her copper hair and brushed it across her cheek. She let the wind take it; her gaze still fixed on the shifting lake.

"I was not brave," she said. "I was frozen. My legs would not move. My voice would not work. My brother had to drag me away because I could not make myself run."

Nicholas blinked. "But you are never scared now."

Anna let out a breath that trembled at the edges, the first crack in the armor she always wore around him. "That is not true. I get scared all the time."

He turned toward her fully, surprised by the confession.

"Bravery is not the absence of fear," she said. "It is what you do with it. And back then, I did nothing. I just stood there and watched the sky tear open."

The loon called again, a long, low note that echoed across the lake like a memory surfacing from deep water.

Anna's fingers curled slightly in the sand. "The Council came after that first fracture. They sealed it. They saved us. And they saw me, this scared little girl who could not look away from the tear in the sky. They said I had potential."

Nicholas listened, still hugging his knees.

Anna continued, her tone softening into something almost reverent. "They said I had the instincts of a Cura. That I could feel the fractures before they formed. I could sense the way the mist shifted when the Continuum was in pain. But none of that felt like a gift to me. It felt like a burden I did not understand."

"I did not want to be chosen," she said. "I wanted to stay home. I wanted to stay with my brother. I wanted to pretend the sky had never split open."

Nicholas's breath caught. "Then why did you go with them?"

Anna's eyes softened, the gold around her warming like a lantern in the dusk. "Because the fractures do not care what we want. Once they touch your life, pretending they are not there does not make them disappear."

She looked at him then, really looked, her gaze steady and full of something ancient and aching.

"You and I are not so different, Nicholas. The fractures touched you, too. They marked you long before you understood what that meant."

Nicholas drew a slow breath. Something silver-blue stirred beneath his ribs, subtle but unmistakably familiar.

Anna leaned closer, her voice barely above the breath of the reeds. "You ran today. I ran once, too. And just like me, you came back to the place that scares you because you are trying to understand it."

Nicholas's eyes stung. "I did not come back. I just… ended up here."

Anna shook her head gently. "You came here because this is where you feel the world most clearly. The water listens to you. The mist listens to you. And I listen to you."

The breeze shifted, warm and soft, brushing against both of them

Nicholas looked down at his hands, trembling slightly. "I do not feel brave."

Anna's voice was quiet, steady, certain. "You do not have to feel brave to be brave."

The lake shimmered. The reeds bowed. The sky deepened into a richer lavender, as if the world itself leaned closer to hear what came next. Anna rested her hand lightly on his arm, gold meeting silver-blue in a soft, glowing pulse.

"You are not alone in this," she said. "Not now. Not ever."

And for the first time since the Atrium collapsed behind him, Nicholas felt the trembling inside him ease, just enough for him to breathe. The quiet between them settled, warm and fragile, like a blanket laid over a wound.

Anna let that quiet sit for a moment. Then her gaze drifted back to the horizon, and something in her expression shifted. Not away from him, but deeper, as if she were opening a door she rarely touched.

"But I was not chosen yet," she said. "Not then. Not until the next fracture."

The tone of her voice changed. Thinned. Stretched as a thread pulled too tight.

"The one that took my brother."

Nicholas's breath caught.

The sky above them flickered again, a faint gray crack appearing for a heartbeat before fading, as if the Continuum itself remembered the moment she spoke of. The water was still. Even the reeds listened.

Anna did not look away from the horizon. "It happened three months later. Another tear. Bigger. Closer. My brother and I were outside when it opened. He did not hesitate. He grabbed my arm and shoved me behind him."

Her fingers tightened on the driftwood, knuckles whitening.

"I remember the sound," she whispered. "Like the world inhaling. Like everything was being pulled backward. And he pushed me away from it."

A muted lavender-gold shadow spread beneath the surface of the lake, deepening as the silence between them stretched.

Nicholas felt his chest tighten. "Anna…"

"He saved me," she said, voice steady but trembling underneath. "He saved me, and the fracture took him instead."

The wind died. The reeds stilled. Even the lake seemed to hold its breath, as if the world itself bowed its head for the boy it had lost.

Anna blinked once, slowly. "The Council arrived too late to save him. But they saved me. And they said that meant something. That I was meant for this. That I had been spared for a reason."

Nicholas swallowed hard. "That is not fair."

"No," Anna said softly. "It is not."

She finally turned toward him, and for a moment Nicholas saw her not as the guardian who always knew what to do, but as a girl who had once been small, terrified, and alone. A girl who had lost someone, too. A girl who had survived.

Anna's voice gentled. "I do not tell you this to make you sad. I tell you because you need to understand something." She shifted closer, not touching him yet, but close enough that he could feel her warmth. Her gold aura brushed the edge of his silver-blue ripples, smoothing them.

"You are not the only one who has ever felt small or overwhelmed or unprepared," she said. "You are not the only one who has ever been afraid of what the world expects of you."

Nicholas stared at the water, the lavender sky rippling across its surface.

Anna leaned in, her copper bright eyes steady and warm. "I have been where you are. I have felt what you are feeling."

Nicholas swallowed. "But I am not like you."

"You are exactly like me," she said.

He blinked.

"You think you are supposed to be strong all the time," she continued. "You think you are supposed to understand everything that is happening to you. You think you are supposed to carry the weight of the world without letting anyone see you shake."

Nicholas looked down at his hands, the same hands that had made the Atrium tremble, the same hands that had pulled ghost timelines into the air, the same hands Rhet had reached for.

"They expect so much from me," he whispered. "The Council. The mist. Even the world. I do not know how to be what they want."

Anna's expression softened. "You do not have to be what they want. You do not have to be what they fear. Or what they hope. Or what they whisper about when they think you cannot hear."

Nicholas's breath hitched.

"You only have to be Nicholas," she said.

He shook his head. "But that is not enough."

"It is," she said firmly. "It always has been."

The wind stirred again, lifting a ripple across the lake. Anna rested her palm lightly on the driftwood between them, close enough that he could choose to bridge the space if he wanted.

"Tell me what you are afraid of," she said.

The question was not demanding. It was not a test. It was an invitation.

Nicholas drew in a shaky breath. "I am afraid of everything."

Anna nodded once, slow and steady. "Then we will face everything."

She shifted closer.

"Together."

Nicholas did not answer at first. The reeds whispered, urging him gently. The lake exhaled a soft ripple.

"I am afraid of what I saw," he said. "Of what I did. Of what I might do again."

His voice cracked. "I am afraid of Rhet not just because he is dangerous. But because he made it sound easy. Like I would not have to feel all of this if I just..."

He swallowed hard.

"If I just went with him."

A faint gray shimmer rippled across the lake. Anna's breath caught, but she did not interrupt.

"I am afraid of myself," Nicholas whispered. "Of what I am. Of what I am becoming."

The words trembled in the air.

Anna did not hesitate. She slid off the driftwood and wrapped her arms around him in a fierce, full-body hug, warm, grounding and unhesitating. Her gold aura flared, wrapping around his silver-blue ripples and calming them. Nicholas froze. Then something inside him loosened.

Anna pulled back just enough to look him in the eyes.

"You are allowed to be scared," she said. "You are allowed to not know what to do. You are allowed to feel everything you are feeling."

Her voice softened into something steady and unshakeable.

"And you do not have to face any of it alone."

The word settled into him like a promise.

They stood slowly, the driftwood creaking beneath them. Nicholas wiped his face with the back of his hand, and Anna brushed a stray leaf from his hair.

"Come on," she said gently. "Let us head back before Mel decides to drag you by the ear."

Nicholas managed a small laugh. "She would."

"Oh, absolutely."

They started walking along the shoreline, the sky deepening into a dusky violet above them. The lake mirrored the color, turning the world into a soft, shimmering twilight.

They had only gone a few steps when the air behind them shifted. A thin seam of light split the air, vertical and delicate, humming with a faint pink-violet glow. Anna stopped. Nicholas turned.

Melusine stepped through the fold like she had been carved out of the dusk itself. Her bare feet touched the sand without a sound. Her hair lifted in the residual breeze of the seam, catching the lavender light. The fold snapped shut behind her with a soft sigh.

And then the butterflies came.

They rose from the reeds, dozens and then hundreds, drifting toward her in a slow, spiraling dance. Their wings glowed with soft bioluminescent blues and golds and lavenders, pulsing like tiny heartbeats. They did not swarm. They congregated, gathering around her shoulders, circling her arms, hovering in a loose halo above her head.

Melusine lifted one hand, palm up, and a butterfly landed on her finger as if answering a call only it could hear.

Anna exhaled. "Showoff."

Melusine smirked. "I do not control them. They just like me."

Nicholas stared. "Why?"

Melusine stepped toward them, the butterflies drifting with her like a living cloak of light. "Because they know resonance when they feel it."

A faint lavender pulse rippled across the lake. Nicholas's silver-blue ripples answered. Anna's gold aura brightened. Melusine stopped in front of Nicholas.

"You ran fast," she said. "Next time, warn me before you sprint across half of Nirvana."

Nicholas flushed. "Sorry."

Melusine's expression softened, protective and steady. "Do not apologize. Just do not disappear on us again."

Anna crossed her arms. "We are a unit."

Melusine nodded. "A triad."

The butterflies pulsed once, all at the same time, as if echoing the word. A faint hum rose in the air, soft, distant and awakening. The third note.

The butterflies lifted in a single shimmering wave, spiraling upward into the twilight sky.

Melusine glanced at the horizon. "We should get back. The Council will panic if they realize all three of us are gone."

Anna snorted. "They are already panicking."

Nicholas managed a small smile. "Let us go."

The three of them walked back toward Nirvana's heart, Anna on his right and Melusine on his left, the last of the butterflies trailing behind them like drifting embers. Far above the lake, the faint hum of the third note lingered in the air, waiting and growing and calling.

And somewhere deep within the Continuum, a fracture stirred in answer.

CHAPTER 18

As Nicholas, Anna, and Melusine approached the Atrium, the air shifted again. Not with the tremors of collapse, not with the sharp crack of a fracture, but with something subtler. Older. A low, resonant hum vibrated through the ground beneath their feet, as a warning whispered through stone. Nicholas slowed. Anna did too. Melusine's lavender aura tightened around them instinctively, a quiet shield.

The Atrium was no longer sagging or melting. It was not whole either. Instead, it was surrounded by a swirling cloud of tiny golden shapes moving in tight, purposeful patterns. At first, Nicholas thought they were sparks. Then he realized they were bees. Thousands of them. A living swarm weaving in and out of the fractured stone, sealing cracks with shimmering threads of light, stitching the wounded structure back together with impossible precision. Each bee left a faint trail behind it, like embroidery on the air.

Nicholas stared, wide-eyed. "Are they real?"

"As real as anything here," Anna murmured.

A soft voice answered from behind them. "They are Viatori."

Nicholas turned to see Paloma approaching, her steps light, her expression warm but tired. The golden glow of the bees reflected in her eyes. "The Council has recalled every active Viator they can reach," she said. "We need all hands and wings for what is coming."

Nicholas swallowed. "The storm."

Paloma nodded. "It is closer than we hoped."

She rested a gentle hand on his shoulder. "Being a Viator is not only about fighting or traveling through time. Sometimes it means you mend what others cannot. Sometimes it means you hold the world together one thread at a time." She gestured toward the bees. "They are healers. Builders. Memory keepers. They answer when the Continuum cries."

Nicholas watched the bees work, each one moving with a precision that felt ancient and sacred. The Atrium pulsed faintly beneath their touch, as if grateful.

"You three should get to the food court," Paloma said. "Eat. Hydrate. The training ahead will be intense, and you will need your strength."

Anna nodded. "We will."

But Nicholas did not move. His gaze had drifted past Paloma, deeper into the Atrium. The Council was gathered again. This time, they were not arguing. They were speaking to someone. Someone standing at the center of their circle.

Nicholas squinted. "Is that Chase?"

Anna followed his gaze. "It is."

Chase stood tall, hands clasped behind his back, listening intently as the Council spoke to him. Nicholas could not make out the words, but he caught fragments. Lions. Regulatori. Balance. Lineage. Chase nodded once, sharply, like someone receiving orders he already understood.

Nicholas took a step toward him, hope flaring in his chest. Maybe Chase knew something. Maybe he could tell him about home. About the clock shop. About the pink shimmer. About anything.

"Chase," Nicholas called softly.

But Chase did not hear him. He turned, opened a fold in the mist with a practiced sweep of his hand, and stepped through. The fold sealed shut just as Nicholas reached out, fingers brushing only empty air.

The hum of the bees filled the silence.

Anna touched his arm gently. "Come on. Let us eat."

Nicholas stared at the place where Chase had vanished, a knot tightening in his chest. He was not sure if he had missed a chance or if something much bigger had just begun.

The closer they got to the food court, the more the air changed. It was not just noise. It was a charge, a vibration, like the moment a thousand cell phones all buzz with the same notification. A ripple of energy ran through the hallways, through the mist, through the very stones beneath their feet. Nicholas felt it before he heard it.

Then the voices hit.

A wall of whispers. Gasps. Fragments of rumor flying like sparks.

The Atrium is melting. The fracture. The void. The bees. The storm. Rhet. The Equal. The boy who almost. The boy who survived. The boy who ran.

Heads turned as Nicholas, Anna, and Melusine stepped into the food court. The room was packed, students from every when and every discipline clustered around tables, trays forgotten, conversations snapping like static. The air shimmered with tension, fear, excitement, and something else Nicholas could not name.

Anna stepped slightly in front of him, not shielding him, but guiding the energy away from him like a lightning rod. Melusine moved to his other side, lavender aura steady and protective.

The Triad entered the room together.

And the room felt it.

Lazer spotted them first. He stood from a table near the center, posture sharp, eyes scanning Nicholas with a mixture of relief and calculation. Antonia sat beside him, arms crossed, jaw tight, her long mohawk pulled straight back into a knot at the base of her skull in a way that meant she was stressed. Melusine guided Nicholas and Anna toward the table, her lavender aura settling protectively around them as the food court buzzed with rumor and static.

Lazer waved them over. "You three. Here."

Nicholas followed Anna to the table. Melusine slid into the seat beside him, her presence steady. Antonia did not look up at first. She was tapping her fingers against the table in a rapid, irritated rhythm, the kind she used when she was thinking too fast for her own good. When she finally lifted her gaze, her eyes locked onto Nicholas with a strange mix of frustration, fear, and something like resolve.

"You almost died," she said flatly.

Nicholas blinked. "I—"

"And you almost took half the Atrium with you," she added.

Lazer shot her a warning look. "Antonia."

"What," she said, her tone sharp but not cruel. "He deserves honesty."

Nicholas's stomach twisted. "I did not mean—"

"I know you did not," Antonia said, softer now. "But intention does not matter in combat. Survival does."

Anna stepped in. "Antonia—"

"No," Antonia said, sitting up straighter. "He needs to hear this. And I need to say it."

Lazer sighed, but he did not stop her. Antonia leaned forward, elbows on the table, eyes sharp and unflinching. "Nicholas, I do not like this. I do not like that you are thirteen. I do not like that the Council is pushing you. I do not like that Rhet is hunting you. And I really do not like that you are tied to the Continuum in ways none of us understand."

Nicholas's breath caught.

"But," she continued, "I am on your side."

Nicholas blinked. "You are."

Antonia nodded once, reluctantly but firmly. "Yes. I am. Because if you are going to survive what is coming, you need someone who knows how to fight. Someone who knows how to use the Evanidus Sphere without blowing themselves into a different century. Someone who can teach you how to suppress a resonance spike before it kills you."

Lazer added, "And someone who will not sugarcoat anything."

Antonia shot him a look. "Exactly."

Nicholas stared at her. "You are going to train me."

Antonia exhaled sharply, like she had been holding her breath for hours. "Yes. I am your trainer now. Evanidus. Suppressio. Combat basics. How not to get killed in the first five seconds of a fight."

Nicholas swallowed. "Why me?"

Antonia's expression softened, just a fraction. "Because you are important. And because you are not ready. And because if someone does not teach you fast, we are all in trouble."

Lazer nodded. "She is right."

Nicholas looked between them: Antonia's fierce determination, Lazer's steady calm, Anna's quiet support, and Melusine's protective presence. For the first time since the Atrium collapsed, he felt something shift inside him. Not confidence. Not certainty. But direction.

Antonia stood abruptly. "Eat. Hydrate. Meet me in the training hall in thirty minutes."

Nicholas blinked. "Thirty."

"Twenty-nine now," she said, already walking away.

Lazer clapped Nicholas on the shoulder. "Welcome to the team."

Anna smiled softly. "You are not alone in this."

Nicholas slid into the seat beside her, the buzz of the food court still crackling around them like static. His stomach growled loudly, and for the first time since the Atrium collapsed, he realized how hungry he was. He glanced at the table.

"I wish I had a slice of Angelo's," he muttered under his breath. "The pepperoni one. From back home."

Before Anna or Lazer could respond, the air above the table shimmered. Mist curled inward, gathering itself, and with a soft pop of displaced air, a steaming slice of Angelo's pepperoni pizza appeared on the tray in front of him.

Nicholas jerked back. "What… how…"

Anna did not even blink. "It heard you."

Nicholas stared at the slice. It looked exactly right, the crisped edges, the bubbling cheese, the pepperoni curled into tiny cups of oil. He could smell it. He could practically taste it.

And for a moment, the world felt almost steady again.

Nicholas squinted at the pizza. "I need pizza."

Anna shrugged, her gold aura warm and steady. "You need comfort. Familiarity. Something that reminds you of home. The mist knows the difference."

Nicholas leaned back, still unsure. "Alright, but what if I want something else. Like a burrito."

The pizza shimmered. Mist curled around it, folding and unfolding like a breath, and in the space of a heartbeat, the slice collapsed inward, reshaping itself. The cheese dissolved into steam, the crust folded, the pepperoni melted into a swirl of warm spices. A burrito sat on the tray.

Nicholas's jaw dropped. "No way."

Anna smirked. "Told you."

Lazer raised an eyebrow. "Just do not ask for a live tiger. The mist has limits."

Nicholas was not listening. He poked the burrito as it might explode. Around them, the food court's energy shifted again, not quieter but sharper. Students were pretending to leave, but their paths curved closer to Nicholas than necessary. Some slowed their steps, whispering behind their hands. Others angled their phones subtly, snapping pictures as if he would not notice.

A few did not bother with subtlety at all. One girl from a future century held her phone high, capturing a full video as she walked past. Another student from the 1800s stared at the device in awe, whispering, "It captures him. Truly."

Nicholas felt heat rise in his cheeks. "Why are they doing that?"

Anna's expression softened. "Because they are scared. And curious. And because they want to remember this moment in case…"

She did not finish. She did not have to. In case they do not survive the storm.

Nicholas swallowed hard.

A boy from the engineering cohort passed close enough that Nicholas could hear him whisper, "That is him. The one who melted the Atrium."

Another voice followed. "The one who came back from the void."

Another. "The Equal."

Nicholas's stomach twisted. He did not feel like any of those things. He felt like a kid with a burrito he did not ask for.

Anna leaned closer, her voice low and steady. "Ignore them. They do not know you. They only know the stories."

Nicholas nodded, but the knot in his chest did not loosen.

Antonia's gaze found him across the room, her eyes sharp with purpose. She tapped her wrist, the message clear. Twenty-five minutes. Nicholas bit into the burrito, the familiar flavor grounding him even as his stomach twisted. The noise of the food court blurred into a distant hum. For a moment, he simply breathed, aware of Anna beside him, Melusine nearby, and the weight of everything pressing in. The storm was closing in. The world had turned its attention toward him. And the path forward had already begun to take shape beneath his feet.

Chapter 18.5 Interlude

The fracture was wrong.

Rhet felt it the moment he stepped through the seam: a metallic sting in the air, the fracture unsettled around him.

He stood among the drifting shards, coat trailing a fraction behind him. His jagged glass eye caught a dozen broken reflections at once.

He was shaking, though only slightly. Something was rising beyond his control.

A lieutenant approached, a tall, angular figure made of half-formed mist and fractured geometry, its outline glitching with every step. It bowed low, voice crackling like a broken radio. "Commander Rhet. The resonance spike—"

"I felt it," Rhet said, sharper than he intended.

The lieutenant flinched. Rhet rarely raised his voice.

His fingers tapped against his empty holsters. Tap. Tap. Tap.

The lieutenant straightened. "The third—"

"Do not name it." Rhet's voice cut like a blade. "Do not even think it."

The lieutenant froze. Rhet forced his breathing steady.

"He is syncing," Rhet muttered. "He is syncing with them."

The lieutenant tilted its head. "The boy."

Rhet turned sharply.

"He is not a boy," he said, low and dangerous. "He is a hinge. A fulcrum. A threat."

The lieutenant stepped back.

Rhet resumed moving, boots scraping across the fractured ground. "I had him. I had him in my hand. He was right there. He almost…"

He stopped. Jaw clenched.

"He almost chose me."

The admission tasted like rust.

The lieutenant's voice softened. "Commander, the spike destabilized the outer rings. We lost three corridors. The hoppers refuse to enter the lower sectors."

Rhet closed his eyes. For the first time in years, fear felt familiar.

Nicholas was changing. And the effects were spreading through the Continuum.

He opened his eyes, the glass one catching the fractured light in a violent shimmer.

"Prepare the hoppers," he said quietly. "All of them."

The lieutenant hesitated. "For what purpose?"

"For war," he said.

"They will not go."

"Then break them."

The lieutenant hesitated, its outline flickering like a candle in a draft. "They fear the note."

A faint vibration threaded through the chamber, distant but intimate, like the memory of a name.

Rhet staggered and pressed a hand to his chest.

The lieutenant rushed forward. "Commander—"

"Do not touch me."

Rhet shoved the lieutenant back with a burst of fractured force that cracked the ground.

"It is early," he whispered. "Too early for that sound. They are not ready. He is not ready."

The lieutenant flickered uncertainly, its geometry bending in and out of coherence. "What are your orders?"

"Find them," he said. "Find the Cura. Find the dolphin. Find the hinge. FIND THEM!"

"And when you find them, you do not engage."

The lieutenant blinked, its form glitching. "Commander."

"You watch," Rhet said, voice low. "You listen. You report."

He leaned in, the brim of his hat casting a deeper shadow across his face, the glass eye gleaming like a splinter of frozen lightning.

"And if that sound hums again…"

Rhet's smile was thin and sharp, a crack in porcelain.

"…you run."

The lieutenant bowed, glitching violently before vanishing into a seam of static.

Rhet stood alone, fingers tapping once more against his empty holsters.

The vibration returned. Rhet's hand curled into a fist.

"Not yet," he murmured to the empty fracture. "Not him. Not now."

But the sound answered anyway. Soft. Distant. Awakening. It threaded through the chamber with the quiet certainty of a prophecy beginning to stir.

For the first time in years, Rhet was afraid.

CHAPTER 19

The training hall was nothing like Nicholas expected. He thought it would be a gym. Or a dojo. Or maybe some kind of futuristic simulation room with glowing walls and floating targets. Instead, it was a cavern.

A vast cavern opened beneath Nirvana, ribbons of mist drifting along its ceiling like slow comets. Ancient markings shifted across memory-rock walls, and thin lines of light threaded the floor.

Nicholas stepped inside with Anna at his side. His burrito sat uneasily in his stomach.

Antonia stood at the center with arms crossed, one foot tapping. Lazer leaned against a nearby pillar, looking far less concerned.

High above, a dark crystal dome reflected the room slightly out of alignment, shielding the mountain from the distortions of Evanidus practice.

Antonia snapped her fingers with a sharpness that made Nicholas flinch. A sphere of shimmering silver mist appeared in her palm. The Evanidus Sphere pulsed faintly, not like a heartbeat but like a thought forming. Antonia's irritation softened only slightly as she tossed it upward. It hovered above her hand, spinning slowly and leaving a faint spiral of light behind it.

Nicholas reached out and touched the Sphere. The world lurched. The floor seemed to slide slightly to the left while the ceiling shifted to the right. His stomach flipped. His vision blurred. The air tightened around him as if the chamber itself were holding its breath. Antonia stepped forward with the brisk impatience of someone who had explained this a hundred times and expected him to keep up. She reminded him that Evanidus responded to intention and that hesitation only invited disaster.

The Sphere drifted toward him again, silver mist turning slowly inside it. Antonia watched with sharp focus.

Lazer stepped closer. "It wants clarity. Give it one destination and hold it."

Nicholas steadied his breathing. The Sphere brightened in response, as if pleased. Antonia's foot tapped again, faster this time, her impatience returning the moment she sensed hesitation. Anna watched from the far side of the room with her hands clasped tightly, hope and worry tangled together.

Nicholas lifted his eyes. The Sphere pulsed. The hall hummed. The air tightened around him, ready to fold.

Antonia told him again to choose a spot.

Nicholas took a breath and prepared to step.

Nicholas focused on a different platform, this one closer and far less likely to send him tumbling into a chasm. He fixed the image in his mind and stepped. The world contracted sideways, folding in a brief, disorienting twist. He reappeared three feet to the left of his intended mark and slammed shoulder-first into a stone column. The impact echoed through the chamber.

Anna winced and murmured that it looked painful. Antonia did not react at all. She simply told him to try again; her voice clipped with the same impatience that had been simmering since the moment he arrived.

Nicholas groaned and asked if he could rest. Antonia cut him off before he finished the sentence. He tried again. The world collapsed inward. He landed flat on his back. Again. Collapse. He materialized upside down, clinging to a low beam until Lazer gently lifted him down. Again. Collapse. He appeared behind Antonia, who did not bother to turn around. She told him he was drifting and that he needed to stop.

Nicholas's breath came fast and shallow. Sweat slid down his temples. "I can't keep going."

Antonia's stare hardened. "You crossed a fracture without training, survived Rhet, and held the Atrium together while it tried to tear itself apart. Don't tell me three feet of stone gets to beat you."

The realization steadied him. He took a breath and focused. The Sphere brightened in response, sensing his intention with a faint pulse of approval. He chose a spot. He stepped. The world folded cleanly, without distortion or drift, and he landed exactly where he meant to.

Anna clapped with relief. Lazer smiled with quiet pride. Even Antonia's expression softened, only slightly, but enough for Nicholas to notice. He exhaled shakily and said he had done it. Antonia replied that he had done it for now and that he would repeat the process tomorrow and every day after that. Nicholas nodded, knowing she was right. He was not ready, but he was learning.

Nicholas looked down at the Sphere. "Where am I supposed to put this?" A soft stir brushed his ankle. He looked down.

A simple canvas rucksack sat on the floor where nothing had been a moment earlier. Its worn edges and shape reminded Nicholas painfully of the schoolbag he used to stuff with snacks and flashlights for childhood expeditions with Anna.

He opened the flap. The Evanidus Sphere drifted into a padded inner pocket, which tightened neatly around it.

Antonia raised an eyebrow but didn't comment. Nicholas slung the rucksack over his shoulder, and he and Anna headed for the exit.

Antonia watched them go, arms crossed, jaw tight. Lazer drifted to her side.

"He did well," he said.

"He almost died," Antonia replied.

"He didn't."

"That is not the same thing."

Lazer's smile was faint but warm. "It is a start."

Antonia exhaled, the tension in her shoulders loosening. "Do you think he has a chance?"

Lazer watched Nicholas disappear around the corner. "I think we all do. If he keeps learning."

Antonia didn't argue.

Nicholas and Anna walked the long stone corridor in silence. Nicholas rubbed his shoulder and winced. "I think I'm going to sleep for a week."

Anna nudged him. "You'll sleep for an hour. Then Antonia will drag you back."

Nicholas groaned. "She would."

Mist gathered along the corridor floor, brightened, and blossomed into a field of sunflowers. Their golden faces turned toward Nicholas.

He blinked. "Oh, now you're soft," he muttered. "Where was that earlier?"

Anna laughed. Nicholas slowed and took a full breath as the sunflowers swayed around them.

Anna watched him with a small smile. "You're getting better at this."

"I'm not doing anything," Nicholas said.

"Exactly."

They rounded a corner. The warmth tightened. Mel stepped out of the air, not walking but emerging as if space had shaped itself into her. She lifted a hand toward the fading sunflowers.

"Showoff," she said.

For the first time since arriving in Nirvana, Nicholas had a quiet second to really notice Mel. Barefoot, sun-bleached hair in a messy bun, freckles across her nose, she looked more suited to a beach than a magical academy. A dolphin tattoo curled along her thigh, its ink shifting from deep blue to soft lavender.

Mel grabbed both of them by the arms. "Good. You're done. Now we begin."

Nicholas stared at her. "Begin what? I just finished training."

Mel snorted. "That wasn't training. That was Antonia trying not to have a heart attack."

Anna covered her mouth to hide a laugh.

Mel swept her free hand through the air. A fold opened, smooth and shimmering like a vertical pool. "Come on. We're late."

Nicholas threw up his hands. "For a place without time, I'm late a lot."

Anna punched his arm lightly. "Don't encourage her."

Mel smirked. "I don't need encouragement."

She pulled them through the fold. The world snapped back into place with a soft thump. Nicholas blinked in the warm amber glow of the meditation room. The air smelled of cedar, jasmine, and something sweet he couldn't name. Soft mats covered the floor. Candles flickered in carved alcoves. A low hum vibrated through the stone, steady and calm.

Nicholas looked around. "This is… not what I expected."

Anna grinned. "What, were you hoping for more columns to slam into?"

"That happened once."

"Three times."

Mel stepped between them. "Children. Focus."

Nicholas muttered, "We're thirteen."

"Exactly," Mel said. "Children."

She strode to the center of the room. Nicholas and Anna followed.

Mel clapped her hands. "Shoes off. Mats down. We're doing yoga."

Nicholas groaned. "Why does everyone here think I'm bendy?"

Anna snorted. "You're about as flexible as a frozen pretzel."

Nicholas opened his mouth, then closed it. "Fair."

Mel pointed at a mat. "Sit."

Nicholas sat.

She pointed at another. "Stretch."

Nicholas stretched. Anna tried not to laugh.

Then she shrugged. "Or maybe it will."

She knelt with the kind of effortless grace that made Nicholas feel like his bones were made of mismatched parts. Her posture was impossibly straight, her expression shifting into the calm focus she used when she was about to teach something important. "Listen carefully. Evanidus is physical. Suppressio is mental. But the mist is spiritual."

Nicholas frowned. "Meaning what?"

"Meaning," Melusine said, "you cannot control it with brute force. Or fear. Or panic. Or whatever that thing you were doing earlier was."

"That was me trying not to die," Nicholas said.

Melusine nodded. "Yes. And you did a dramatic job of it."

Anna laughed, bright and unrestrained.

Melusine continued, "Flexibility is not only about your body. It is about your mind. Your breath. Your ability to shift when the world shifts. To bend when the Continuum bends. To stay soft when everything around you hardens."

Nicholas blinked. "So, yoga helps me not explode."

Melusine beamed. "Exactly."

Nicholas sighed dramatically. "I miss the pit. The pit was simple. The pit wanted me dead. This makes me calm."

Anna fell over laughing.

Melusine pointed at Nicholas. "Breath first. In through the nose. Out through the mouth. Slow. Steady."

Nicholas tried. He inhaled too fast, choked on his own breath, and coughed so hard he nearly toppled sideways.

Anna wheezed with laughter.

Melusine sighed. "This is going to take a while."

Nicholas glared at both of them. "I survived Antonia today. I can survive yoga."

Melusine's smile softened. "Good. Because you will need both. Flexibility and focus. Breath and movement. Strength and softness. Without them, the mist will eat you alive."

Nicholas froze. "Eat me alive."

Melusine waved a hand. "Metaphorically."

Anna whispered, "Mostly."

Nicholas groaned. "I want a refund."

Melusine clapped her hands. "Too late. You are enrolled."

She straightened, expression shifting from playful to serene. "Now," she said softly, "let us begin."

Nicholas swallowed, then closed his eyes and tried, truly tried, to follow Melusine's breathing pattern. In through the nose. Out through the mouth. Slow. Steady. No rushing. No bracing for impact. Just breath.

The air around him shifted. Not wildly. Not dangerous. But with recognition. A soft stir. A faint warmth. A whisper of something aligning, not outside him but inside, like a door he had never known was there beginning to crack open.

Anna felt it. Melusine felt it. Nicholas did not, not fully, yet. But the room did. The candles flickered, their flames leaning toward him. The stone deepened its hum, a low resonant vibration that settled beneath his ribs. The air leaned in, attentive, almost curious.

Far away, in the fracture between moments, something answered. A note. Soft. Distant. Awakening.

CHAPTER 20

Nicholas woke with the distinct feeling that someone was staring at him. He blinked. Someone was staring at him. Antonia. Standing at the foot of his bed, arms crossed, expression carved from stone.

"Up," she said.

Nicholas groaned. "Is it morning?"

"There is no morning," Antonia replied. "There is only training."

"That is worse," Nicholas muttered.

Anna snorted from the bed across the room. "Told you."

Nicholas pushed himself upright, rubbing sleep from his eyes. His shirt twisted awkwardly as he sat up, yesterday's training shirt, sweat stiff and wrinkled. He tugged it off and reached for a clean one from the foot of the bed.

"Breakfast would help," he mumbled. "You know, the most important meal of the day. And I am a growing boy."

Anna laughed into her pillow. "You are always a growing boy."

Antonia did not respond at first. She had turned away out of habit, but not fast enough to miss the bruises blooming across Nicholas's ribs and shoulder. Dark, uneven marks from the column, the beam, the overshot landing. Evidence of every mistake he had made trying to survive Evanidus.

For a fraction of a second, something flickered across her face. Not pity. Not softness. Recognition. A memory she did not want: another student, another set of bruises, another morning she had pushed too hard and been too late. A hand slipping from hers. A fracture collapsing too fast. A scream cut short. The smell of scorched stone. Silence. She swallowed it down, spine straightening.

Then, with a small, almost irritated flick of her fingers, two warm bagels appeared on the nightstand, each wrapped in paper and smelling faintly of toasted dough and strawberry cream cheese. Two chilled orange juices materialized beside them, condensation already forming on the bottles.

"You can eat yours on the way," Antonia said, voice clipped. "Quickly."

Nicholas blinked. "Wait, did you just…"

"No," she said immediately.

Anna sat up, grinning. "Thank you."

Antonia ignored her. "Move."

Nicholas tugged the clean shirt over his head, grabbed his bagel and juice, and followed her out the door, still not entirely sure whether she had done it out of practicality, pity, or because she did not want him fainting in the Suppressio chamber. Maybe all three.

The Suppressio chamber was nothing like the Evanidus cavern. It was small. Circular. Silent. Except the silence was not empty.

As Nicholas stepped inside, something brushed the edge of his awareness, a faint, almost melody woven into the stillness. Not music exactly, but the shape of music. A soft hum threaded through the air, like distant voices singing from behind a wall of time.

Not loud. Not clear. But present.

Ancestors.

The thought was not his, but it settled in him all the same.

The walls were smooth stone, etched with spirals that drifted like slow galaxies. The air was dense, not heavy but full, like standing inside a held breath. The silence pressed gently against his skin, vibrating with that faint ancient harmony.

Nicholas swallowed. "Do you hear that?"

Anna frowned. "Hear what?"

Antonia did not answer. But her eyes flicked toward the spirals, and for a heartbeat her expression softened, as if she too remembered the voices that once guided her.

A single sphere hovered in the center of the room, dark and smoky, its surface expanding and contracting in slow pulses. At first, the rhythm was uneven, like a heartbeat out of sync with itself.

But as Nicholas stepped closer, the sphere's cadence shifted. Slowed. Aligned with him.

And the faint melody in the silence shifted with it, as though the ancestors themselves were adjusting their breath to match his.

Antonia noticed.

Her jaw tightened, but not in anger.

In awe.

"Sit," she said.

Nicholas sat.

The sphere drifted toward him, its smoky surface pulsing in slow, deliberate breaths. He tensed. "Is it going to…"

"Yes," Antonia said.

The sphere touched his forehead.

The Silence.

The world went silent. Not quiet. Silent.

Nicholas gasped, but even the gasp made no sound. His heartbeat thudded in his chest, but he could not hear it. His breath rushed in and out, but it made no sound. The chamber swallowed everything, even the smallest noise, until the only thing left was the pressure of his own thoughts.

Then he noticed something else.

The ringing in his ears, the constant high-pitched whine he had carried since the Atrium collapse, did not vanish. It was unwound. Thread by thread. Layer by layer, like someone pulling apart a tangled knot.

And inside the ringing were thoughts. Not words. Impressions. Fear. Memory. Pressure. The echo of Rhet's influence. The echo of his own panic. He could see them, almost thin strands of soundless thought drifting through the Silence like smoke.

I cannot do this. I am not ready. I am going to hurt someone. I am going to—

The sphere darkened, reacting to his panic.

Lazer's device flickered sharply. He stepped closer, voice low but urgent. "Antonia, his levels are spiking. He is not just overwhelmed. He is spiraling."

Antonia did not look at him at first. Her jaw clenched, eyes fixed on Nicholas as his shoulders trembled and his breath came in short, silent gasps.

Lazer softened his tone. "He is fighting everything at once. He cannot hold it."

A muscle in Antonia's cheek twitched, the only sign she had heard him.

Then she knelt in front of Nicholas, her voice cutting through the unraveling with a steadiness that felt almost like a hand on his back. "Nicholas," she said, firm but not harsh. "Suppressio is not about shutting down your thoughts. It is about choosing which ones you listen to."

Nicholas squeezed his eyes shut. "They are all loud."

"Then quiet them," she said.

"I do not know how."

Antonia leaned in, her voice dropping to something almost gentle. "Start with one. One thought. One fear. Hold it. Look at it. Then let it go."

Nicholas tried. He grabbed onto the loudest fear, I am going to hurt someone and held it in his mind like a burning coal. His chest tightened. His breath hitched. The sphere dimmed. The ancestral melody pressed closer.

Antonia heard it too, clearer than Nicholas did. She always had. The song of the ancestors was not comforting to her. It had never been. It was a reminder. A reminder of the boy with a quick smile who had slipped from her grasp in a collapsing fold. A reminder of the girl who had steadied her breath too late. A reminder of the silence that followed each loss, the same silence that hummed now, threading through the chamber like a ghost of every mistake she had ever made.

She inhaled through her nose, slow and controlled, forcing the memory back into its place.

"Nicholas," she said quietly. "Stay with me."

He forced himself to exhale. The fear loosened. The sphere steadied.

Nicholas opened his eyes, shaking. "That was awful."

"That was progress," Antonia said.

The second attempt was worse. The third was better. The fourth nearly knocked him unconscious. By the fifth, Nicholas was sweating, trembling, and barely holding himself upright. Antonia watched him with the intensity of someone who had trained dozens of students and lost more than she cared to admit. Nicholas did not know that, not yet, but the chamber did.

The spirals shifted. The melody deepened. The air leaned in.

Nicholas closed his eyes. The sphere drifted toward him again. His breath hitched. His pulse spiked. His thoughts spiraled.

I cannot do this. I am going to fail. I am going to…

A soft voice cut through the tension.

"Enough."

Nicholas's eyes snapped open. He felt her presence before he saw her.

Melusine stood in the doorway, half hidden by the shadows, as if she had been there longer than anyone realized. Her expression was calm, but her eyes were sharp, reading Nicholas's fear as if it were written on the air itself.

Antonia stiffened. "Melusine, this is my…"

"Your training," Melusine finished gently. "Yes. And he is drowning."

Antonia bristled. "He needs discipline."

"He needs connection," Melusine said.

Lazer did not intervene. He simply stepped back, giving Melusine space.

Melusine crossed the room with quiet, fluid steps. She knelt beside Nicholas and placed a hand lightly on his shoulder. "May I help?"

Nicholas nodded, breath shaky.

Melusine turned to the doorway. "Anna."

Anna hurried in, worry etched across her face. "Is he alright?"

"He will be," Melusine said. "Sit."

Melusine guided Anna to the floor beside Nicholas, then positioned herself opposite them. The three formed a triangle, close and grounded, the shape settling into the room with a quiet inevitability.

Nicholas froze for half a heartbeat. The shape. The spacing. The quiet gravity of it. It tugged at something deep in him, a memory of his basement back home. The old clock on the shelf. The carved wooden bird with the chipped wing. The little house-shaped lamp that always glowed warmer than it should. Three objects he had never thought twice about. Three points forming a triangle. He had never realized he had been sitting inside of one his whole life.

A shiver ran through him, not fear, not exactly, but recognition.

Melusine's voice softened. "Hands."

Nicholas blinked, pulled back into the moment. Anna placed her palm against his. Melusine placed hers against his other. Their hands formed a small circle between them, warm, steady and alive.

Nicholas swallowed. "What is this?"

"Support," Melusine said. "The mist listens to your heart. But your heart listens to the people you trust."

Anna squeezed his fingers lightly, not gripping, just presence.

Melusine inhaled slowly. "Breathe with me."

Nicholas tried.

"No," Melusine said gently. "Not like that. Like this."

She breathed again, slow and deep and steady. Anna matched her. Their chests rose and fell in unison. Nicholas followed. For the first time all day, his breath did not catch.

Melusine closed her eyes. "Good. Again."

They breathed together. Slow. Steady. Unified.

A soft ripple of mist curled around their joined hands. Nicholas felt something warm settle in his chest. Not power. Not fear. Something quieter. Connection.

Anna's steadiness and Melusine's calm gave him something solid to follow. The trembling in his hands eased.

A faint shimmer brushed his skin. Nicholas glanced down and caught a glimpse of the dolphin tattoo on her thigh. It had always faced forward, swimming ahead. Now it curved the other way, silver bright, as if turning toward the center of the triangle.

He blinked, startled.

Melusine opened her eyes. "Now try."

The sphere drifted toward him again, its smoky surface moving in time with their breath.

Nicholas inhaled, steady and sure, held by the two people beside him.

And for the first time, the Silence did not swallow him.

It listened.

Nicholas nodded. The Suppressio Sphere drifted toward him again. It touched his forehead. Silence. But this time, he was not alone in it. He breathed with them, not against himself. The fear rose, then softened. The panic flickered, then dimmed. The thoughts swirled, then drifted away like leaves on water.

The sphere steadied.

Nicholas opened his eyes. Antonia stared at him, stunned. Lazer smiled.

Mel squeezed his hand gently. "Better."

Nicholas exhaled shakily. "Not perfect."

"No," Mel said. "But close."

Anna grinned. "And close is amazing."

Nicholas looked at both of them, really looked, and felt something he had not felt since the Atrium collapsed. Hope.

Antonia saw it too—not the hope exactly, but a faint alignment around the three of them that brushed the edge of her awareness. Her jaw tightened. Something had happened in this room that did not belong to Suppressio alone.

Far above the chamber, the Council room shuddered. Not violently. But unmistakably.

Asiza dropped her quill. "What was that?"

Bharati's eyes widened, her hand pressing to her sternum. "A resonance."

The suspended fire twisted, its flame narrowing into a thin spiraling thread of light. Shadows recoiled from it, as though the hall itself leaned in to listen.

Chanotedah gripped his staff. "From where?"

Paloma whispered, "It feels close."

Chittaswarup closed his eyes, breathing steadily as he reached into the Continuum. The mist around him brightened, then dimmed, then brightened again, as if unsure how to respond. He inhaled slowly. When he spoke, his voice carried a weight the others had not heard in centuries.

"It feels ancient," he said. "But new."

The Council fell silent.

Chittaswarup opened his eyes. "Someone has touched a thread older than Nirvana. Older than the Council. Older than any of us."

Bharati swallowed. "Who?"

Chittaswarup's gaze drifted downward, toward the training chambers far below.

"Nicholas," he said softly. "Something around him is changing."

The fire flared. The hall trembled.

And none of them, not even Chittaswarup, understood the full meaning of what had just awakened.

Back in the Suppressio chamber, Antonia watched Nicholas, Anna, and Melusine seated in their quiet triangle. Nicholas's silver-blue aura brushed the edges of Anna's gold and Melusine's lavender without merging.

Antonia felt the hum. She did not understand it. She did not like not understanding.

But she could not deny it.

Far from Nirvana, in a fractured pocket of the Continuum, the hoppers trained with hunger rather than discipline. They moved like a hunting pack across jagged shards of broken timelines, lunging through unstable folds and striking targets with brutal coordination. Every movement was built for pursuit.

Their commander barked orders, but the pack barely needed them. Above, Rhet watched from a jagged outcropping, coat snapping in the unstable wind. Then he felt it: three distant notes, separate but beginning to align. An unfinished chord.

Rhet froze.

A shiver ran down his spine—not fear, not yet, but recognition. The kind a wolf feels when another pack howls on the ridge. The kind that says you are not alone in this territory anymore.

His jaw tightened. The hoppers below sensed the shift in him. Their frenzy slowed, heads lifting, nostrils flaring as if they smelled something new in the wind too. Rhet exhaled once, sharp and controlled.

"Prepare them," he said quietly.

The commander bowed. "For what, sir?"

Rhet's smile was thin and humorless.

"For something that thinks it can challenge me."

The hoppers roared as one; a guttural, animal sound that shook the fractured ground. The Continuum trembled.

And far away, three hearts beat in unison, unaware that their unfinished chord had caught a predator's attention.

CHAPTER 21

The Great Hall of Nirvana was never silent.

Even when empty, the air hummed with the low vibration of the Continuum—a sound felt more than heard. Tonight, the hall was full, and the hum carried a faint melodic undertone, the same ancestral whisper Nicholas had felt in the Suppressio chamber. It threaded through the air like a distant choir, soft enough to doubt, ancient enough to fear.

Every Council member stood in a wide circle around the suspended fire, their faces lit by its shifting gold-and-blue glow. The fire burned in midair, untethered to wood or stone. It twisted slowly, as if stirred by an invisible hand, casting shadows that moved like living things across the carved walls.

Nicholas, Anna, and Melusine stepped into the hall, and the air changed.

The suspended fire pulsed once, a soft, resonant thump that rippled through the chamber.

Nicholas felt it. Anna felt it. But Melusine felt it most. The moment her foot crossed the threshold, the mist moved.

A thin ribbon of mist slid across the stone floor and brushed Melusine's bare feet. It rose around her ankles, waiting.

Mel looked toward the Council circle, then back at Nicholas and Anna. For a long moment she stood between the two. Finally, she stepped back beside them. The mist followed her decision, weaving itself upward into the robes of a Sustentet.

Her hair, normally pulled into a messy bun loosened all at once, falling in soft waves to her shoulders as if the Hall itself had decided she should be seen.

Melusine stared at herself, stunned.

"This… isn't normal," she whispered.

Antonia's eyes widened. "No. It isn't."

"Wait," she whispered. "I'm… I'm supposed to…"

Mel's breath trembled. "No," she said softly. "I'm choosing."

Antonia watched her with a rare softness, understanding the weight of divided duty better than anyone.

Mel squared her shoulders, the Sustentet robes settling around her.

"I'll stand where I'm placed," she said quietly. "And right now… that's here."

Nicholas nodded, relief softening his features. Anna slipped her hand into Mel's. The three stepped forward together.

Bharati stepped forward first, her shawl still slightly askew from her earlier sprint through the corridors. "We must speak of Rhet," she said, voice trembling with urgency. "The children deserve to know what they are facing."

Nicholas stiffened. Anna reached for his hand. Melusine shifted closer, her presence steady and warm.

Chittaswarup nodded. "A resonance has awakened. The Continuum has shifted. The time for secrecy is over."

The fire brightened, swirling into a slow spiral. Shadows pulled away from the flare, and an expectant hush settled over the hall.

Antonia exhaled sharply. "Very well. Let it be told."

Chittaswarup raised his hands. The fire responded instantly, stretching upward, then folding inward, forming images within its core. The flames shaped themselves into a young man, sharp-eyed and intense, standing at the edge of a fracture. His aura shimmered with precision and hunger.

"Rhet was once one of us," Chittaswarup began.

Nicholas's breath caught. The fire shifted, showing Rhet as he had been before the fractures claimed him, before the glass eye, before the shadows clung to his coat like loyal ghosts.

"He was a Viator of extraordinary talent," Lazer said quietly. "Gifted. Precise. Brilliant."

"And dangerous," Bharati added.

The fire twisted, showing Rhet reaching into a fracture and pulling something out. A hopper. Then another. Then dozens. Their forms flickered like broken reflections, half-formed and trembling.

"He believed the Continuum was flawed," Chittaswarup continued. "That time should not flow freely. That it should be controlled."

"By him," Antonia muttered.

The fire dimmed, as if recoiling from the memory.

"He learned to manipulate the hoppers," Bharati said, voice tight. "To command them. To weaponize them."

Nicholas swallowed. "Why?"

Chittaswarup looked at him with deep, ancient sadness. "Because he feared chaos. And in his fear, he became the very thing he sought to control."

The fire flared violently, showing Rhet tearing open a fracture too wide, too fast. The Continuum shuddered. The hall trembled with the memory.

"He broke the first great fracture," Lazer said. "The one that nearly collapsed the Atrium."

Anna's eyes widened. "The one Nicholas fell through."

"Yes," Bharati whispered. "That one."

Nicholas felt the room tilt slightly. Anna caught his arm, steadying him, but before she could fully anchor him, Melusine moved. A soft ripple of mist rose from the floor, drawn to her like metal to a lodestone. She lifted her hands without thinking, and the mist obeyed, weaving itself into a thin shimmering shroud that unfurled across her palms. She stepped behind Nicholas and draped it gently over his shoulders.

Warmth spread through him at once, grounding and steadying. The shroud tightened just enough to anchor him, its weight settling across his collarbones like a reassuring hand. Nicholas exhaled shakily, leaning into the support.

Melusine blinked, startled. "I did not do that. It just happened."

Anna smiled softly. "Mel, it is all right."

Melusine did not correct her. For the first time, she let the shortened name settle between them without resistance. Antonia noticed the shift, a flicker of something she could not name brushing the edge of her awareness.

Chittaswarup continued, "When we tried to stop him, he fled into the fractures. There he learned to move between damaged timelines, twist their seams, and gather hoppers to his cause."

The fire showed Rhet in the fractured realm, surrounded by flickering hoppers.

"And now," Bharati said, voice trembling, "he has felt the resonance."

The fire pulsed again, three synchronized beats of light. Nicholas's heart matched them. Anna's breath matched theirs. Melusine's aura brightened in time with them.

Antonia felt the pulse too. It brushed her skin like a whisper, like a warning, like a truth she was not ready to understand.

Asiza stepped forward, her voice soft but steady. "A triad is the rarest phenomenon in the Continuum. Three auras, three souls, whose frequencies align so perfectly that they form a single harmonic chord."

The fire responded with a soft three-note hum. Nicholas felt it in his ribs, the same chord he had felt in the Suppressio chamber, the same one that had steadied the sphere.

"It should not happen," Asiza continued. "Not naturally. Not mathematically. The probability is so low that most believed it impossible."

Chittaswarup nodded. "True Triads are extraordinarily rare. Most exist only in fragments of our oldest records."

Nicholas hesitated. "Why us?"

"We don't know why," Bharati said. "Your signatures are compatible in a way we have almost no record of. When the three of you work together, they begin to resonate as one."

Anna whispered, "The perfect chord."

Asiza nodded. "Yes. Alone, each of you is strong. Together, you create a resonance we have not seen in generations."

Nicholas drew a slow breath. "And hoppers… what are they?"

Asiza inhaled, a breath taken before delivering a painful truth. "Hoppers begin as individuals born with the gift to become Viatori, but who were never found by us. Unidentified. Untrained. Vulnerable. In fractured timelines, that uncontrolled ability can consume them. Their connection to the Continuum twists without guidance, warping body, instinct, and resonance. Rhet learned how to accelerate that corruption, shaping them until very little of the person they were remains."

The fire showed silhouettes falling through fractures, reaching out, and Rhet's hand reaching back.

"He took them in," Asiza said. "Promised them power. Purpose. Freedom from our rules."

"And now they answer to him," Antonia said bitterly. "They jump without discipline. They tear at timelines like children ripping pages from a book."

Nicholas felt a chill. "So, they are dangerous."

"Extremely," Lazer said. "A single hopper can destabilize a century. A legion can collapse a world."

"And Rhet commands them all," Bharati added.

The fire dimmed, as though bracing for what came next.

The fire flared, forming a crest: a lion on one side, an eagle on the other. The image shimmered in the suspended flame, ancient and deliberate.

Nicholas stared. "What is that?"

Chittaswarup stepped closer. "The original sigil of the First Council. Two bloodlines. Two gifts. Two destinies."

He pointed to the lion. "The Line of the Lion. Our oldest records associate it with strength, grounding, and stability."

Then to the eagle. "The Line of the Eagle. The surviving accounts speak of speed, precision, and an unusual affinity for moving through timelines."

Nicholas felt his heart thud. A memory flickered, his father's steady hands, the way he always calmed a room simply by entering it. The way Nicholas had always felt safest was when he was near.

"And what does that have to do with me?" Nicholas asked, voice barely above a whisper.

Chittaswarup turned to him, eyes soft with both pride and sorrow. "We believe the Continuum is telling us that you are the child of the Lion."

The suspended fire pulsed warmly, a deep grounding glow.

"And Rhet," Bharati whispered, "is believed to be the child of the Eagle."

As the words settled into the air, the hall shifted. The fire dimmed to a molten glow. Shadows along the walls stretched, then lifted, rising from the stone as if waking from a long sleep.

Two shapes emerged. Not solid. Not fully formed. Silver silhouettes woven from mist and memory. A lion, massive and regal, its mane rippling like starlight, padded silently along the curve of the chamber. An eagle, sharp-winged and fierce, its feathers glinting like shards of moonlight, soared above it in a slow circling glide.

They crossed paths in the center of the hall. The lion's shadow brushed Nicholas's feet. The eagle's wings passed over his head. The air hummed, a low harmonic vibration that resonated in Nicholas's bones.

Anna gasped softly. Mel's breath caught. Even Antonia's eyes widened, awe breaking through her composure.

The shadows dissolved as quickly as they had formed, fading back into the stone as if they had never been there. But the echo of them, the weight of them, lingered.

Nicholas swallowed hard. "So, he and I are related."

Chittaswarup nodded. "Distant cousins if the signs are true. Descendants of the two brothers, Aerelion and Abbadon."

Nicholas staggered again, but the shroud tightened around his shoulders, steadying him. The fire flickered, a brief, sharp tremor, as if echoing Rhet's distant fear.

Bharati stepped forward, voice low and steady. "The old records place the Lion and Eagle in opposition more than once. Beyond that, much of what we know is fragmentary."

"Yes," Chittaswarup said. "And that is why he fears you."

The hall fell quiet. Nicholas stepped back and turned toward the carved stone wall. His hands trembled as the truth settled over him.

Anna watched him carefully. Mel moved closer without speaking.

Nicholas closed his eyes. He saw the Atrium collapsing, Rhet's shadow in the mist, the lion and the eagle crossing above him.

He breathed. Slow. Unsteady. Human.

Then he turned back. Not quickly. Not dramatically. But with a quiet, deliberate resolve that made the air shift.

He walked toward Antonia. She straightened, something like pride flickering behind her stern expression.

And then something else happened.

A ripple of mist curled around Nicholas's ankles, then rose, slow and deliberate. The air thickened with a soft vibration, like the Continuum exhaling.

Nicholas blinked. "Uh… guys."

The mist tightened, weaving itself into fabric. His clothes shifted into worn gray sweats and a zip-front warm-up jacket that settled comfortably across his shoulders.

He looked down.

He was wearing a warm-up suit, the kind Rocky Balboa wore in the first Rocky.

Anna burst into a grin. "Oh, my god. Nicholas, you look like you are about to chase chickens."

Nicholas flushed. "I did not do this."

Mel tilted her head, studying the outfit with the seriousness of a monk evaluating ceremonial robes. "It is fine," she said slowly. "But a Gi would be more appropriate for centering. Breath alignment. Rooting the stance."

Nicholas stared at her. "Mel, I do not even know how to tie a Gi."

Mel shrugged. "Apparently the mist does."

Antonia pinched the bridge of her nose. "Of all the things it could have made." But a tiny thread of relief softened her voice. The clothes were familiar, grounding, human.

Lazer stepped closer, eyes bright with curiosity. "It responded to his intention. His emotional state. His need for familiarity."

Anna elbowed Nicholas lightly. "Honestly, it suits you."

Nicholas groaned. "Please do not say suits you."

Mel crossed her arms. "I still think a Gi would have been better."

Antonia exhaled sharply. "At least he looks like he is ready to work."

Nicholas straightened, tugging the jacket zipper up with a small, determined motion. The fabric felt warm. Solid. Like armor made of memory instead of metal.

He looked up at Antonia, bruised, scared, but standing. "Time to train."

Antonia's expression flickered, surprise, pride, and something like relief breaking through her usual steel. She gave a single sharp nod.

And then the Hall shifted. The suspended fire stretched upward, thinning into a tall, wavering column of light. The carved walls dimmed in response, as though the Hall itself were bowing to the Council's next task.

Bharati approached the archway first. She paused, fingers brushing the edge of the fire as if seeking reassurance. The flame recoiled, then softened, pulsing once in sympathy. Asiza followed, her gaze lingering on Melusine, on the silver-blue robes, on the Triad formation, on the future she could no longer predict. She pressed a hand to her heart before turning away.

Lazer hesitated behind them, torn. His eyes stayed on Nicholas, on the boy he had monitored, measured, and quietly believed in. He opened his mouth as if to speak, then closed it and followed the others.

As each Council member passed through the archway, the mist parted for them, drawing back like a curtain. Their robes stirred in an unseen wind, threads of gold and silver lifting as if pulled by the Continuum's breath.

The air tightened. The walls hummed. The fire dimmed to a thin trembling thread of light.

Chittaswarup was the last to leave. He looked back at the Triad, not with fear, but with reverence.

"The Continuum has chosen you," he said softly. "Now choose each other."

Then he stepped into the mist. The hum cut off. Silence fell like a dropped curtain.

Nicholas exhaled, squared his shoulders, and turned toward the training chambers. Anna and Mel fell into step beside him.

The Triad walked as one.

CHAPTER 22

Morning in Nirvana felt wrong. Not loud. Not violent. Just… off.

Nicholas woke with a start, the kind that left his heart beating a little too fast for no reason he could name. He swung his legs over the side of the bed and stumbled toward the old wooden chest beneath his window, rubbing the sleep from his eyes. The lid creaked softly as he lifted it, digging blindly for a T-shirt.

Nothing looked different.

But it sounded different; the air outside carried a faint, metallic hum, like the world was tuning itself to a new frequency.

And it felt different; a heaviness in the mist, a pressure behind the morning light, as if Nirvana itself was bracing for something it couldn't name.

Nicholas pulled the shirt over his head slowly, pausing halfway as the unease settled deeper in his chest.

Something was wrong.

When he stepped outside, the courtyard mist curled around his ankles in tight, restless spirals instead of drifting lazily the way it usually did. A few Viatori hurried past him, shoulders tense, eyes unfocused, as if they were listening to something he couldn't hear.

Anna met him halfway down the path, or rather, she appeared there, moving with a lightness that made it hard to tell when her feet touched the ground. Her senses were sharpened, every line of her body alert, protective. The orange-and-gold shimmer of her Oriole colors flickered beneath her skin, brightening and dimming in soft pulses as if her aura were testing the air.

She didn't look like she was walking. She looked like she was one breath away from taking flight.

"You feel it too," she said, voice low, eyes scanning the courtyard as though expecting something to leap from the mist.

Nicholas nodded. "Yeah. I don't know what it is, but… something's wrong."

Mel joined them a moment later, pulling her damp, salt-tangled hair back into a messy bun as she walked. She still carried the hint of ocean and sand, the faint shimmer of sea-mist clinging to her skin. Her energy was darker than usual, pulsing in slow, uneasy waves, as if the shoreline itself had whispered something to her before she left it.

She didn't speak. She didn't need to. The look in her eyes said she felt it too. They walked together toward the training halls. The closer they got to the training halls, the stranger the air became.

The mist thickened around their ankles, slow and velvety, as though trying to cling to them. Hints of chocolate and strawberry drifted through the air; faint, sweet, familiar in a way that made Nicholas's stomach tighten. Anna inhaled sharply, confused by the scent; Mel frowned, trying to place it. But Nicholas knew it instantly.

The fragment. The walls themselves leaned inward as they walked past, the stone bending with a subtle, unnatural tension—not threatening, but waiting, as if the entire corridor were holding its breath.

Nicholas swallowed. "Why does it feel like the whole place is… bracing?"

Anna didn't answer. Mel's breath hitched. And when they stepped through the archway into Evanidus Hall, the truth hit them all at once: The world wasn't waiting anymore. Evanidus Hall was louder than usual.

Not in sound. The jumps themselves were silent. But in energy. The air crackled with it, sharp and restless, like static before a storm. Nicholas felt it the moment he stepped inside. The mist did not drift lazily here; it snapped in tight, controlled currents, pulled taut by something he could not name.

A young Viator named Jalen blinked out of existence, then reappeared three feet too far to the left, slamming shoulder-first into a stone pillar.

"Focus," the instructor barked. "Your intention determines your landing point, not your panic."

Jalen groaned, clutching his arm, but forced himself upright.

Nicholas winced. "They are pushing them harder than yesterday."

Anna scanned the room, jaw tight. "Everyone is on edge."

Melusine did not answer.

Her breath hitched, barely, but enough for Nicholas to notice. Her knees softened for a moment, as if the floor had shifted beneath her. The violet in her aura pulsed once, then again, darkening at the edges like a bruise blooming under the skin.

The mist near her ankles smoothed out, its currents flattening around her, as though trying to steady her—or as though she were steadying the room without meaning to.

Nicholas watched her more closely, a chill settling in his chest. Melusine was not reacting to the room. The room was reacting to Melusine.

Another student, Mara, executed a perfect jump, smooth and clean, landing on the narrow platform with barely a wobble. The instructor nodded once. "Good. Again."

But even Mara's aura flickered with strain.

Nicholas stepped farther into the hall, watching the jumps more closely. The platforms were spaced farther apart. The instructors' tones were sharper. The students' movements were tight, rushed, and desperate.

"Why is it like this?" Nicholas asked quietly. "Why does it feel like everyone is training for something that is already happening?"

The nearest instructor, a stern woman with white streaks in her hair, turned toward him. Not with curiosity. Not with sympathy.

With accusation.

"You want to know why," she said. "Because you are here."

Nicholas blinked. "Me."

"The Continuum woke up the moment you arrived," she said, stepping closer. "It is stirring. Shifting. Pressing against the walls of Nirvana. And every Viator in this hall can feel it."

Anna stiffened. Melusine's breath caught.

Nicholas swallowed. "I did not mean…"

"It does not matter what you meant," the instructor cut in. "Your presence is accelerating everything. The training. The tension. The fear."

Her voice dropped, low and cold. "You are the reason we do not have time."

Her eyes locked onto his, and in that instant, Nicholas felt the heat of a thousand years of unrest and fear burning through him. It was not just anger. It was history. It was every sleepless night, every fracture tremor, every whispered warning the Council had ignored. It was the weight of a world that had been waiting too long for a storm it could no longer outrun.

The words hit Nicholas like a physical blow.

And the Triad reacted.

Not consciously. Not deliberately. But instinctively.

Melusine's aura surged toward him in a protective sweep, like a warm tide rising to shield him. It was not aggressive. It was not loud. It was simply there, placing itself between him and the accusation without her even realizing she had moved.

At the same moment, Anna's Oriole colors simmered beneath her skin, a flash of gold white heat bright enough to pulse through her aura for a single heartbeat. Not a transformation. Not a shift. Just a warning flare, the instinctive spark of a guardian bird bristling at a threat.

The instructor did not notice.

But Nicholas did.

And the mist did.

And somewhere deep in the Continuum, something old and waiting stirred in answer.

The damage was done. And the Triad had felt every word. They didn't just hear the accusation; they absorbed it. The weight of it slammed into them like a sudden shift in gravity, a responsibility they had never asked for settling across their shoulders all at once. For a heartbeat, all three of them buckled under it. Anna's breath caught, Mel's aura dimming at the edges, Nicholas's knees softening as if the floor had tilted beneath him.

The burden wasn't his alone anymore. It belonged to all of them.

Suppressio Hall was a different kind of chaos.

Rows of Viatori sat cross-legged with spheres pressed to their foreheads. Some breathed steadily. Others shook violently, their auras flickering like old Christmas lights struggling to stay lit. One boy whimpered, "I cannot quiet it." His sphere pulsed dangerously bright, the glow stuttering like a neon sign with too little charge.

"Release it," the instructor snapped.

"I am trying."

"Release it."

The boy gasped and dropped the sphere just before it overloaded. It clattered across the floor, dimming in a weak, sputtering flicker.

Across the room, even Sera, the calmest of them, sat with a posture so rigid it looked painful. Her breathing was steady, but too steady, the kind of practiced calm that came from trying far too hard. And though she was doing everything right, the sphere pressed to her forehead flickered with a faint, stubborn hesitation, pulsing in uneven beats that betrayed her effort. It was as if the sphere itself doubted her control, resisting her discipline with a quiet trembling refusal.

Paloma noticed. Chittaswarup noticed. They stood in the shadowed alcove, watching the students struggle.

"They are trying," Chittaswarup murmured.

"Trying to be quiet in a world that is turning the volume up," Paloma whispered.

A sphere across the room flickered violently, a sudden blinding flare that lit the hall in a harsh burst of white. For a heartbeat, every shadow vanished. Then the sphere dropped, striking the floor with a sharp crystalline shatter that reverberated through the chamber.

"They are not being given a fair chance," she said softly.

The crack of the shattering sphere hit like a whip. Paloma flinched, her shoulders tightening, a sharp inhale catching in her throat. Her fingers curled reflexively against her robes, as if bracing for an impact that never came. For a heartbeat, the mist around her trembled in sympathy.

Chittaswarup's eyes darkened. "It is not the Continuum that accelerates," he murmured. "It is the battle horns calling in the distance. The Continuum only answers."

He exhaled slowly, the mist around him tightening in a faint spiral. "And it cannot wait for readiness. Not now. Not with what approaches."

Paloma's jaw tightened. "Then we must."

But neither said the truth aloud.

This was only the beginning.

The next chamber was sharp, disciplined, physical. Mist shields shimmered across the room in staggered rows, each one flickering under the pressure of impact drills. Nicholas paused.

These Viatori were older, taller, broader in the shoulders, their movements more practiced. They carried themselves with the confidence of people who had been training for years, yet they were even learning something new.

Their shields were not the standard forms. These were tighter, more angular, but also longer, extending down past the ribs and wrapping subtly around their sides. The design did not simply protect; it redirected, catching incoming force and channeling it away in controlled arcs. Each shield curved like a hardened ribbon of mist light, built not to endure impact but to turn it aside, preparing them for a kind of energy they clearly expected to face.

Every Viator had short hair. Cropped close, practical, efficient. As if hair itself were a liability in battle. Something to be grabbed in a struggle or burned in a resonance blast. A weakness no one here could afford. The close cuts were not a style. They were a survival choice, a quiet acknowledgment that the world they were training for had no patience for anything that could be used against them.

Nicholas swallowed. These were not ceremonial Viatori. These were soldiers.

And they were being reshaped for a fight no one understood. A battle that lived only as footnotes in the archives, half-forgotten warnings from a time when the world still believed it could survive such things. A force no one alive could truly imagine, though every Viator in this hall tried to anyway, straining to picture the shape of a threat their ancestors barely survived.

High above the halls, Asiza and Bharati watched in silence.

"They are children," Bharati whispered. "And we are asking them to stand against a monster."

"We are not asking," Asiza said. "We are forcing."

A shield shattered below.

"They are not ready," Bharati said. "Not even close."

Asiza's jaw tightened. "Rhet grows reckless when he senses weakness. And right now, all he would see is weakness."

Bharati's voice trembled. "We should have had more time."

"We were never going to have more time," Asiza said. "But this..." She gestured to the hall below, where instructors barked orders and students fought to keep their auras from collapsing. "This is not training. This is desperation."

Bharati swallowed hard. "At least we have the legions. The trained Viatori, the ones who have seen real battle. Maybe that will be enough."

Asiza did not answer immediately. She drew in a slow breath; her eyes drifting closed for a moment as if she were searching for the archives of her own faith. When she finally spoke, her voice carried the steadiness of someone who had spent a lifetime believing in the strength of those who came before her.

"The legions are strong," she said at last. "Stronger than most remember. They can hold back a tide."

For a heartbeat, she seemed to believe it, her shoulders settling, her jaw unclenching, the faintest flicker of hope softening her expression.

Then her eyes opened again.

And the hope vanished.

"But Rhet…" Her voice thinned, the words pulled from somewhere deeper, older. "Rhet will not come with a tide."

She looked down at the trembling students below, her face hollowing.

"He will come with a storm. And storms do not care how many stand in their path."

Another sphere sputtered out.

"We are sending them into a storm with no shelter," Bharati whispered.

"And Rhet," Asiza said, "is the storm."

Neither said the truth aloud.

Their fear was not that the Triad might fail. It was that all their faith now rested on a prophecy they had long dismissed as myth, a story meant to comfort children and steady the archives, not shape the fate of a world. And now that the Triad stood before them, real and breathing, the question neither dared voice was the one that hollowed them.

Would the prophecy hold? Would the Triad become what legend promised? Or had they placed their hope in a story that was never meant to come true?

Cura Hall thrummed with instinct.

Curas shifted into their bird forms, goldfinch, red-tailed hawk, barn owl, golden eagle, reacting to their Viatori with protective urgency. The air shimmered with shifting colors, gold, blue, red, and white, as the Curas mirrored every flicker of fear, doubt, or strain.

Nicholas watched, mesmerized.

"They are instinct made flesh," said a voice behind him.

Master Kaelen approached, leaning on a crooked walking stick, his face young, his eyes impossibly ancient. The cane looked as if it had been carved from the root of a tree older than Nirvana itself, polished by centuries of storms.

"A Cura's form is a mirror," he said. "Fear sharpens the talons. Confidence steadies the wings. Instinct guides the shift."

A girl flinched as her Viator stumbled, and her body ripped into a goldfinch, feathers bright as sunlight.

Across the room, a boy's Viator hesitated, and the Cura beside him elongated into a red-tailed hawk, tail flaring. A barn owl hovered protectively over a trembling Viator. A golden eagle unfurled its wings with a low resonant cry, reacting to a spike of fear.

Nicholas swallowed. "They react to everything."

Kaelen nodded. "A Cura feels what their Viator feels. Sometimes, before the Viator feels it themselves."

A Viator across the room stumbled, aura flickering, and their Cura snapped into the form of a sparrowhawk, feathers bristling.

Kaelen's expression darkened, the change subtle but unmistakable. He shifted, leaning more of his weight onto the crooked cane, as though the truth of what he sensed pressed heavier against him than he let on. The movement was not weakness. It was memory, the body of a man who had weathered storms no one else in the room could name.

"And today," he said quietly, "there is much to react to."

Nicholas felt the truth settle in his bones. No one was ready. Not the students. Not the instructors. Not even him.

No matter how hard they trained, Nicholas could not shake the feeling that none of them were ready for what was coming.

Jalen sat on the floor, shoulders shaking, his sphere dimming in weak, uneven pulses.

Nicholas knelt beside him. "You are all right. Just breathe."

Jalen did not look up. "I cannot get it to settle."

Nicholas opened his empathy, quietly, instinctively. The mist rose around him in a soft curl, drifting toward Jalen, smoothing the air between them. Across the chamber, Anna's aura brightened. Melusine's aura pulsed once. And then the mist around Nicholas blended with the edges of their auras, a shimmering bridge stretching across the room.

Jalen's sphere steadied.

Nicholas felt the connection like a warm hand on his back.

Antonia whispered, almost to herself, "That wasn't part of the exercise."

Deep in his chamber, Chittaswarup's eyes snapped open.

"The lion is ready to roar."

Nicholas stood in the Evanidus chamber with Antonia when the song began. Soft. Ancient. Everywhere.

"Antonia… do you hear that?"

Her face paled, the color draining so fast it looked as if the song itself had pulled the blood from her skin. Antonia's spine straightened, every nerve in her body snapping to attention. The fine muscles along her jaw tightened. Even her breath changed, shallow and controlled, the way a soldier breathes when instinct takes over before thought can catch up.

Her aura, normally a steady red ember, darkened into a deep cardinal, pulsing once in a sharp warning flare.

The sound threaded through her bones, through her lineage, through every memory she had ever inherited. It was not just a song to her. It was a summons.

"That song has only been recorded before periods of widespread fracture and war."

The melody swelled again, louder, older, undeniable.

"And the ancestors only sing that loud when war is imminent."

A chilly wind swept through the room. In the corner, unnoticed by Nicholas, her battle gear formed from the mist, piece by piece, silent and inevitable.

"War," she whispered. "Not someday. Now."

Anna felt the song in Cura Hall. Mel felt it on the beach. Both moved instantly.

Nicholas staggered into the corridor, the melody pulling at him like a thread woven through his ribs. Anna arrived from the left. Mel from the right. The moment they saw each other, the mist surged upward, weaving their auras together in a soft braid of gold, lavender, and blue.

Antonia stared at them, then at her battle gear in the corner.

"The ancestors are calling you," she said.

Something in her face changed as she spoke. Not fear. Not shock. But recognition. If there had been even a flicker of doubt left in her about the prophecy, the song erased it completely.

Antonia straightened, her aura deepening into that fierce cardinal red, and the soldier in her gave way to something older, more resolute.

From this moment on, she was no longer their instructor.

She was their protector.

Her stance shifted, her jaw set, and a quiet, unshakable vow settled behind her eyes, a promise carved from lineage and war and the weight of every ancestor who had ever stood where she now stood.

Whatever was coming, Antonia knew exactly where she would stand.

And if it took a thousand legions to keep them alive, she would summon every last one.

CHAPTER 23

The chamber felt close to breaking, pressure trembling through the air like glass under strain.

Shadows slipped out of sync with the bodies that cast them. One peeled away entirely, drifting in a confused arc before collapsing into mist.

Nicholas's pulse spiked, a tremor running through his hands before he could stop it. "Did you see that?"

Anna's posture sharpened, instinct pulling her a half step closer to Nicholas. "It is like the shadow forgot where it belonged."

Melusine inhaled sharply. Her breath trembled, her energy flickering in jagged pulses of lavender. "The fractures are bleeding through."

The mist jittered around their feet as the floor hummed with a faint murmur of lost voices. Light bent through invisible cracks.

Melusine's breath hitched. "It is not just the fractures. It is the lost moments inside them. They are reaching out, trying to find where they belong."

The mist surged around them. Lavender bands formed across Mel's arms and shoulders; gold shaped itself into Anna's chest piece and bracers; silver-blue plates settled over Nicholas, shifting with his breath.

The armor settled around them, each set carrying the color and rhythm of its wearer: Nicholas in silver-blue, Anna in gold, Mel in lavender touched with bronze.

A low resonant hum rippled through the chamber. The mist brightened.

Antonia's breath caught. "This is not possible."

Lazer entered and stopped, eyes fixed on the three of them.

"It's not reacting," Lazer said. "It's aligning."

The three held formation, their breathing settling into the same rhythm.

Antonia swallowed hard, her throat working. Her voice came out low, reverent, shaken. "the Triad."

Nicholas felt the weight of the word settle across him. Antonia straightened.

"Suppressio. Now."

Nicholas stepped forward without hesitation.

Anna and Mel did not move with him this time, not the way they usually did. Instead, they shifted outward, taking measured steps to widen the formation. Antonia had drilled this into them: support at a distance, close enough to anchor him, far enough not to interfere if the sphere lashed out.

Anna's breath steadied into a slow deliberate cadence, her hands hovering just off her sides, golden light held tight and controlled. Melusine mirrored her on the opposite flank, shoulders squared, her lavender shimmer dimmed to a focused pulse. Their breaths synced with Nicholas's, the same instinctive rhythm that had begun in the fractured hallway, but now it carried discipline, intention, training.

The Triad did not simply stand together.

They resonated.

The Suppressio sphere rose from the rucksack, drawn upward as if answering a summons. It hovered before Nicholas's forehead, its light flickering in sharp, testing pulses.

He did not brace. He did not fear. He simply breathed.

And in that breath, he felt them.

Anna's steady cadence pressed gently against the edges of his inhale, a grounding counterweight, a quiet reminder that he was not standing alone. Melusine's softer rhythm threaded through his exhale, smoothing the jagged places before they could form, her presence settling the emotional tremors he used to fight by himself.

The sphere touched his forehead.

Pressure surged. Nicholas exhaled into the shared rhythm and held.

Nicholas did not waver.

His aura settled into a calm silver-blue. The sphere dimmed.

"Again," Nicholas said quietly.

The sphere responded.

Fear rose, then doubt. Anna and Mel held the rhythm while Nicholas let both pass without chasing them.

The sphere's light flickered, then stabilized.

Nicholas lowered his hand, breathed steadily, shoulders loose. "It is done."

Antonia stared, the color draining from her face. "That was full intensity."

Lazer stepped closer, eyes wide, voice barely holding steady. "He did not suppress fear," he murmured. "He redirected it. He turned it into control."

The mist pulsed once, a quiet acknowledgment, as if agreeing with him.

Nicholas blinked. "We did."

Before anyone could respond, Evanidus pulsed. Suppressio answered, then Defensio and Stabilis. Thin strands of mist flashed between them.

The temperature dropped as a column of light rose around Nicholas.

Anna stepped back, instinct overriding curiosity. "What is that?"

Melusine's voice barely carried. "Resonance. But not ours."

Blue flame folded around the spheres, sealing them inside a bright barrier.

Inside the boundary, the mist convulsed. Not violently, but in a sudden, focused contraction. It folded inward, collapsing on itself as if the rules of gravity had reversed.

Nicholas felt the pull in his chest. Not physically. Not emotional. Something deeper. A chord tightening. A summons. A recognition.

The kind of pull that did not ask. It's called.

The flames rose. The Seer Orb coalesced—not assembled, but drawn into being.

Gold, silver-blue, and lavender spiraled inside the blue flame boundary, each color moving with its own rhythm, yet pulsing together like a single ancient heartbeat.

Nicholas stepped closer, drawn by a pull he did not fully understand. The orb flared, a sharp, blinding flash that sent ripples through the mist.

The barrier snapped shut around Nicholas.

Something was waking.

"Nicholas."

Anna lunged forward, but the flames surged upward, swallowing him whole and sealing him inside their shimmering dome before she could take another step.

Melusine reached for her. "Anna, wait."

Too late.

Anna's essence detonated outward in a burst of gold, fierce and instinctive. Her form shimmered, edges blurring as her body folded inward, reshaping with a speed that bordered on violent. Feathers erupted from her shoulders in a radiant flare. Light wrapped around her like a tightening cocoon, pulsing with her panic.

In a breath, she was gone.

An oriole shot upward in a streak of molten gold. She darted toward the flames, over, around, through, desperate angles, frantic wings, every motion a single thought made flesh: reach him.

But the flames rose with her.

She struck the boundary, not with a crash, but with the sickening softness of a bird hitting a pane of glass that had not existed a heartbeat before. The blue fire rippled outward in concentric rings of silver and cobalt, humming with a resonance that vibrated through the chamber.

The impact threw her back, tumbling her through the air in a blur of gold and panic. Antonia caught her midfall. The oriole trembled violently in her hands, wings fluttering in frantic, uneven bursts. Her tiny heart hammered against Antonia's palm, a rapid, desperate rhythm that did not belong to a creature built for fearlessness.

Melusine dropped to her knees beside them, breath shaking. "He's terrified."

Antonia stiffened. "What do you mean?"

Melusine's face went pale. "I can feel him. He thinks he can't stop what's happening."

Anna shrieked, a sharp, broken sound that cut through the chamber, carrying more emotion than any human throat could hold. The sound vibrated through Antonia's bones.

For a heartbeat, Antonia froze. Commander, instructor, guardian, all of it warring with the unfamiliar ache rising in her chest. Then she lowered herself to the floor beside Melusine. It was awkward. Stiff. Not her. But she wrapped one steady arm around Melusine's shoulders, pulling her close, grounding her with the same fierce steadiness she used to anchor recruits in panic drills. Her other hand cupped the trembling oriole, thumb brushing gently over Anna's feathers.

Melusine leaned into her, trembling hard enough that Antonia felt it through her own ribs. "He is trying to hold everything together," Melusine whispered, voice cracking. "He is trying so hard."

When one of them broke, all of them bled.

Anna pressed her tiny head against Melusine's knee, shaking uncontrollably. Lazer stood behind them, pale and silent, unable to look away from the flames.

Inside the fire, Nicholas fell to his knees.

Inside the vision, Rhet's realm opened around him.

Frigid air slapped his face, sharp and metallic. At the same time, radiant heat rolled off the collapsing tower in suffocating waves, baking his skin. The contrast made his nerves scream, freezing and burning at once, as if his body could not decide which agony to register first.

He staggered forward, boots crunching on broken shards of timeline glass. Each step sent a brittle crack echoing through the empty streets. Dust swirled around him in choking spirals, gritty and bitter. It clung to his lips, coated his tongue, stung his eyes.

Then the smell hit.

Burnt barbecue. Charred wood. Scorched meat. Smoke curling through the air. A backyard memory twisted into something monstrous.

Nicholas gagged, doubling over as the heat and cold collided in his lungs. The tower groaned, a deep resonant sound like a dying animal, and another section sheared away, collapsing in a plume of dust and flame.

The shockwave hit him a second later, slamming into his chest, rattling his bones. Something inside him cracked. Not physically. Emotionally. Primally.

A voice whispered through the dust, not spoken, not heard, but felt.

You are too late.

Nicholas's breath hitched. His vision blurred. His knees buckled.

Outside the flames, Anna shrieked. Melusine trembled. The Triad resonance strained like a rope pulled to breaking.

The tower groaned again, fractures spider-webbing across its surface, glowing with unstable light. Echoes flickered inside the structure, silhouettes trapped in collapsing timelines, each one a moment that once belonged to someone.

He felt them. Their panic. Their confusion. Their desperate reaching for someone who could anchor them.

Nicholas reached out, hands shaking. "Please."

A massive shard of the tower sheared off, crashing downward in a cascade of glowing debris. Heat blasted across his face, searing his skin. The air rippled with the force of it, a shockwave that punched the breath from his lungs.

He stumbled backward, coughing as dust clawed its way into his throat. The ground trembled beneath him, a deep rolling quake that made the world feel hollow.

A fracture split open at his feet, glowing with violent, unstable energy. Freezing air roared upward from the void, chilling his bones even as the radiant heat from the collapsing tower scorched his skin. The contrast tore through him, a war of temperatures that made his nerves scream.

Nicholas screamed as the tower finally gave way.

It folded inward, collapsing like a dying star, crushing the echoes inside it. Their light flickered, a thousand tiny flares of memory, then extinguished in a wave of collapsing timelines that rippled outward like a shockwave.

The sound, not audible but felt, tore through him as a blade dragged through the center of his chest. He fell to his knees, hands pressed to the fractured ground, breath ragged, vision swimming.

"No. No, no, no."

The word was not a denial. It was grief. It was recognition. It was the unbearable weight of watching something die that should never have been alive in the first place.

Dust settled on Nicholas's face, gritty and bitter. It clung to his eyelashes, his lips, the corners of his mouth. He tasted despair in the air, metallic and sharp, like breathing in the death of a world.

A shadow moved behind him.

Nicholas turned slowly.

Rhet stood on a raised platform of fused fractures, coat whipping in the unstable wind. His aura flickered violently, too bright and too sharp, as if his very existence strained against the rules of the realm. His living eye glowed with fractured light while the jagged glass of the other scattered broken timelines in sharp, shifting reflections.

"He grows stronger," Rhet murmured, voice low and reverent.

Nicholas's breath froze in his chest.

Rhet stepped forward, boots crunching on broken timelines that shattered like brittle glass beneath him. "And so must we."

A hopper materialized beside him, flickering with fear, its form glitching at the edges. "The first wave is ready."

"Not yet," Rhet said.

He lifted his hand.

The fractures around him trembled, a deep bone rattling vibration that crawled up Nicholas's spine and settled in his teeth. Rhet's field flared, a violent burst of light that cracked the ground beneath him, sending fissures racing outward in jagged lines.

"He feels me," Rhet whispered. "And I feel him."

His gaze snapped toward Nicholas. Through the vision. Through the Continuum. Through the Seer Orb. Through every fracture that connected them.

"You cannot hide from me, cousin."

Nicholas staggered backward, breath ripped from his lungs as if the realm itself had punched the air out of him.

Rhet smiled, a sharp, broken thing that did not reach his eyes. "the Triad awakens. The Lion roars. The Continuum bends."

The fractures behind him pulsed in agreement, light rippling outward like a heartbeat.

"And soon," Rhet said, lifting his hand, "it will break."

The fractures exploded outward.

A legion of hoppers surged forward, hundreds, maybe thousands, flickering like dying stars. They leapt in unison, tearing the air, ripping open new fractures with every jump. The realm shook. The sky wound widened. The light grew violent.

Nicholas felt himself being pulled backward, ripped from the vision, dragged through the mist, through the light, through the collapsing realm.

Back in the chamber.

Nicholas slammed onto the stone floor, gasping, fingers clawing at the ground as if trying to hold onto a world that no longer existed. The blue flames vanished in an instant, snuffed out like a candle in a storm.

Anna burst from Antonia's hands, shifting midair back into human form, landing hard on her knees beside him. She grabbed his shoulders, breath breaking. Melusine threw her arms around both of them, sobbing into his chest, her aura flickering in frantic pulses.

Antonia knelt behind them, one hand still on Melusine's back, the other braced on the floor as if the chamber itself had tilted beneath her. Her eyes were wide, unfocused, trying to process what she had just witnessed.

Lazer stared at Nicholas, voice barely a whisper. "What did you see?"

Nicholas lifted his head. Dust clung to his lips. Ash streaked his cheeks. His eyes were red, raw, and haunted.

"Rhet," he whispered. "He is building an army."

Anna cupped his face, trembling. "Nicholas."

He swallowed hard, voice cracking. "And he is coming."

The mist shuddered, a full-body tremor that rippled across the chamber like a living thing recoiling from the truth.

Silence fell. Not empty. Not peaceful. A silence with weight. A silence that listened.

And somewhere deep in the Continuum, in the fractures, in the timelines, in the places where memory and reality blurred, something trembled in answer.

The world had shifted.

The Triad had awakened.

And nothing would be the same.

The Continuum trembled, as if recognizing the storm now set in motion.

Chapter 23.5 Interlude

The collapse settled into silence. Not peace. Never peace. But the heavy, smoldering quiet that follows catastrophe.

Dust drifted through the fractured air like ash shaken loose from a dying star. The tower Nicholas had watched crumble was now a jagged skeleton, its remaining shards jutting upward like broken ribs clawing at the sky.

At the center of the ruin, where the ground still glowed with unstable light, Rhet sat upon a throne.

It was not carved. It was not built. It was formed.

A jagged seat of fused fractures and crystallized timelines, pulled together by the violent gravity of his aura. The throne pulsed faintly beneath him, threads of broken possibility weaving through its structure like veins.

Rhet leaned back, one elbow resting lazily on the armrest, his round-brimmed hat tilted just enough to shadow half his face. The other half, the one with the glass-shard eye, gleamed with fractured light. It caught the chaos around him and scattered it in sharp, violent angles.

A hopper limped toward him, aura flickering. "The collapse is complete, my lord."

Rhet did not look at him. "I can see that."

The hopper bowed its head, trembling. "The echoes inside are extinguished."

Rhet's lips twitched, not quite a smile. "Nothing is ever gone. It simply becomes available."

He lifted a hand. The air rippled. A faint echo drifted toward him; the last dying resonance of the timelines crushed in the collapse. It was not spirit or soul, but the raw imprint of extinguished moments, the emotional residue of everything that had been erased.

Rhet inhaled slowly, savoring the taste of it. Fear. Confusion. Desperation. The lingering aftershock of a thousand collapsing histories. It settled into him like fuel.

He gestured lazily at the ruins around them. The fractured sky flickered with unstable light, each pulse sending ripples through the broken horizon. The ground beneath the throne radiated residual heat, glowing faintly where timelines had burned themselves out. The air tasted of dust and burnt chronology, the acrid tang of histories collapsing in on themselves. The crater stretched outward in every direction, so vast it warped perspective, as if the world itself struggled to comprehend what had been taken from it.

Rhet tapped a finger against the throne's armrest, the sound sharp in the smothered quiet.

"Nicholas saw it."

He did not say it with anger. He said it with certainty, with the satisfaction of a man who knew exactly which domino had just fallen.

The hopper swallowed. "Yes, my lord."

"And the Triad felt it."

"Yes."

"And the Council…" Rhet tilted his head, listening to something distant, a tremor in the Continuum, a whisper only he could hear. "…they tremble."

He leaned forward slightly, elbows resting on his knees, posture relaxed in a way that made the ruin around him feel even more precarious.

"But trembling is not action."

A slow smile crept across his face, thin and dangerous, the kind of smile that belonged to a man who had already calculated the next ten moves.

"If this does not spur them to move," he murmured, "then time will be mine for the taking."

He lifted his hand again.

The fractures around him responded instantly, rising like serpents from the ground, twisting and coiling in the air. They pulsed with violent light, awaiting command, not summoned, but eager, as if the realm itself recognized him as its rightful master.

Rhet flared, casting jagged shadows across the ruin. The fractures leaned toward him, bending like metal drawn to a magnet.

"Do you feel it?" he asked softly, though the hopper dared not answer. "The Continuum shifting. The balance is tilting. The old rules are cracking."

He closed his fingers slowly, and the fractures tightened in unison, constricting the air with a sound like glass screaming.

"Fear is a beginning," Rhet whispered. "But fear alone cannot stop what is coming."

He opened his hand. The fractures exploded outward in a silent burst of light, rippling across the crater like a shockwave. Rhet watched the horizon distort, watched the broken sky ripple, watched the last remnants of the collapse settle into stillness.

Then he exhaled, a long, satisfied breath. He leaned back into the throne of fused timelines, the ruin stretching before him like a kingdom waiting to be claimed.

"Because I am done waiting."

The fractures roared in response. The throne of ruin pulsed beneath him like a heartbeat.

Rhet inhaled, slow and deliberate, syncing himself to the rhythm of the broken world around him. From his throne, the devastation radiated toward every horizon, a wound carved through the Continuum with Rhet sitting calmly at its center.

He lifted his chin, the glass-shard eye catching the unstable light.

"Let them scramble," he murmured. "Let them cling to what remains."

The fractures leaned toward him, drawn by the gravity of his intent.

"Because the next move is mine."

The wind shifted, a low resonant hum rolling across the ruin, carrying the faint tremor of distant timelines buckling under the weight of what he had set in motion.

Rhet's smile sharpened. "And I do not intend to be gentle."

The fractures flared once more, answering him like loyal hounds. In the smoldering quiet of the collapse, the Continuum seemed to draw away from Rhet, as if even the broken places between worlds understood what he had unleashed.

CHAPTER 24

Nicholas did not remember standing.

One moment, he was on the chamber floor, dust still clinging to his lips, Anna's hands on his face, Mel's arms around him, Antonia kneeling behind them like a pillar trying to hold up a collapsing world.

Next, he was walking. Or being walked. He was not sure.

The corridor blurred around him, mist drifting low, walls pulsing faintly with blue veins of light. His senses were still flickering between worlds. Every breath tasted like dust. Every blink brought flashes of collapsing towers. Every shift of air carried the phantom heat of destruction.

Then the mist moved.

Not drifting. Not swirling. Responding.

A thin ribbon of silver vapor curled around Mel's ankles first, rising in a soft, deliberate spiral. Her breath hitched as the mist climbed her legs, her waist, her shoulders, weaving itself into the familiar robes of a Conclave Sustentet, lavender threading the fabric with faint copper at the edges.

It did not stop with her.

Another ribbon of mist slid across the floor toward Anna, brushing her bare feet with a cool, testing touch. She gasped as it rose, wrapping around her in gentle, fluid motions, forming robes that shimmered with faint gold undertones, the color of her aura when she was steady.

Nicholas staggered.

A third ribbon of mist reached him.

It touched his ankle like a pulse. Then it rose, slowly and hesitant, as if the Continuum itself were unsure whether he could bear the weight of recognition. The mist climbed his legs, his torso, his shoulders, weaving into deep blue robes threaded with silver fractures that glowed faintly beneath the fabric.

Anna stared at him. Mel's hand tightened around his arm.

The robes were not ceremonial. They were not decorative. They felt like armor, soft and woven from light, but heavy with meaning.

Antonia inhaled sharply behind them. Lazer froze mid-step. The mist settled. The Triad stood in the corridor wrapped in robes they had not earned, had not asked for, had not been prepared to wear. As if the Continuum had decided before the Council ever could.

Anna stayed pressed against Nicholas's side, one hand gripping his arm as if afraid he would vanish. Mel hovered on his other side, trembling, her eyes red from crying but steadier now, anchored by the robes that had formed around her.

Antonia walked behind them, silent, jaw tight, her expression flickering between awe and fear. Lazer led the way, his slate clutched to his chest like a shield.

They entered the Council Chamber.

The temperature dropped instantly. The chamber felt colder than the corridors, not physically, but in the way a place feels when too many eyes are waiting for you to speak. The suspended blue fire cast long shadows across the floor, and the mist pooled low, as if holding its breath.

Nicholas stood before the semicircle of Council members, Anna and Mel flanking him like anchors. The new robes still shimmered faintly, as if the Continuum had not finished deciding what they meant. Antonia and Lazer took their places beside the Triad, silent but watchful.

Chittaswarup stepped forward. "Nicholas. Tell us what you saw."

Nicholas swallowed. His throat felt raw, coated in dust that was not really there. His hands shook. Anna slid her fingers into his. Mel touched his back, grounding him with a steady pulse of warmth through her aura.

He nodded. And began.

"At first, it was just fractures. Everywhere. The air was cold, but the heat from the collapse burned my face. Both at once. Cold and heat. I could not breathe."

A ripple passed through the chamber, not movement, but stillness tightening, as if the room itself braced. The suspended fire dimmed a fraction. The mist at their feet curled inward, listening.

Nicholas continued, voice trembling. "There was a tower. Huge. Made of timelines. Echoes inside it, thousands, reaching for me."

His voice cracked.

A faint shimmer crossed his vision, the chamber walls bending for a heartbeat into the jagged silhouette of the collapsing tower. Anna's grip tightened instantly. Mel's aura flared in a protective pulse, brushing against his.

Nicholas blinked hard, forcing the room back into focus.

"They were not just reaching," he whispered. "They were begging. Pulling. Like they thought I could help them."

A murmur of breath passed through the Council, not a sound, but a shift in the air, a collective tightening of shoulders.

Nicholas swallowed again. "I could feel them. All of them. Their fear. Their confusion. Their endings."

The mist around the Triad rose slightly, brushing Nicholas's ankles like a sympathetic touch.

"The tower started collapsing. Slowly. Like it wanted me to watch. I could taste the dust. It stuck to my lips. My tongue. I could not get it out."

The chamber flickered, a shimmer of fractured light, the Continuum echoing his panic. The air tightened around him, not trapping him, but breathing with him.

Nicholas's voice cracked. "It smelled like burnt barbecue. Not fire. Not smoke from a fireplace. Just burnt. Familiar. Wrong. Like something that should not be burning was burning."

His throat closed. Tears blurred his vision.

"I tried to stop it," he whispered. "I tried to reach them. But I could not touch anything. I could not save anyone."

Anna's eyes filled with tears. Mel pressed her forehead to his shoulder, her energy folding around him in a soft protective pulse.

Nicholas's breath trembled. "And then Rhet appeared."

The room stilled.

The mist stopped drifting. The suspended fire dimmed. Even the faint hum of the chamber's wards fell silent.

"He floated through the fracture as he owned it. The hoppers moved for him. He raised his hand, and they tore the world apart. He did not even look at the destruction. He just watched me."

Nicholas's voice dropped. "He saw me. Through the vision. Through the orb. Through everything."

Chittaswarup's aura tightened.

Nicholas continued, shaking. "He said the Triad awakens. The Lion roars. The Continuum bends. And then he said soon it will break."

Silence followed. Heavy. Charged.

Nicholas wiped his face. "He is building an army. A legion. And he is coming."

He waited for outrage, fear, urgency.

None came.

Only the quiet weight of the Council's measured breathing.

Instead, the Council exchanged measured glances, not unified, not aligned, but split cleanly down an invisible fault line.

Bharati folded her hands. "This confirms our projections."

Asiza's jaw tightened. "The escalation is worse than projected. Rhet is accelerating."

Paloma exhaled sharply. "Which is why we must proceed with caution."

Lazer countered immediately, eyes flashing. "Caution is how timelines collapse. We need action."

Antonia stepped forward, voice low. "We need protection. For them."

The chamber vibrated with tension, two factions forming, neither willing to yield.

Nicholas stared at them, stunned. "Caution?"

Chittaswarup stepped forward. "Nicholas. What you saw was horrific. But we must respond with clarity."

Nicholas's breath hitched. "Clarity? I watched a timeline die."

Anna stepped closer. "Nicholas."

He shook his head, voice rising. "I smelled the burning. I tasted the dust. I felt the heat on my face. I heard the fractures screaming. I felt them reaching for me."

His voice broke.

"And you are talking about clarity."

Mel's aura flared. "He is traumatized."

Anna's voice cracked. "He almost died in there."

The Council remained composed, but their pulse betrayed them, flickers of fear, anger, guilt.

Nicholas's knees buckled. Anna caught him. Mel wrapped her arms around both of them. Nicholas leaned onto Anna's shoulder, shaking.

The breakdown hit all three at once. Anna sobbed into his hair. Mel clung to him, trembling. Nicholas gasped for breath, the dust of the vision still choking him. Their breathing synced without meaning to, three rhythms collapsing into one.

Mist rose around the three of them in a soft luminous veil as they clung to one another.

They collapsed to the floor in a tangle of arms and tears.

The Council watched. Not coldly. Not dismissively. But helplessly, torn between fear and duty, between caution and action, between protecting the Triad and needing them.

The fracture between them widened in silence.

Chittaswarup stepped forward, kneeling slowly before the Triad. Not as a Council elder. Not as a leader. But as someone who acknowledges a truth older than titles.

He placed a hand on Nicholas's back, gentle and steady. "We are steady," he said softly, "so that you may fall."

Nicholas sobbed harder.

"You carry the weight of what we cannot see. You feel what we cannot bear. You break so that we may stand." Chittaswarup bowed his head. "And now we stand so that you may break."

For the first time since the vision, Nicholas let himself fall apart completely, held by the two people who refused to let him fall alone.

The chamber doors closed behind the three of them, leaving the Council alone in the dim blue glow of the suspended fire.

Chittaswarup stood at the center of the semicircle. "We must proceed."

Bharati exhaled slowly. "We knew Rhet was escalating. But the scale of the collapse Nicholas described exceeds our projections."

Asiza's voice was quiet, but her aura flickered sharply. "Thousands of echoes extinguished. A timeline erased. And Rhet did not hesitate."

Lazer tapped his slate, the sound sharp in the charged air. "He is accelerating. The second wave is already forming."

Paloma folded her arms. "And the Triad is not ready. We are not ready."

Antonia's jaw tightened. "They are unseasoned, not unworthy."

Chittaswarup shook his head. "Whatever is happening around them, we cannot ignore it."

"Choice or not," Bharati said, "they are fragile."

"Fragile," Lazer echoed, "but necessary."

Silence settled over them, stretched thin with everything unsaid.

Chittaswarup finally spoke, voice steady but heavy. "We must decide our next step."

Chapter 25

Night met the sea in a wash of lavender and gold. Nicholas, Anna, and Mel sat where the surf met the sand, the waves rolling steadily around their feet.

Nicholas let the cool water ground him. The salt air stung his nose, clean and sharp, nothing like the dust of the vision, and he breathed until the last trace of burnt air seemed to leave his lungs.

Anna sat beside him with her knees pulled to her chest, damp hair clinging to her cheeks. She did not speak.

Mel sat on Nicholas's other side, legs stretched into the surf, her aura faint and shaken as she watched the horizon.

Nicholas closed his eyes. For the first time since the vision, he felt something quiet.

A soft crunch of sand behind them broke the silence.

Anna turned first.

Bharati stood a few paces away, her robes gathered in one hand to keep them from the tide, her hair loose in the breeze.

She looked smaller than she ever had in the Council Chamber, not diminished, but human.

"May I join you?" she asked quietly.

Nicholas nodded. Bharati lowered herself into the sand beside them with a slow, careful motion.

For a long time, she said nothing. The waves washed in and out in a steady rhythm. Finally, she exhaled.

"I have watched you both for many years," she said softly. "Long before you knew who you were. Long before you knew who I was."

Nicholas blinked. "Miss Carter."

Bharati smiled faintly. "Yes. Miss Carter. The woman who manned the office and watched you come in after your daydreams. The one who called your parents and kept them calm. The one who watched over you and made sure the school was safe."

Anna's breath caught. The surf stilled for a heartbeat.

"You knew."

"I knew everything I was allowed to know," Bharati said. "And far more than I wanted to."

She looked out at the ocean, eyes distant, the silver-blue threads in the sky reflecting in her gaze.

"When I was assigned to watch over you, Nicholas, I thought it would be simple. Keep you safe. Keep you hidden. Keep you unaware until the time was right."

Her voice tightened.

"I never imagined the time would come so soon."

Nicholas swallowed. "I am not ready."

Bharati turned to him, her expression softening in a way he had never seen. "No one is ever ready to carry the weight of one world, let alone the many collapsing around you."

Anna leaned forward, voice trembling. "You should have shared with me. I was his protector."

Bharati's eyes glistened. "I wish I could have. It was incredibly unfair. But I did not have the right to tell you. Not until circumstances forced the truth into the open."

She looked between Nicholas, Anna, and Mel.

"You were a child," she whispered. "And I was preparing you for a burden no child should ever bear."

Nicholas stared at the sand. "And now you are asking us to put our lives on the line."

Bharati's voice cracked. "I know."

The waves rolled in, brushing against her knees.

"I never wanted this for you," she said. "Not for either of you. I wanted you to grow up. To have choices. To live without fear. But Rhet has forced our hand, and whatever is happening around the three of you can no longer be ignored."

She reached out and placed a gentle hand on Nicholas's shoulder.

"You carry a weight no one else can carry. Not because you are stronger. Not because you are destined. But because you are willing."

Nicholas's breath trembled. "I do not know if I am."

Bharati squeezed his shoulder. "You are. Because you are still here."

Anna wiped her eyes. "We are scared."

"So am I," Bharati whispered.

The admission hung in the air like a fragile truth.

Mel leaned closer, voice soft. "Then why us?"

Bharati looked at them, really looked.

"I don't know why you," she said. "Anyone who tells you they do is pretending certainty we don't have. But I know what I've seen in you: courage, loyalty, and the refusal to leave each other behind."

She stood slowly, brushing sand from her robes.

"When dawn comes, the Council will call for you. But tonight…" She looked at the three of them sitting in the surf, wrapped in mist and moonlight and a faint silver-blue glow. "…tonight, you are allowed to be young. You are allowed to be afraid. You are allowed to breathe."

She stepped back, letting the waves wash over her feet.

"And know this," she added, voice steady. "I watched over you for years. But now... now I stand with you."

She bowed her head, not as a Council member, not as Miss Carter, but as someone who loved them.

Then she turned and walked back up the beach, her silhouette framed by the lavender and gold horizon.

As she moved away, a single firefly blinked into existence above the surf.

Then another. And another.

Within seconds, dozens of fireflies floated around the Triad, their tiny bodies pulsing with warm light. They did not flicker randomly. Their glow rose and fell in a steady, measured rhythm, a rhythm Nicholas recognized, but half a beat off, the same subtle wrongness he had felt in the collapsing tower.

Anna whispered, "Is that..."

Mel nodded, eyes wide. "Time."

The fireflies drifted outward across the shoreline like stars spilled onto the sand, their synchronized glow reaching toward the dark water.

Nicholas exhaled, the tension in his chest easing. Anna leaned against him. Mel took his hand.

The fireflies pulsed again, soft and steady.

Time was still moving.

CHAPTER 26

Nirvana did not wake gently.

The suspended fire in the Great Hall burned in jagged pulses, flaring and dimming as though struggling to hold its shape. The mist along the floor trembled in thin, nervous ripples. Even the walls, normally serene and unchanging, seemed to hum with a low, uneasy vibration.

Nicholas felt it the moment he stepped inside.

The Council was already gathered. Antonia stood rigid, arms crossed, jaw tight. Bharati paced in sharp, clipped steps. Lazer scribbled frantic notes on a floating slate. Asiza whispered to the mist itself, listening for something only she could hear.

And Paloma looked heartbroken.

Chittaswarup raised a hand. "We begin."

The suspended fire steadied, barely.

Paloma stepped forward first. "Eunomia was one of Arotza's greatest works—a harmonic structure designed to stabilize the early Continuum."

Nicholas frowned. "A structure?"

Paloma tilted her head. "The early Viatori described it more like a harmony than a machine."

Lazer snorted. "A poetic oversimplification."

Paloma did not flinch. "And your equations are a clinical oversimplification."

Lazer finally looked up, eyes sharp. "Eunomia was a stabilizing field. A self-correcting harmonic lattice that maintained structural coherence across the Continuum."

Paloma raised an eyebrow. "A song."

"A mechanism," Lazer corrected.

"A presence," Paloma countered.

Nicholas glanced between them. "You are both saying the same thing."

They both turned to him.

Mel whispered, "Careful."

But Paloma smiled. "He is right."

Lazer sighed. "He is partially right."

Paloma gestured, and a crystalline tablet projected a shimmering sphere of resonance into the air.

Lazer tapped his slate, splitting the image into an interlocking lattice. "This is how it behaved: a stabilizing matrix across timelines."

Anna leaned forward. "What happened to it?"

Paloma's expression dimmed. "It shattered."

Lazer nodded. "Under stress."
"What kind of stress?" Nicholas asked.
Lazer hesitated. "Unknown."
Paloma added quietly, "Or unspoken."
The room fell still.
Mel's voice was barely a whisper. "How many pieces?"
Paloma and Lazer exchanged a look, not disagreement, but caution.
"Many," Paloma said. "Scattered across timelines."

Lazer added, "Each fragment retains part of Eunomia's original frequency. Enough to affect the stability around it."

Paloma touched the projection. "Fragments become active during periods of severe instability."
Nicholas felt the Seer Orb pulse faintly in his rucksack.
Anna noticed. "Nicholas."
He shook his head. "I am fine."
Lazer's eyes flicked to the rucksack. "The Seer Orb reacted when this fragment became active. That may be why it formed."

Nicholas rubbed his temples. "So the fragment triggered the Seer Orb?"
Paloma knelt in front of him. "That is one possibility."
Lazer added, "the Triad resonance may be amplifying whatever sensitivity you already had."
Anna stiffened. "Connected how?"

Mel exhaled. "That is comforting."
Lazer muttered, "It is also mathematically improbable."
Paloma smiled. "And yet here they are."
Nicholas looked at the projected sphere again. "The fragment in the clock shop… why there?"

Lazer said, "Our records suggest someone placed it there intentionally."

Nicholas's breath caught. "Someone."

Paloma nodded. "Possibly a Viator who understood what could happen if a fragment fell into the wrong hands."

Nicholas felt the room tilt slightly. "So, we are not the first to deal with this."

"No," Paloma said.

Lazer's voice dropped. "One active fragment may affect others. We do not yet know how far that effect reaches."

Nicholas felt the weight of what they were walking into.

Chittaswarup entered the chamber. His presence shifted the room, not with force, but with gravity.

"You have learned what Eunomia was," he said. "Now you must understand what it is becoming."

Nicholas straightened. Anna and Mel flanked him instinctively.

Chittaswarup gestured, and the suspended fire flared to life. Its flames twisted into shapes, a clock face, a pendulum, a gear turning in slow, heavy arcs.

Nicholas's breath caught.

His dream. The Seer Orb's vision. The mantle clock at home. The dusty shop he had stumbled into by accident.

Chittaswarup watched him carefully. "You recognize it."

Nicholas nodded. "I have seen it. In the dream. In the vision. And once… in real life."

Anna frowned. "Real life."

Nicholas swallowed. "When I fell through the fracture the first time. I landed on a street. A small town. There was a clock shop at the end of the block."

Mel's eyes widened. "The same one from your dream."

"Yes," Nicholas whispered. "Exactly the same."

Chittaswarup stepped closer, the firelight reflecting in his eyes. "The Seer Orb does not show illusions. It reveals intersections, places where the Continuum thins, where past and future brush against the present."

He raised a hand, and the flames shifted again.

Now the clock shop appeared more clearly, shelves of clocks frozen at various times, dust motes drifting through still air, a faint shimmer around the back room.

Nicholas felt the pull in his chest.

"A fragment lies within a clock shop," Chittaswarup said. "That much is certain."

Anna leaned forward. "But where is it?"

Chittaswarup's expression darkened. "That is what we do not yet know."

Lazer stepped in, adjusting his slate. "The Seer Orb gave us imagery, not coordinates. It showed a location, but not a timeline. The clock shop could be anywhere, any world, any era, any branch."

Paloma added, "Fragments hide themselves. They distort perception. They blur memories. They resist being found."

Nicholas's pulse quickened. "But I have been there. I saw it. Does that not mean…"

"It means," Chittaswarup said gently, "that you are connected to it. Not that you know where it is."

Nicholas felt the floor tilt beneath him. "So, the dream and the vision are clues, but not directions."

"Precisely," Lazer said. "The Continuum isn't a map. It's a pattern."

Mel frowned. "Then how do we find the shop?"

Chittaswarup turned to the suspended fire. The flames twisted again, this time into a swirling pattern of mist and light, like a compass made of breath.

"We follow resonance," he said. "The fragment calls. The Seer Orb listens. And you, Nicholas…" He placed a hand over Nicholas's heart. "… you feel."

Nicholas's breath hitched.

Anna touched his arm. "We will find it together."

Mel nodded. "Wherever it is."

Chittaswarup stepped back. "The Seer Orb will guide you. But be warned. Fragments attract more than seekers. They attract danger. They attract hunger."

The flames flickered, forming the silhouette of a wide-brimmed hat. A drifting coat. A single jagged eye.

Nicholas shivered.

"And you are not the only one searching," Chittaswarup said. "Now you must train."

The Resonance Hall was already restless when they arrived, mist swirling in agitated spirals and lights flickering along the walls.

Antonia stood in the center of the chamber, arms folded, jaw tight.

"Positions," she barked.

Nicholas, Anna, and Mel scrambled into formation.

Antonia snapped her fingers. A shockwave of mist surged toward them. Nicholas barely had time to raise Defensio. The barrier flickered, thin and unstable. Anna tried to reinforce it with Suppressio, but her focus slipped. Mel reached for Nicholas's arm to anchor him, but her timing was off.

The shockwave hit. Nicholas staggered backward. Anna stumbled into him. Mel nearly fell.

"Again," Antonia snapped.

Another wave.

Nicholas raised Defensio too late. Anna's aura flared unevenly. Mel's stabilizing touch missed its mark.

The wave slammed into them. Nicholas hit the floor hard.

Antonia's voice cut through the chamber. "You are thinking. Stop thinking."

"We are trying," Nicholas began.

"Trying is hesitation," Antonia said. "Hesitation gets you killed."

She flicked her wrist. Three mist constructs materialized, hopper silhouettes, flickering and unstable, but fast.

"Defend."

The constructs lunged. Nicholas raised Defensio, but fear spiked, and the barrier wavered. Anna tried to suppress the constructs' jumps, but her timing was off. Mel attempted to stabilize Nicholas, but her hand slipped through unstable mist.

The constructs broke through.

Nicholas ducked. Anna tripped. Mel's sphere belt clattered against the floor.

"You are not children," Antonia shouted. "You are a Triad. Act like one."

Nicholas's breath came fast and shallow. His aura flickered wildly.

Anna's voice cracked. "We are doing our best."

"Your best is chaos," Antonia shot back. "Your best is fear. Your best is three people acting alone."

Mel's eyes glistened. "We are trying to work together."

"Then stop trying," Antonia said. "And be together."

Nicholas clenched his fists. "We do not know how."

Antonia stepped forward, fierce but kind. "You're rushing. You're letting urgency become panic and fear become noise. Stop fighting the room and listen to each other."

She pointed between them. "Find Anna. Find Mel. Let them find you."

Nicholas swallowed. "Then what do we do?"

"You stop."

The Triad froze.

"You breathe."

Nicholas blinked. "What?"

"Sit," Antonia ordered.

They hesitated.

"Sit."

Nicholas, Anna, and Mel lowered themselves to the floor, forming a small triangle.

"Close your eyes."

Nicholas did.

"Start with your breathing," Antonia said. "Then feel each other."

Nicholas inhaled slowly.

Nicholas reached out with his awareness. Anna's presence was sharp, bright and determined. Mel's was warm, steady, grounding. His own was turbulent, flickering and afraid.

"Let the noise fall away," Antonia whispered. "Let the urgency fall away. Let the fear fall away."

Nicholas exhaled. The chamber quieted. For the first time since the Seer Orb's vision, he felt something like stillness.

"Now listen."

Nicholas listened. Anna. Mel. Three breaths settling toward one rhythm.

"Good," Antonia said. "Now rise."

They stood together.

Antonia snapped her fingers. A shockwave surged. Nicholas raised Defensio, and this time Anna and Mel were already there. Their auras synced. Their timing aligned. The barrier formed clean, strong, luminous.

The shockwave hit. The barrier was held.

Antonia's eyes softened. "Again."

And this time, they were ready.

The Resonance Hall still hummed with the echo of the Triad's training when the alarm struck.

A deep resonant chime rippled through Nirvana, not a sound, but a vibration that passed through bone and breath. The mist recoiled. The suspended lights flickered. Every Council member froze.

Bharati's eyes widened. "No."

Lazer's slate lit up with frantic pulses of red. "A fracture. A large one."

Nicholas's stomach dropped. "Here."

"No," Antonia said, already moving. "Worse."

The Great Hall doors burst open as Asiza sprinted inside, her breath sharp, her aura flaring with urgency.

"It has opened in a metropolis," she said. "A dense one. Thousands nearby."

Chittaswarup's expression hardened. "Where."

Asiza shook her head. "The coordinates are unstable. The fracture is distorting the reading. But it is a major city, with tall structures, heavy traffic, and high population density."

Nicholas felt cold. "People are there. Right now."

"Which is why we move," Antonia said.

She snapped her fingers. Sixty Viatori appeared within seconds, cloaked, armed, sphere belts gleaming. Their Curas followed, hands already glowing with stabilizing mist.

Antonia addressed them with clipped precision. "Your objective is containment. Push the hoppers back. Seal the fracture if possible. Minimize civilian exposure."

One of the Viatori bowed. "Understood."

Nicholas stepped forward. "Should we not…"

"No," Antonia said sharply. "You three are not ready for a live breach."

Nicholas's jaw tightened. "But…"

Chittaswarup placed a hand on his shoulder. "This is not your battle. Not yet."

The Viatori formed a circle. Their Curas stepped into the center. Mist surged upward, swirling into a vortex of light.

In a flash, they were gone.

Nicholas paced the Great Hall while Anna watched the suspended fire and Mel stood nearby, hands clasped. Minutes dragged.

The Council waited in tense silence.

Then a tear opened in the air.

The Viatori stumbled through. Two collapsed immediately. One Cura fell to her knees, coughing violently. Another clutched his arm, blood seeping through his sleeve. Their cloaks were torn, scorched and stained with fracture residue.

Antonia rushed forward. "Report."

The lead Viatori, a tall woman with a cracked visor, struggled to speak. "We contained it. Barely."

Asiza knelt beside a wounded Cura, her hands glowing as she stabilized his aura. "How many hoppers breached?"

"Too many," the Viatori whispered. "They poured out like a flood. They were coordinated. Faster than usual. Aggressive."

Bharati's face drained of color. "Coordinated."

The Viatori nodded weakly. "They moved with purpose. As if they were being directed."

Nicholas felt his chest tighten. Rhet.

Antonia's voice sharpened. "Did you close the fracture?"

The Viatori hesitated.

Antonia stepped closer, aura flaring. "Did you close it?"

The lead Viatori swallowed. "We did not."

Paloma's breath hitched. "Then it is still open."

The Viatori shook her head. "No. It closed."

Relief flickered until she added, voice cracking, "It closed itself?"

A cold, heavy stillness fell over the Great Hall.

Lazer's slate chimed violently. "That is not possible. Fractures do not self-seal. They collapse, or they are forced to shut. They do not…"

Asiza whispered, "Unless something on the other side wanted it closed."

The mist recoiled sharply, pulling tight against the floor like a frightened animal.

Nicholas felt the sensation inside him pulse, a sharp warning throb beneath his ribs.

Anna stepped closer. "Nicholas."

He shook his head. "Something is wrong."

Mel's aura flickered. "The resonance is off. Like something is pulling on it."

Chittaswarup stepped forward, voice low and grave. "What did you encounter?"

The Viatori trembled. "Not a creature. Not a hopper. A presence."

Antonia's jaw tightened. "Describe it."

The Viatori's voice dropped. "It was watching us. Directing the hoppers. And when we pushed back…"

She shuddered.

"…it pushed harder."

Nicholas's pulse hammered. "Rhet."

The Viatori nodded weakly. "He did not step through. But he was there. Close. Too close."

Bharati pressed a hand to her mouth. "He is accelerating."

Lazer's slate projected a jagged waveform, unstable, spiking, violent. "The Continuum is destabilizing faster than predicted. If Rhet is coordinating hopper behavior, then the next fracture—"

"—will be worse," Asiza finished.

The suspended fire guttered, shrinking to a thin trembling flame.

Chittaswarup closed his eyes. He stood perfectly still, as if listening to something deep beneath the surface of reality, not sound, not vision, but the subtle shift of a world holding its breath. The mist around his feet tightened, then loosened, then tightened again,

Chapter 27

They reached the rooftop's edge, the city stretching out beneath them in a maze of lights and motion. Neon signs flickered. Cars crawled along distant streets. The air tasted like rain and electricity.

Nicholas lifted the rucksack and unfastened the top flap.

The Seer Orb pulsed faintly; uncertain, like a compass struggling to find north.

Anna frowned. "It's weaker here."

Mel nodded. "The fragment's resonance is muffled."

Chanotedah kicked a loose piece of gravel off the roof. "Or we're in the wrong timeline entirely. Wouldn't be the first time someone misjumped with an Evanidus sphere."

Nicholas ignored him.

He reached into the rucksack and pulled out the Regulatori.

The metal was cool against his palm. The glass face shimmered faintly, as if remembering something. The gears inside didn't tick; they shifted, breathed and aligned.

Nicholas stared at it.

He'd carried it for days. He'd felt it watching him. Waiting.

He lifted the Seer Orb in his other hand.

The moment the two objects were close, the air changed.

The mist around them tightened. The rooftop lights dimmed. The city noise softened to a distant hum.

Anna stepped back. "Nicholas…"

Mel whispered, "It's reacting."

Chanotedah's eyes widened. "Oh, that's not normal."

Nicholas held the Regulatori closer to the Seer Orb.

The Orb pulsed not once, but twice, then flared with a soft, golden light.

The Regulatori answered.

Its hands spun wildly, then stopped. The gears shifted into a new configuration. A faint hum vibrated through Nicholas's bones.

And then…

The two devices synced.

The Seer Orb projected a faint shimmer into the air; a translucent map of overlapping timelines, branching like veins of light. The Regulatori's hands twitched, aligning with one of the branches.

Nicholas felt a pull in his chest.

A direction. A certainty.

He whispered, "It's pointing."

Anna stepped beside him. "To the fragment?"

Nicholas nodded. "Yes. The Orb can sense it… But the Regulatori can translate it."

Mel's eyes widened. "It's like the Orb is the signal, and the Regulatori is the tuner."

Chanotedah muttered, "Great. We're following a cosmic radio station."

Nicholas adjusted the Regulatori's crown.

The Seer Orb brightened. The map sharpened. One branch glowed brighter than the rest, a thin line of gold cutting through the haze of timelines.

Nicholas felt the pull again, stronger this time.

"There," he said. "That's the direction."

Anna leaned in. "How far?"

Nicholas turned the Regulatori slightly.

The hands spun, then locked into place.

"Not far," he said. "A few jumps. Maybe less."

Mel exhaled. "Then we follow it."

Chanotedah groaned. "Of course we do."

Nicholas lowered the Regulatori and the Seer Orb. The map faded, but the direction remained—a tug in his chest, a whisper in the mist, a certainty in the air.

He tightened his grip on both artifacts.

"Let's go."

But the mist didn't let them move.

It thickened around their ankles, not restraining but waiting.

The rooftop lights dimmed further. The air vibrated. And then a shape stepped out of the fading map. Silver-blue mist coiled upward, gathering, thickening, taking form. A mane. A broad chest. A long, sweeping tail made of drifting light. A lion.

A lion made of silver-blue resonance, its presence pulling at something deep inside Nicholas.

Anna inhaled sharply. Mel's aura flared in awe. Chanotedah muttered, "Great. A cosmic housecat. Sure. Why not?"

The lion turned its massive head.

And swatted Chanotedah squarely in the shoulder with one luminous paw.

Chanotedah stumbled. "HEY. I was respectful. Mostly."

The lion's mane rippled in a silent, radiant huff.

Nicholas felt the pull in his chest sharpen, aligning with the lion's gaze. The Regulatori hummed. The Seer Orb brightened. The map collapsed into a single glowing path.

The lion stepped onto it. The path unfurled beneath its paws; a bridge of light suspended in the void between worlds.

Nicholas tightened his grip on the artifacts. "We follow it."

Anna and Mel stepped beside him.

Chanotedah sighed. "If this thing eats me, I'm haunting all of you."

They stepped forward. The rooftop dissolved. The city fell away. The world folded.

They landed in a narrow alley; dim, damp, flickering with unstable light.

Chanotedah groaned. "Ugh. Perfect landing. Ten out of ten. Really enjoying the ambiance."

The lion padded past him. And flicked him in the hip with its tail, a smooth, dismissive swipe of glowing mist.

Chanotedah yelped. "Okay! Rude. Cosmic and rude."

Anna snorted. Mel covered a laugh. Nicholas felt the first real breath of relief since Nirvana.

The lion paused at the mouth of the alley, looking back at Nicholas. Its silver eyes glowed. Then it stepped forward, dissolving into mist, leaving only a faint shimmer in the air. Nicholas felt the pull in his chest again.

"Left," he said. "A few blocks."

They stepped out of the alley. The city felt alive, but not in the way cities usually did. The air shimmered faintly, like heat rising off asphalt. Streetlights flickered in uneven rhythms. A passing bus distorted at the edges, as if reality were struggling to hold its shape.

Anna noticed it too. "Is that… normal?"

Chanotedah snorted. "No. That's what happens when a fragment wakes up in a timeline that can't manage it."

Mel's eyes widened. "It's destabilizing the city."

Nicholas tightened his grip on the Regulatori. "Then we need to move."

They walked quickly, weaving through crowds of people who didn't seem to notice the distortions. A man's shadow lagged half a second behind his steps. A street vendor's umbrella flickered between colors. A digital billboard glitched, showing three different ads at once.

Mel whispered, "They don't see it."

"They can't," Chanotedah said. "Their minds smooth it over. Humans are great at ignoring things that would break them."

Nicholas checked the Regulatori again. The hands twitched. The Seer Orb pulsed.

"We're close," he said.

Anna pointed ahead. "That street looks familiar."

Nicholas's breath caught. It did. Brick buildings. Dim sky. A narrow road sloping downward. A faint smell of rain on old pavement. His heart hammered.

"This is it," he whispered. "This is the street from my first fracture."

Mel stepped closer. "Nicholas…"

He didn't hear her. He was already moving.

The fragment's pull grew stronger with every step, a pressure behind his ribs, a whisper in the mist, a tug in the air like gravity shifting sideways.

Nicholas turned the corner. And froze. There it was. The clock shop.

Dusty windows. Faded wooden sign. Door slightly ajar. A faint shimmer around the frame, like the air was holding its breath.

Anna exhaled shakily. "It's real."

Mel whispered, "It's waiting."

Chanotedah muttered, "I hate this. I hate all of this."

Nicholas stepped toward the door.

The Seer Orb pulsed violently. The Regulatori's hands spun in a frantic circle. The mist around the shop rippled outward, distorting the street like a heat mirage.

Anna grabbed Nicholas's arm. "Wait."

Nicholas turned. "What?"

Mel pointed at the ground. A crack in the pavement; thin, jagged, glowing faintly with fractured light.

Chanotedah swore under his breath. "Oh, that's bad."

Nicholas swallowed. "What does it mean?"

Chanotedah's voice dropped.

"It means the fragment isn't just calling."

He looked at the shop.

"It's waking up."

Nicholas stared at the door, the same door he'd stumbled through once before, terrified and alone. This time, he wasn't alone. He tightened his grip on the Regulatori. Anna and Mel stepped beside him.

Chanotedah sighed and moved behind them, muttering, "I swear, if a hopper jumps out of a cuckoo clock, I'm quitting."

Nicholas pushed the door open. The bell above it chimed. Not a normal chime, not metal striking metal, but something deeper, rounder, like a ripple moving through a pond.

And the world inside the shop shifted.

CHAPTER 28

The sound moved through the mist, through the floorboards, through the very air, a soft resonant thrum that felt less like a greeting and more like a recognition.

Nicholas stepped inside.

The air was thick with dust and old wood and something else metallic and sweet, like the scent of a storm trapped in a bottle. Beneath it lingered a faint trace of old candy, vanilla and strawberry, the kind of sweetness that should not have survived decades of neglect, yet somehow clung to the room like a memory that refused to fade.

Clocks lined every wall. Mantle clocks with cracked faces that watched them. Grandfather clocks leaning like tired giants, shadows pooling at their feet. Pocket watches dangling like frozen raindrops, suspended mid-fall. Cuckoo clocks with birds that never emerged, their doors slightly ajar as if listening.

All of them were still. All of them were wrong.

A faint shimmer drifted through the room, not light, not mist, but a subtle distortion, like the air was remembering how to move and getting it slightly wrong. Dust motes hung too long in the space between breaths. The silence was not silence at all, but a held note stretched thin.

And that sweetness, the vanilla and strawberry, did not fade. It deepened as if the room itself were exhaling a memory.

Nicholas felt the mist lean toward him, not touching, not pulling, simply attentive, as if the shop welcomed him back, not with warmth, but with the quiet certainty of a place that had been waiting for an old friend to return.

Anna whispered, "It feels like time is holding its breath."

Her shoulders were tight, barely rising with her inhale. She kept one hand near Nicholas's back, not touching him, but close enough that she could close the distance in an instant. Her eyes tracked every shadow, every unmoving clock hand, pupils wide as if she were bracing for something to leap.

Mel nodded, voice soft. "Or like it is waiting for someone to exhale."

She stood a little too close to Nicholas, fingers brushing the hem of his sleeve as if grounding herself. Her aura, normally a calm, steady glow, flickered in thin nervous pulses along her arms. She kept swallowing, the kind of small, tight motion people make when their throat has gone dry.

Chanotedah stepped in last, letting the door fall shut behind him. His hoodie hung crooked, his hair stuck up in chaotic tufts, and his expression hovered somewhere between terror and irritation.

But his body told the truth. Shoulders hunched, elbows tucked in, weight balanced on the balls of his feet like he was ready to bolt. He kept glancing over his shoulder even though the door was already closed, as if expecting it to open on its own.

"Fantastic," he muttered. "A cursed antique shop. My favorite. Really puts me at ease."

His voice was steady enough, but his fingers fidgeted with the zipper of his hoodie, tugging it up, then down, then up again, a nervous tic he did not realize he had.

Nicholas did not answer.

The mist drifted toward him, the way dawn fog gathers around a lone figure in a field, drawn by something older than wind. Dust motes slowed near him, caught in a subtle shift in the room's rhythm, as if time itself adjusted to his presence.

Anna noticed. Mel felt it. Chanotedah pretended not to.

But all three of them leaned subtly toward Nicholas, the way people do when the room feels wrong, and instinct tells them to stay close to the one thing that feels anchored.

He moved deeper into the shop.

Each step stirred dust that drifted too slowly, as if gravity were optional here. The floorboards creaked, but the sound lagged behind the movement, arriving a heartbeat late.

Anna noticed. "Nicholas, the sound is delayed."

Her voice was quiet, but her posture sharpened, shoulders tightening, chin lifting, eyes narrowing as she scanned the shadows. She shifted closer to him, her hand hovering near his arm, instinctively protective.

Mel opened her mouth to speak, and she even seemed startled by the half-beat lag between her lips forming the word and the sound reaching the air. She blinked, throat tightening, as if her own voice had stepped out of sync with her.

Chanotedah frowned, touching his throat, then his ear, like he could not tell whether the delay was in the room or in him.

"Great," he muttered, though the word arrived just a fraction after his mouth moved. "Love that. Nothing screams safe environment like physics giving up."

Nicholas reached the counter. Behind it, a narrow hallway stretched into shadow, the same hallway from his dream, from the Seer Orb's vision, from the day he first fell through a fracture. The air around it shimmered faintly, like heat rising off pavement, though the room was cold.

The mist leaned toward him, drifting in soft spirals, the way sugar folds toward the center of a cotton candy machine, as if remembering where it belongs.

Mel's breath caught. Anna's hand hovered even closer to Nicholas's arm.

Chanotedah froze. "Is it just me," he whispered, "or is the light literally getting out of your way?"

Nicholas glanced back. He had not noticed it, but Chanotedah had. The light around him did not fall evenly. It curved, softened, parted just slightly as he moved, like the room was adjusting itself to make space for him.

Chanotedah touched his throat again. "Cool. Great. Love that for you. Really enjoying this whole physics optional vibe."

Mel shot him a warning look, but even she could not hide the way her pulse jumped.

Anna's voice was barely above breath. "Nicholas."

He did not answer.

"It is in the back room," he said.

And the hallway seemed to deepen at the sound of his voice, as if it had been waiting for him to say exactly that.

Anna stepped beside him. "Then we go together."

Her voice was steady, but her stance shifted, feet planted, shoulders squared, the quiet readiness of someone who had already decided she would take the hit first if anything went wrong.

Mel reached for Nicholas's hand out of instinct, the same instinct that had saved him more than once, but stopped herself halfway. Training overrode impulse. She pulled back a few steps, positioning herself where she could see the whole room, where she could intercept anything that moved. Her fingers curled and uncurled at her sides; the only sign she hated the distance.

Chanotedah immediately slid behind her, using her as a human shield without shame. "If a clock starts talking, I am leaving. I do not care if it is prophetic."

Nicholas pushed open the backroom door.

The Fragment.

The room was small, cluttered, and humming with a faint unnatural vibration. Shelves sagged under the weight of gears, springs, and half-repaired clocks. A single workbench sat against the far wall, covered in brass scraps and tools older than the building itself.

And in the center of the bench, there is a pocket watch.

Small. Brass. Simple. Unassuming. But glowing.

A soft golden pulse radiated from it, not light, not heat, but resonance. The air around it shimmered, bending the edges of the room. Dust motes circled it in slow, deliberate ribbons, caught in an invisible current that seemed to draw everything in the room toward its center.

Mel's breath hitched. She took another step back, widening her stance, eyes locked on the watch as if it might leap. Her aura flickered along her arms, thin and restless.

Anna moved in the opposite direction, closer to Nicholas, closer to the danger, her hand hovering near his back, ready to pull him behind her or push him forward, whichever moment demanded.

Chanotedah peeked around Mel's shoulder, then ducked back behind her. "Nope. Absolutely not. That thing is glowing like it knows my birthday."

Nicholas did not speak. The room had gone too quiet for words. Even the clocks seemed to be listening. Nicholas felt the Continuum shift around him, not inside him, but toward him. A slow, inevitable tilt. The vessel recognized him.

Anna exhaled, the sound thin. "It is beautiful." Her fingers trembled where they hovered near his arm, torn between pulling him back or anchoring him in place.

Mel whispered, "It feels alive." She remained several feet behind him, lavender-copper light flickering along her arms as she watched the vessel closely.

Chanotedah took a step behind her. "It feels like a cosmic landmine. Please do not touch it."

Nicholas stepped forward anyway.

The Regulatori warmed through the fabric of his front pocket, a rising hum, a shifting resonance, the mist threads within it trembling like something inside was answering a distant call. The Seer Orb pulsed through the rucksack in uneven searching beats, syncing with the vessel's glow like two signals trying to find each other across a widening gap.

Nicholas reached out.

The room shuddered. Not a tremor. A recoil.

A crack split across the ceiling, thin and jagged, glowing faintly with fracture light, like lightning trapped in plaster.

Anna lunged in from the side, grabbing his wrist. "Nicholas, stop." Her voice arrived half a beat late, the delay sharper now, like the room was struggling to keep up.

Mel's aura flared in a sudden protective burst, a thin shimmer rippling through the air between Nicholas and the vessel, a veil snapping into place. "It is destabilizing," she called out, her voice tight.

Chanotedah flattened himself against the wall. "Oh great, she is doing the sparkly force shield thing. That is never a good sign."

The vessel pulsed again, brighter and stronger, and the clocks on the walls began to tick.

All at once. All at different speeds. Some racing. Some dragging. Some ticking backward.

The sound layered over itself, a chaotic, impossible chorus, until it felt less like clocks ticking and more like time itself grinding its teeth or tripping over its own feet.

Nicholas's breath hitched. "It is reacting to us."

"No," Chanotedah said, voice tight. He lifted both hands, shaking his head. "Not us. I am just here. It is answering you."

Nicholas stared at the vessel. It pulsed again, a deep resonant thrum that rippled through the floorboards and up his spine, bending the air around it in a widening ring. The lights flickered. The mist recoiled, then surged forward. The crack in the ceiling brightened, fracture light bleeding through like something on the other side was pressing its face against the world. A thin crust of frost crept across the glass faces of the clocks, spider webbing outward as the temperature dropped in a breathless, unnatural wave.

And then the air behind them tore open.

Not a pop. Not a flash. A rip, a jagged vertical tear splitting the room with a sound like fabric and thunder being pulled apart at the same time. Cold rushed out of it, sharp enough to sting skin, and the edges of the tear glowed with the same impossible light as the vessel.

Anna's wings twitched beneath her skin. Mel's aura flared. Chanotedah swore under his breath.

Nicholas did not move.

The tear widened.

Something was coming through.

A shape flickered within the rift, jittering and stuttering, its outline refusing to settle.

Then another.

Two hoppers stepped through, their bodies glitching in and out of alignment, edges fractured like shards of broken glass, trying to remember how to be a creature. Their movements were too fast, too sharp, too wrong. Their eyes burned with cold predatory hunger, the kind that did not see people, only targets.

Anna's breath caught. "Scouts."

Mel's aura flared in a violent surge of lavender and copper light. "Rhet sent them."

Chanotedah backed toward the wall, hands still raised. "Of course he did. Why would he not?"

The temperature plunged again, a sudden, brutal drop that stole the air from their lungs.

The first hopper lunged.

Nicholas raised Defensio instinctively. The barrier snapped into existence with a sharp resonant crack, stronger than before, steadier, as if the mist itself surged up to reinforce it. The first hopper slammed into the shield, claws screeching across the mist surface, sparks of fractured yellow-green light scattering like broken embers.

The second hopper darted toward the vessel.

Anna moved before Nicholas even registered the motion. She thrust her palm forward, releasing a burst of Suppressio. The creature's leap faltered midflight, its intent suddenly severed from its movement. Its body twisted off course and crashed into a shelf of clocks. Brass gears and glass faces exploded across the floor.

Mel's aura snapped out to Nicholas, a stabilizing band of deep bronze that reinforced his center of gravity. The mist heaved, but her resonance held him steady. "Nicholas, now."

He reached for the mist. An Evanidus sphere formed between his fingers. He did not think; it was as natural as breathing.

He threw.

The sphere struck the first hopper square in the chest. Light detonated outward, a burst of white mist and spiraling glyphs, and the creature vanished with a sound like a violin string snapping under too much tension.

Gone. Relocated.

The second hopper recovered with a guttural hiss, its fractured outline stuttering as it prepared to lunge again.

Anna's aura flared gold. Mel's surged a deep copper-bronze. Nicholas's mist snapped toward them like a drawn breath.

The three currents braided together, not planned, not spoken, simply instinct.

Their three resonances braided together, forming a whip of gold, lavender, and silver-blue mist. It cracked through the air with a sound like thunder being folded in half.

They struck as one.

The whip snapped across the hopper's torso, the impact shattering its form into glitching shards of light. It shrieked, a broken digital sound, before collapsing into a smear of dissolving mist.

The tear behind them pulsed again.

A third hopper stepped halfway through, its head emerging first, eyes glowing with that same predatory hunger.

It froze.

It looked at the fading remains of its companions. At the Triad whip still crackling in the air. At the vessel pulsing like a heartbeat about to detonate.

It made a low, uncertain clicking sound.

Then it stepped backward. Slowly. Deliberately. Never breaking eye contact.

And slipped back through the tear, its fractured outline dissolving into streaks of yellow-green light.

Nicholas lunged after it. "No."

He reached the tear just as the creature slipped through, its form scattering like broken pixels.

Nicholas did not stop. He ran. Straight toward the tear. Straight toward the void. Straight toward Rhet.

Anna screamed, "Nicholas!"

Mel did not reach him. She did not have to. Her aura flared outward in a sweeping surge, indigo-violet currents spiraling around his legs, slowing his momentum as if the room itself had bent to her will.

Anna dove in from the other side, her hand closing around his wrist with a burst of gold. Their grips landed at the same instant.

Behind them, the Triad whip still crackled in the air, a fading ribbon of gold, lavender, and silver-blue mist.

Chanotedah staggered back, visibly shaken. "What was that? You did not tell me you had an all-powerful friendship braid. I feel a little left out now. No, not really, but still."

The tear pulsed violently, red and yellow green light spiraling outward like a warning flare.

Nicholas strained toward it anyway, breath ragged, every instinct screaming to finish what he started.

Anna held on. Mel's aura anchored him. The mist surged around all three of them, folding inward like a held breath.

And the world changed.

The Triad Chord.

A chord rang through the shop, not sound, not exactly, but resonance. A Triad pulse. Gold, lavender, and silver-blue light burst outward from where their hands met, rippling through the air like a shockwave.

The clocks reacted first.

Every ticking, stuttering, broken clock in the shop froze.

They all clicked at the same time.

Every face. Every hand. Every pendulum. Every gear.

All aligned. All synchronized. All pointing to 11:30.

Chanotedah's breath hitched. "Oh, that is not good. Eleven thirty is never good. That is the brace yourself time. Something is coming, and it is not sending a courtesy text." He blinked, touched his jaw, and added, startled, "Oh. My voice and mouth are finally back in sync. Perfect timing."

The vessel pulsed once, a deep resonant thrum, and the fracture snapped shut like a slammed door.

Nicholas stumbled backward, breath ragged.

Anna caught his arm. "Do not ever run into a fracture alone."

Mel's voice trembled. "You scared us."

Chanotedah exhaled shakily. "You scared me, and I do not even like you that much."

Nicholas stared at the now silent clocks. All of them frozen. All of them unified. All of them are waiting.

The vessel glowed softly on the workbench.

And far away, in Nirvana, the chord kept traveling.

CHAPTER 28.5

The Great Hall trembled. Not violently, but with a deep harmonic vibration that passed through stone, mist, and bone. The suspended fire spasmed white, then dimmed sharply, as if ducking for cover. The mist recoiled from the center of the room, curling against the walls as though the Hall itself remembered the Atrium's collapse.

Bharati staggered, gripping the railing as the vibration rolled through her. It hit her like a memory, the Atrium tearing, the scream of the Continuum, the moment she thought they had lost Nicholas forever. Her breath caught. "That was not a fracture. That was a cry. What just happened?"

Lazer's slate spasmed with light, readings spiking so fast the device struggled to keep up. "A resonance event. Enormous. It echoes the Triad signatures I recorded during meditation, but twisted and amplified beyond anything they should be able to generate. This is not just stronger. It is different."

Paloma pressed a hand to her chest, eyes widening with awe and fierce, trembling relief. She felt the chord in her bones, recognized the shape of it, the stubborn will behind it. "It is them," she breathed. "They are alive, and they are fighting." Pride flickered across her face, chased immediately by worry. "But they should not have had to do this alone."

Asiza's voice trembled. "the Triad has struck a chord." Her eyes flicked to Bharati, searching for agreement. "Their resonance is evolving faster than anything we have recorded. This is not the guidance they need. This is containment."

The doors slammed open.

Antonia stormed in at a near run, jean jacket half zipped, baseball cap askew, breath sharp as if she had sprinted the entire way. She took in the chaos of the Hall, the fear on every face, the trembling fire, the recoiling mist, and stopped mid-stride. Her expression hardened instantly, sharpening into something lethal.

"Where?"

Chittaswarup closed his eyes, not in meditation, but in recognition. The mist surged toward him as if drawn by gravity, coiling around his feet, then rising in slow spirals. It thickened, darkened, and then unfurled across the chamber floor, forming a trembling map of the Continuum. Lines of light spiderwebbed outward, branching timelines flickering like nerves firing under skin. Nodes pulsed in uneven rhythms, some bright, some dim, all unstable.

The Hall fell silent. Even the suspended fire shrank to a thin, frightened thread.

One point on the map convulsed, gold, violet, and silver flaring in frantic overlapping bursts, beating like a heart under duress.

Chittaswarup exhaled, the sound soft but heavy enough to bend the room. "There," he said, voice low with awe and dread. "A small human world town. The vessel is active."

He opened his eyes. They were darker than before. Older. Knowing.

Lazer's voice cracked. "The vessel is resonating. The fragment is trying to heal, but something is stopping it. It is pushing through them to reach equilibrium."

The words hit the chamber like a blow.

Bharati's face drained of color. Her hand flew to her mouth, her breath shuddering. "They are alone." Her eyes darted across the trembling map, the pulsing node, the recoiling mist. "Against hoppers? Without a strike team? Without even a stabilizer." Her voice splintered. "We should have been with them. We should have…"

Paloma stepped forward, guilt twisting her features. "They were not supposed to leave yet. We were still preparing them. Still teaching them. They were not ready for this." She swallowed hard, eyes shining with a mix of pride and terror. "And they still went. They still fought."

"We built those protections to contain fractures, echoes, things that do not belong in this timeline." Her eyes moved slowly around the chamber. "If the three of them can pass through those barriers without breaking them, then we are no longer dealing with something the Council understands."

"Enough."

Antonia's voice cut her off like a blade. Sharp. Final. She was not entertaining fear, blame, or theory.

"They are in the field," she said, fury simmering beneath every syllable. "They are facing hoppers. And if the Triad's chord was strong enough to reach Nirvana, then Rhet felt it too."

The suspended fire flickered again, not just agreeing, but warning.

Asiza swallowed hard. "If Rhet senses them, he will not send hoppers. He will go himself."

A silence fell over the chamber, heavy and suffocating, thick with the unspoken truth:

They had failed the Triad. They had let them walk into danger alone. And now the effects were spreading across the Continuum.

Antonia's voice snapped the room back into motion. "Viatori, arm yourselves."

The Viatori surged into action, shaken, furious, terrified, boots pounding against trembling stone as they scattered to gather weapons, armor, and stabilizers.

Lazer hesitated only a heartbeat before running with them, slate clutched tight, already shouting for stabilizer packs and resonance dampeners as he disappeared into the chaos.

But Antonia did not move with them.

She was already moving somewhere else.

Her eyes snapped toward a narrow, half-hidden passageway where the air had begun to thin.

Chittaswarup opened his eyes, calm but grave. "Go," he said softly. "But remember. You are not rescuing them."

Antonia paused, jaw tight, breath sharp, every muscle coiled. "I am joining them."

Cold bled into the air. A thin breath of frost drifted across the stones near the passage, the temperature dropping sharply enough that her exhale fogged in front of her. Then a silver shadow rippled through the mist.

It took shape beside her, fluid and luminous, the faint outline of a lion pacing at her flank. Its mane shimmered like moonlit smoke. Its eyes glowed with quiet ancient certainty. It did not roar. It did not speak. It simply turned toward the passage and waited.

Antonia did not hesitate.

She sprinted toward the opening. The mist parted. The stone thinned. The cold deepened, biting into her skin. A gust of frigid air rushed out, carrying the metallic tang of a wound in the Continuum.

The lion stepped forward. Antonia followed.

The seam opened.

And she slipped through, jean jacket, baseball cap, fury, fear, and all, vanishing into the fold with only one desperate hope burning in her chest: that it would spit her out where her charges were, and that she would not be too late to reach them.

Far away, the Triad stood together as the first shockwaves spread across the Continuum.

CHAPTER 29

The clock shop held its breath. Every clock sat frozen at 11:30, pendulums motionless, gears locked in place. The vessel glowed steadily on the workbench. Nicholas stood between Anna and Mel, their hands still trembling from the chord that had ripped through the room. Chanotedah hovered near the door, hoodie half zipped, eyes darting like a cornered cat.

"Nicholas," Mel whispered. "Do you feel that?" He did. The air had weight, and the shadows near the far doorway stretched too deep. Something had followed the chord.

Chanotedah swallowed hard. "Okay. Hypothetically. If a terrifying void cowboy is about to walk in here, what is our plan?" Anna did not answer because the lights flickered once, twice, then died. Darkness swallowed the shop. Only the vessel glowed, a faint golden heartbeat in the black. Nicholas froze. Mel inhaled sharply. Chanotedah whispered, "Oh, that is subtle. Love that. Really calming."

Anna did not speak. Nicholas felt her hand slip from his. A soft rustle of feathers brushed the air, followed by a warm pulse of golden mist shimmering beside him. Then a small weight landed on his shoulder. He turned his head just enough to see her. An oriole, feathers glowing faintly with golden resonance, gold threaded with soft amber, perched against his neck. Her eyes were bright and sharp and fiercely alert. Her wings were tucked close but ready. Her presence was a steadying warmth against his cheek. Even in this form, he felt her resolve, protective and unyielding, already bracing for whatever stepped out of the dark.

Mel exhaled in awe. "Anna." Chanotedah whispered, "Okay, that is actually adorable and terrifying at the same time." The oriole clicked her beak softly, a warning. A sound drifted from the hallway, a slow, deliberate footstep, then another, then the soft scrape of a boot heel dragging across warped floorboards. Nicholas's pulse hammered. The oriole stiffened, feathers lifting in a silent threat. Mel's fingers tightened around his sleeve.

The footsteps stopped just outside the back-room door. Silence followed, thick and waiting. Then a voice, low, smooth and wrong, drifted through the dark. "Peekaboo, cousin… found you." The doorframe darkened as a silhouette stepped inside. A wide-brimmed hat. A long coat drifting like smoke. One eye hidden beneath shadow. The other gleamed like a shard of broken glass. Rhet.

The shadows did not fall around him. They bent toward him, as if gravity itself leaned in to listen. The oriole hissed, wings flaring in a sharp electric warning. Rhet's glass eye flicked toward her. "Well," he murmured.

"Isn't that precious?" He advanced with the silence of a predator who already knew the outcome. The mist recoiled from him. The air tightened. The room seemed to shrink around his presence.

His gaze slid to Mel. "A chord strong enough to wake the dead. Well, well… Melusine. I did not know you had it in you. I always figured you for the kumbaya and flower power type." Mel stiffened. Her aura rose like a tide, lavender and copper spiraling upward, swirling around her in luminous coils. Then the scent hit, warm, sweet and intoxicating, chocolate-covered strawberries blooming from her aura like heat from a flame. Her eyes sharpened. Her breath steadied. She lifted her hand with a fluid, practiced motion. She spun her wrist. The mist followed the motion.

A tight whirling funnel of air and light coiled into existence, a miniature tornado, sharp and fast, its edges crackling with concentrated resonance. It shot across the room toward Rhet with a shriek of displaced air. Chanotedah whispered, "Oh, that is new." Rhet did not flinch or brace or blink. He simply lifted his hand and swatted. The tornado collapsed instantly, snuffed out like a candle flame, scattering into harmless mist that drifted to the floor. Rhet looked almost bored. "A tantrum, Melusine. How adorable."

The oriole on Nicholas's shoulder flared her wings, golden light shimmering across her feathers. Rhet's smile sharpened. "And here I thought the Council might give you something respectable, cousin. A hawk. An eagle. A creature with some teeth." His gaze lingered on the oriole. "But no. They saddled you with a watercolor sparrow." Nicholas's jaw tightened. The oriole's feathers bristled, glowing brighter in a silent, furious rebuttal. Mel stepped closer, aura flaring hotter. Chanotedah muttered, "Oh, he is going to regret that."

Nicholas did not wait. His hand shot to his belt. A Suppressio sphere. He hurled it across the room with every ounce of force he had. The ringing in his ears, always faint and always present, spiked sharply. Faster. Louder. A warning. A countdown. The sphere ignited midair, a burst of violet and white mist spiraling outward, a suppression wave designed to break concentration, arrest momentum, and silence directed power. It streaked toward Rhet like a comet.

For the first time, Rhet's expression shifted. Not fear. Annoyance. He snapped his fingers. A single sharp crack. The world convulsed. Every clock in the shop screamed, a metallic grinding wail that tore through the air like tortured steel. Pendulums jerked violently. Clock faces split down the center. Gears spun backward in frantic, impossible spirals. Time itself recoiled.

The Suppressio sphere froze midair, then unraveled into dust, its mist sucked backward into its own collapsing core. Nicholas staggered as the floor lurched beneath him. Mel grabbed his arm. The oriole shrieked, wings flaring wide. Chanotedah clapped his hands over his ears. "Nope. Absolutely not. Time should not make that sound."

Rhet lowered his hand, the echo of the snap still vibrating through the room. He smiled, slow, cruel and inevitable. "Suppressio? Cousin… you are going to have to do better than that."

Nicholas's ears rang harder, a frantic rising alarm. Mel and Anna moved instinctively. The oriole launched from Nicholas's shoulder, shifting midair into a streak of golden mist. Mel's lavender aura surged, copper-bronze spirals tightening. Together, they reached for Nicholas's hands, forming the braid, the whip, the weapon they had made once before. It sparked. It hummed. It began to take shape.

Rhet rotated his hand, just a small, lazy turn of his wrist. The braid unraveled instantly, threads of gold and lavender and silver-blue snapping apart like cut strings. The backlash hit them like a shove. Anna stumbled. Mel gasped. Nicholas's ears screamed. Rhet stepped forward, coat drifting like smoke. "Now," he murmured. "Where were we?"

He reached for the vessel. His fingers brushed the pocket watch. The world detonated.

A blast of golden resonance tore through the room. Rhet was launched backward into the far wall with a crack that shook dust from the rafters. Shelves collapsed. Clocks shattered.

Every clock in the room lit up, not with light but with time. Hands spun wildly, then snapped to 11:30. Pendulums swung in perfect unison. Gears locked into alignment. A single unified tick echoed through the room.

A protective sphere of golden mist formed around the Triad and the vessel, shimmering and humming around them like a cocoon.

Rhet staggered to his feet. For the first time, he looked shaken. His coat hung in tatters. His hat lay crushed on the floor. His glass eye flickered like a dying star. He stared at the Triad, at the shield, at the vessel. Then he laughed, low, delighted and unhinged. "Oh," he whispered. "It chose you."

Nicholas's heart pounded. Anna's wings glowed brighter. Mel's breath steadied. Chanotedah whispered, "That is not good, right?"

Rhet rose slowly, dust drifting from his coat. His glass eye burned. "This changes everything." He lifted his hand. The fracture behind him tore open, wider, brighter and hungrier. Hoppers swarmed at the edges, their silhouettes twitching in anticipation. Rhet stepped backward into the light. "We will finish this soon," he said. "All of us." He paused, gave a slow mocking bow. "I will see you at high noon."

Then he vanished into the fracture. The tear snapped shut. Silence crashed over the room.

Nicholas exhaled shakily. Mel touched his shoulder. "Nicholas." Anna fluttered from his shoulder to his hand, shifting back into human form in a shimmer of golden mist. Chanotedah collapsed onto a broken stool. "I am filing a complaint with the Continuum. That was traumatic."

Nicholas stared at the vessel, still glowing on the workbench. Rhet was not retreating. He was preparing.

CHAPTER 30

The silence after Rhet vanished felt heavier than the fight itself. Dust drifted through the air in slow spirals. Shattered clock faces lay scattered across the floor like broken moons. The golden protective sphere around the Triad flickered once, then dissolved into mist. Nicholas exhaled shakily.

Mel rubbed her arms, still trembling. "Is everyone… okay." Anna nodded, though her voice was thin. "I think so." Chanotedah raised a hand from the broken stool he had collapsed onto. "Define okay. Physically? Emotionally? Spiritually? Because I am quite sure I lost at least one of those."

Nicholas did not answer. His attention was locked on the vessel. The pocket watch still glowed faintly on the workbench, steady and warm. It looked harmless, ordinary, like something a grandfather might pass down to a child. But Rhet's words echoed in Nicholas's skull. It chose you.

Nicholas swallowed hard. "We need to hide it." Mel blinked. "Hide it? Where." "Anywhere Rhet cannot find it." Chanotedah threw his hands up. "Fantastic. The cosmic pocket watch…" He stopped, pointed at it accusingly. "Actually, no. Not just cosmic. It is haunted. It has opinions. And it is choosing a kid to talk to."

"I am not a kid," Nicholas snapped. Chanotedah gestured wildly. "Tell that to the sentient time bomb that just imprinted on you like a baby duck." Anna tried not to smile. Mel failed. Nicholas groaned. "You are not helping." "I am not trying to," Chanotedah said.

Nicholas stepped toward the vessel. "We need to get it out of here. Somewhere…" He stopped. A sharp metallic ringing pierced his ears, faint at first, then rising like pressure inside a sealed chamber. The hairs on his arms stood straight up. The air thickened, charged, humming with a frequency only he seemed to feel.

Mel frowned. "Nicholas." He did not answer. His pulse quickened. The room tilted—not physically, but in the familiar way that told him a seam was forming.

"Get behind me," he said quietly.

Anna did not hesitate. Mel grabbed Chanotedah by the sleeve and pulled him back. The three of them clustered behind Nicholas as he stepped forward, placing himself between them and the center of the room. The ringing intensified. The mist shifted. A blast of chilled air knifed through the room, sharp enough to sting their skin. Frost dusted the broken floorboards. Their breaths fogged.

A thin vertical line of white light split the air like a blade. The seam tore open, widening with a low resonant hum that vibrated through the floorboards. Dust lifted from the ground. Shattered clock faces rattled. The air bent inward, pulled toward the tear as if gravity itself were being rewritten.

Chanotedah whimpered. "No. No more void cowboys. I am done."

But the figure who stepped through was not Rhet.

It was Antonia.

She wore a denim jacket, the collar turned up against the cold of the seam. A black t-shirt clung to her frame beneath it, and her baseball cap was still askew from the sprint. Her boots were scuffed. Her breathing was sharp. But her eyes, fiery, focused, laser precise, swept the room like she was clearing a battlefield. She took in the shattered clocks, the buckled floorboards, the scorch marks and the Triad huddled behind Nicholas. She exhaled a long, shaky breath.

"Thank the Continuum," she muttered. "You are not dead." She paused. "Yet."

Nicholas opened his mouth. "Antonia…" She cut him off with a glare sharp enough to slice steel. "Do not 'Antonia' me. You three vanish into a fracture, trigger a seismic spike big enough to wake the Archivists, and then I walk into this." She gestured broadly at the wreckage. "This looks like the aftermath of a toddler with a flamethrower."

Nicholas winced. "We did not…" "Save it," she snapped. "You are thirteen. You do not get to improvise with Continuum anomalies."

Mel stepped forward, trying to smooth things over. "Antonia, we did not plan for Rhet to…" Antonia rounded on her. "Oh, Melusine. Sweetheart. You sit on the Council. You should absolutely know better." Mel's mouth fell open. "I… what… I do know better." "Do you?" Antonia asked, eyes narrowing. "Because from where I am standing, it looks like you let a thirteen-year-old Viator and his Cura walk into a fracture without backup."

Chanotedah raised a timid hand. "Technically, I walked in too." Antonia did not even look at him. "Yes. And that was also a mistake."

Nicholas stepped forward, bristling. "Antonia, we handled it." She barked a laugh. "Handled it? Nicholas, the room looks like time had a nervous breakdown." She pointed at the vessel. "And that thing is glowing like it is about to file a complaint."

Nicholas opened his mouth again, but she jabbed a finger at him. "Do not go anywhere. I mean it. If you so much as breathe in the wrong direction, I will personally drag you back to the Hall by your ear."

She stepped closer to the Triad, lowering her voice. "You are with me now. Chittaswarup said I am not rescuing you. I am joining you. So, nobody moves alone. Nobody acts alone. Nobody touches anything glowing unless I say so."

Chanotedah raised his hand again, hopeful. Antonia sighed. "Yes, Chanotedah." He pointed at the sealed seam. "If you are staying… can I go back to Nirvana?" "No," she said instantly. He deflated like a punctured balloon. "Worst timeline."

Mel closed her eyes, exhaled, then flicked her fingers. A ribbon of mist curled upward from the floor, coiling around Chanotedah's mouth and snapping into place like a soft, shimmering gag. "Mmph," he protested, pointing at it indignantly.

Mel did not even look at him. She sagged backward until her spine hit the workbench, sliding down until she was half sitting, half leaning against it. Her breath shook. Her hands trembled. The adrenaline was wearing off, and the crash was brutal.

Anna knelt beside her. "Mel…" "I am fine," Mel whispered. "Just… give me a second."

Nicholas stood in the center of the ruined shop, staring at the vessel. The glow had dimmed, but a faint pulse remained. He did not touch it. He did not dare.

Antonia stepped beside him, her voice low. "Do not even think about it." Nicholas swallowed. "I was not." "You were," she said. "And you are going to stop."

Chanotedah paced in frustrated circles, still gagged, still gesturing wildly.

Then a flash of colored light spilled through the cracked front windows. Blue. Red. White. Gold. The Triad froze. A low thunderous whump-whump-whump rolled through the street outside, rhythmic, mechanical and unmistakable.

Helicopters. More than one. A squadron.

Mel's eyes snapped open. "Oh no." Anna grabbed Nicholas's arm. "They found us." Chanotedah stopped pacing mid-step, eyes wide above the mist gag. Nicholas swallowed hard.

Antonia stepped in front of all three of them, shoulders squared, jaw set, eyes burning. "Stay behind me."

None of them moved. None of them breathed. They did not know who was landing out there. The Council. The Viatori. The Continuum Guard. Or something else entirely. The lights outside flared brighter. The sound grew louder.

All five stood tense, bracing for whoever came through the door.

CHAPTER 31

The colored lights outside the clock shop did not simply pulse. They shattered across the broken windows like living constellations, splintering into jagged ribbons of blue, red, white, and gold that danced over the ruined floor. Each rotation of the helicopter blades sent a fresh wave of light rippling through the shop, strobing across toppled clocks and fractured gears as if the whole room were caught inside a heartbeat of war. The whump of the rotors became more than sound. It became pressure, a physical vibration that crawled up the walls, rattled the rafters, and made the dust itself tremble as if it knew something powerful was closing in.

Nicholas stood in the center of the wreckage, the fractured light strobing across his face as he stared at the vessel lying on the workbench. The metal glowed faintly, warm, steady, and pulsing, as if each breath in the room made it pulse in answer. Anna hovered just behind him, her golden aura flickering at the edges like a heartbeat she was trying to steady. Her eyes never left Nicholas's hand, her whole body coiled between protectiveness and fear. Mel stood to his right, arms wrapped around herself, violet mist trembling around her like static caught in a storm. Every shift of the vessel's glow made her aura twitch, colors rippling through it in nervous, involuntary waves.

Antonia planted herself between the Triad and the door, denim jacket still dusted with frost from the seam she had crossed. Her stance was pure battlefield instinct, weight forward, jaw set, one hand hovering near the hidden blade she always carried. She did not trust the silence. She did not trust the helicopters. And she certainly did not trust the steady pulse of the vessel beside Nicholas. Chanotedah crouched behind a toppled grandfather clock, hoodie pulled tight around his ears, eyes darting between the vessel and the windows as if he expected either one to explode. "Just saying," he whispered to no one in particular, "this feels like the part in the movie where the glowing thing either grants wisdom or vaporizes everyone."

And in the middle of all of them stood Nicholas. Drawn forward. Compelled. As if the vessel were a magnet and he was the only piece of metal in the room. He reached for it. The air tightened, not just around the vessel but around him, as if the room itself were holding its breath. His fingers hovered over the metal, trembling, suspended in a pocket of charged stillness. The hum around the vessel deepened, shifting from a faint vibration to a low resonant thrum that crawled up his arm like recognition. The glow brightened. The temperature dropped. A single grain of dust drifted sideways, tugged toward the watch as though gravity had changed its mind.

Nicholas's breath hitched. The vessel was not simply waiting. It was listening.

The moment his skin brushed the metal, the world did not tilt. It lurched.

Light fractured. Sound folded. The floor dropped away like a trapdoor. A flash came, not of the shop or the Viatori or the present, but of one of his daydreams. One of the early ones, back when the pull of the unknown was just a whisper. He was in his bedroom at home. Sunlight slanted across the carpet in warm honey-gold bands, catching dust motes that drifted like tiny planets in a quiet universe. His posters were still crooked on the walls. His backpack lay half unzipped at the foot of his bed. The air smelled like laundry soap and old books and the faint citrus of his mother's cleaning spray.

He remembered pressing his palm to the window, forehead resting against the cool glass, staring out at nothing in particular. Wondering why he felt like he was supposed to be somewhere else. Wondering why something he could not name tugged at him from far beyond the horizon.

How did I end up here?

Here, in a ruined clock shop. Here, with a vessel that was never supposed to exist. Here, being treated as an equal to Anna and Mel when, half the time, he still felt like a kid pretending he understood any of this. He appreciated them. He needed them. But right now, he wanted his mother. He wanted her arms around him, the way she would hug him tight and run her fingers through his hair, brushing it back from his eyes like she was smoothing the universe into place. He wanted the warmth of her cheek against his forehead, the soft hum she made when she was worried but trying not to show it.

He wanted his father too, the soft crackle of the needle dropping onto an old LP, the way the room would fill with music as his father pulled his mother into a slow dance in the kitchen. Nicholas used to watch from the doorway, pretending he was not watching, pretending he did not love it. He missed that sound. He missed that life. He missed them. And now he was supposed to be… what? A fulcrum. A Viator. Someone expected to stand against Rhet. Someone who could stand against Rhet. He did not feel ready.

But the vessel pulsed in his hand, warm and steady and almost reassuring, like a heartbeat pressed into his palm. Nicholas closed his eyes.

Am I ready to be who I need to be?

He did not know. But he tightened his grip anyway. Whether he was ready or not, the world outside was waiting.

Anna stepped closer, the golden shimmer along her spine brightening in sharp pulsing flashes. Her shoulders squared, her breath steadied, and the faint outline of feathers rippled beneath her skin. She was one heartbeat away from shifting into her oriole form, waiting only for the threat to reveal itself. Mel steadied herself beside her, but her eyes had already gone distant. Her aura thinned, then stretched, then folded inward as she slipped into a meditative state, the one Antonia had drilled into her for emergencies. Her breathing slowed. Her fingers curled into a loose mudra. The lavender mist around her tightened into a controlled spiral, ready to snap outward the moment she needed it.

Chanotedah whimpered behind the toppled grandfather clock, hoodie pulled over his head like it was armor. He peeked over the edge, eyes huge. "Nope. Nope. Nope. This is how horror movies start. This is exactly how they start."

Antonia did not flinch. She moved. One smooth, practiced step forward, placing herself between the Triad and the front of the shop. Her denim jacket creaked as she lifted both hands, palms outward, fingers splayed. A thin arc of blue-white mist snapped into existence, stretching from her fingertips to the shattered doorframe. A Defensio shield, small, focused and personal. A focused barrier of blue-white resonance between her kids and whatever was about to walk in. Her jaw clenched. Her breath fogged in the frigid air still leaking from the seam she had crossed. "Stay behind me," she murmured, voice low and steady and lethal.

Nicholas did not move. He could not. The vessel's glow strengthened against his palm, alive with a rhythm he could feel all the way into his bones. He wasn't just holding it. He was connected to it. The hum vibrated through his bones, through his ribs, through the ringing in his ears. He felt like he was standing at the center of a storm that only he could hear.

The door handle twitched. Just once.

In the silence that followed, it felt like the entire world held its breath. Dust hung suspended in the air, shimmering in the fractured light like the glitter Nicholas had glued onto his caterpillar art project in second grade, the one his mother kept on the fridge for years. A loose pendulum from a shattered wall clock teetered on its hook, swinging out of rhythm. Tick… tick. Then it dropped, hitting the floor with a tiny metallic clink that sounded impossibly loud.

Nicholas's heart hammered so violently he could not tell if the vibrations were coming from his chest or from the vessel pulsing in his hand. The glow throbbed against his palm, warm and insistent, syncing with the ringing in his ears until he could not separate one from the other. His breath came shallow. His fingers trembled.

A hundred pairs of boots struck the pavement in unison.

A hundred pairs of boots struck pavement in perfect unison, a deep commanding rhythm that rolled through the street like a living war drum. The vibrations climbed the walls and traveled through the floorboards into Nicholas's bones. Outside, shouted commands cut through the rotor wash. Dust sifted from the rafters. Even the broken clocks seemed to twitch with every approaching step.

Mel's aura flared, then shifted, then flared again. The colors spun around her like a frantic shimmering wheel, lavender deepening to copper, flashing bronze-white, then snapping back again, her emotions ricocheting too fast to land on anything stable. The scent of chocolate-covered strawberries flickered in and out of the air, sharp and sweet, a byproduct of her power struggling to find a center. Anna's breath hitched. The golden shimmer along her spine brightened, feathers rippling beneath her skin. She was seconds from shifting, one wrong sound away from unleashing her oriole form in full.

Chanotedah pressed himself flatter behind the toppled grandfather clock, hoodie cinched tight around his face. "Nope," he whispered. "Nope, nope, nope. This is above my pay grade. I do not even have a pay grade."

Antonia did not move. She stood like a wall between them and the door, denim jacket dusted with frost, hands raised, palms outward. The thin arc of her Defensio shield shimmered in front of her, a curved barrier of blue-white mist that hummed with quiet, lethal promise. Her jaw was set. Her stance was unshakable. "Stay behind me," she murmured.

Nicholas barely heard her. The vessel pulsed again, harder and brighter, and the world outside seemed to pulse with it, as if the helicopters, the boots, the lights, the entire street were syncing to the beat in his hand.

The door handle twitched again. Antonia's Defensio shield flared brighter, the arc of blue-white mist sharpening like a blade. Nicholas tightened his grip on the vessel, the pulse in his palm syncing with the pounding in his chest until he could not tell which was which. Mel's aura spun faster, a frantic cyclone of lavender and copper, colors stuttering like a glitching star. Her breath hitched, her fingers trembling in their meditative pose as she fought to keep her center. Anna's eyes narrowed, golden light rippling beneath her skin. Her muscles coiled, feathers threatening to break through. She was one heartbeat away from oriole form, waiting for the slightest confirmation of danger.

Chanotedah whimpered, sliding lower behind the grandfather clock. "Nope. I reject this timeline," he whispered.

Outside, the boots stopped. All at once.

The silence that followed was not silence. It was pressure. It was gravity. It was the world holding its breath so tightly the air itself seemed to shrink. The flashing lights outside strobed harder, casting jagged ribbons of color across the walls. The helicopter rotors thumped in slow, heavy pulses, each one vibrating through the floorboards like the countdown of something ancient waking up.

Dust hung suspended midair, frozen in the fractured light. A single gear rolled an inch across the floor, then stilled. Nicholas swallowed. No one else moved.

Then the door handle turned. Slowly. Deliberately. As if whoever stood on the other side wanted them to feel every second of it.

Antonia braced. Anna tensed. Mel's aura snapped tight. Chanotedah squeaked. Nicholas held the vessel as if it was the only thing keeping him upright.

The door swung open.

A figure stepped inside. Not rushed. Not cautious. Simply inevitable.

Tall. Armored. Helmeted. A silhouette carved out of shadow and fractured light, filling the doorway as if it had been built for him alone. The weapon in his hand hummed with a low predatory vibration, the kind that made the air tighten and the mist recoil. He did not speak. He did not need to. The room reacted to him.

The fractured lights from outside bent around his armor, catching on the etched lines of Viatori insignia and scattering across the floor in sharp, trembling shards. Dust drifted sideways, tugged by the pressure of his presence. Even the broken clocks seemed to hesitate, as if time itself were waiting for permission to move.

The figure paused. The visor swept across the wreckage, the shattered gears, the trembling triad, the vessel glowing in Nicholas's hand, and Antonia braced like a shield in front of them. The air thickened. Then the figure lifted a hand to the helmet. A soft click. A hiss of decompressing air. The visor retracted in a slow, deliberate slide.

Lazer's voice cut through the tension like a blade. "Stand down," he said. "They are ours."

Behind him, the street erupted into controlled chaos, a storm of Viatori precision. Teams jogged in formation, sweeping rooftops and alleyways with machine-like synchronicity. Others cleared buildings, weapons raised, searching for hoppers. Farther down the block, another unit guided terrified residents toward helicopters, ushering them up ramps with firm protective hands.

Closest to the clock shop, a squad of Viatori in golden armor broke off from the main force. They moved as one. No words. No hesitation. Just a fluid circular motion as they positioned themselves around the Triad, forming a perfect perimeter. Their armor caught the streetlights and fractured them into shimmering halos, as if they were forging a pocket of safety out of pure light.

Nicholas stared, breath catching in his throat.

Lazer stepped fully inside, helmet tucked under one arm, the fractured lights sliding across his armor like liquid gold. His expression was a perfect storm of irritation, disbelief, and the kind of exhausted resignation only someone who has cleaned up a thousand disasters could wear. "You three," he said, voice flat with incredulity, "have a talent for making a mess."

He stepped over a shattered clock gear, and the gear moved out of his way, skittering an inch across the floor as if even the debris respected his boots. Lazer did not acknowledge it. He muttered under his breath, just loud enough for Nicholas to hear, "Glad I am not the one who has to clean it up."

Nicholas blinked, stunned. Anna snorted, a sharp, involuntary burst of laughter she immediately tried to smother. Mel groaned, dragging her hand down her face. "Please do not encourage them." Chanotedah peeked out from behind the grandfather clock, eyes wide. "Honestly? Same. Deeply same." Antonia did not smile, but the corner of her mouth twitched, the tiniest crack in her battlefield mask.

Outside, the Viatori continued to move like a living machine, precise, unstoppable and mythic. Inside, for the first time since Rhet appeared, the Triad felt the smallest flicker of something they had not felt in hours.

Safety.

Lazer jerked his chin toward the street, fractured light flashing across his armor. "Come on," he said, voice low but carrying the weight of command. "We are getting you out of here before Rhet decides round two sounds fun."

The Triad did not hesitate. They stepped into the golden perimeter, Anna first with her jaw tight, Mel next with her aura flickering in nervous spirals, Nicholas last with the vessel pulsing in his hand like a second heartbeat. The Viatori closed around them instantly, shields angled outward, formation tightening with a precision that felt almost supernatural.

The vessel throbbed again, warm and insistent, and Nicholas's breath caught. Lazer moved to him, placing a steady hand on his shoulder. The contact grounded him, cutting through the chaos like a lifeline.

"Listen," Lazer said quietly, leaning in so only Nicholas could hear. "What you are seeing out there, the precision, the formation, the sweep teams, that is not just training. That is a millennium of Viatori expertise. Generations of warriors who have held the Continuum together with their bare hands." His grip tightened, firm and reassuring. "The best of the best. And all of it, all of them, are here for one reason."

Nicholas swallowed, the vessel pulsing harder.

"To protect the Triad."

The words hit like a physical force. Anna's breath hitched. Mel's lavender aura warmed toward copper, steadier now. Chanotedah peeked out from behind a Viator's shield, whispering, "Okay, that is actually kind of epic."

Nicholas stared up at Lazer, feeling the enormity of the moment settle across his shoulders. It was still too much to carry alone, but for the first time, he realized he might not have to. "But… am I ready for this?"

Lazer did not hesitate. "I am ready to face Rhet again."

The words slipped out before he could stop them, sharp and unguarded and too honest. A blade falling from a sheath.

Nicholas blinked. "Wait… you."

Lazer froze. Just for a heartbeat. A tiny fracture in his armor. Then he coughed, straightened, and forced a shrug that did not reach his eyes. "I meant you are ready to face Rhet. That is all."

Anna's brow furrowed, golden light rippling along her spine. Mel's lavender aura flashed with a sharp bronze edge, the tell Nicholas was beginning to associate with suspicion. Chanotedah whispered, "Oh, he definitely did not mean that," then immediately pretended he had not spoken.

Nicholas stared at Lazer. "You have faced him before."

Lazer did not answer. His jaw tightened. His eyes flicked away. And for the first time since he had arrived, he looked haunted. Antonia's gaze cut toward him, quick, sharp, and knowing, but she said nothing.

"Point is," Lazer said, voice firm but thinner than before, "you are not alone. Not tonight. Not ever."

Nicholas wasn't sure he believed that. A steady warmth spread from the vessel into his palm, strangely resolute, as though it believed for him when he couldn't quite believe for himself.

Then the air changed. Not a breeze. Not a shift. A pressure drop, like the Continuum itself, had taken a step closer.

The vessel pulsed again, harder this time, a sharp jolt against Nicholas's palm that made his fingers twitch. A warning. A recognition. A name whispered without sound. Nicholas turned slowly, scanning the rooftops, the alleyways, the shadows between the helicopters. The world outside felt stretched thin, as a sheet pulled too tight.

"He is here," he whispered.

Every Viator within earshot reacted instantly. Weapons lifted in perfect unison, a single fluid motion that rippled through the street like a wave snapping into place. The sound of metal aligning with purpose cut through the air, crisp and lethal. The golden armored unit slammed their palms outward, fingers splayed, boots anchoring into the pavement. A ring of blue-white mist erupted around them, spiraling upward in a perfect arc.

The energy leapt from soldier to soldier, linking their shields into a single seamless dome.

A unified Defensio Shield snapped into existence with a deep resonant hum that vibrated through the ground, through the air, through the Triad's bones. The dome shimmered like a constellation forged from a thousand tiny stars, each point of light flickering in its own rhythm, a living barrier, ancient and unbreakable. Air rushed inward in a sudden, sharp pull, a vacuumed gasp that stole the breath from their lungs for half a second. Dust spiraled upward in tight vortices before slamming flat against the inside of the dome, as if gravity had momentarily forgotten which direction to obey.

Nicholas staggered, the vessel jerking in his hand as if it felt the shift. Anna grabbed his arm, eyes wide as the golden shimmer along her spine flared in shock. Mel's aura snapped tight around her, instinctively forming a protective spiral as she braced against the sudden heaviness pressing down on her shoulders. Chanotedah yelped, dropping into a crouch as the floor seemed to tilt beneath him. "Nope. Shields should come with warning labels."

The pressure settled, not crushing, but denser, like the air inside the dome had thickened into something with weight and intention. Every breath felt a fraction heavier. Every sound carried a faint echo, as if the Continuum itself were listening.

Antonia did not flinch. She was already in front of them, feet planted, shoulders squared, hands raised, her Defensio shield angled toward the front of the shop like a blade waiting to be swung. And as the Continuum pressure spiked, her armor answered. The denim jacket dissolved into a shimmer of blue-white mist, reforming around her in overlapping plates of matte silver and deep indigo. The transformation was silent and efficient, the kind of shift that came from decades of training and a lifetime of readiness. Her boots anchored into the floor. Her gauntlets locked into place. A faint hum radiated from the seams of her armor, the sound of a Guardian preparing for war.

Her visor had not dropped yet. Not until she saw the threat.

Anna stared upward, eyes wide. Mel exhaled shakily, her lavender aura settling, threaded now with faint copper. Chanotedah crouched lower, whispering, "Okay. This is fine. This is probably fine."

Nicholas drew the vessel closer to his chest. The mist thickened. The air tightened. A ripple of sickly green and red energy crawled across the pavement like a tide, bending the light around it, warping the shadows into impossible angles.

The haze parted.

Rhet stepped out as if he had been there the whole time, simply waiting for the world to notice him. His wide-brimmed hat sat low over one eye. His long coat drifted like smoke, except the edges did not merely fray into mist. They bled into green and red tendrils, twisting like corrupted auroras, the colors pulsing in slow, sick rhythms that made the air shiver. His glass shard eye gleamed like a dying star, fractured and furious and hungry.

He did not walk. He glided, the mist curling around his boots as if it recognized him, as if it obeyed him. Then the sound hit. A single spur clink. Just one. On his right boot. Sharp and metallic, a sound that cut through the dome like a warning bell from a forgotten world.

He paused, lifted two fingers, and touched the brim of his hat, straightening it with a slow, mocking flourish. "Well now," he drawled. "Howdy, cous…" He stopped mid-word, patting his coat until he found the battered pocket watch he always carried. He flipped it open, squinted at the face, then gave it a little shake as if the gears inside had betrayed him.

A razor-thin smile cut across his face. "Huh. Looks like high noon came early."

He snapped the pocket watch shut with a soft metallic click.

The haze parted again, and Rhet stepped fully into the open, as if the world had no choice but to make room for him. His coat bled color into the air. His aura warped the light. His presence bent the mist.

For a heartbeat, the world held still. Then every bell in town began to toll. Not in unison. Not in harmony. But in a staggering, discordant cascade. Church bells. Shop bells. School bells. Warning bells. All of them ringing at once, as if the entire city had been yanked into the moment with him. The sound rolled through the streets like a shockwave, rattling windows, vibrating through the dome, shaking dust from the rafters.

Rhet smiled.

The single spur on his right boot scraped against the pavement with a slow, deliberate clink.

A heartbeat later, something slammed into the barrier. Strikes of red and green. The impact rippled across the dome in jagged pulsing veins. The street erupted into chaos as the Continuum buckled under the force of Rhet's arrival.

And the war began.

CHAPTER 32

The street erupted. Not gradually. Not with a warning. It happened all at once, the kind of silence that might have existed a heartbeat before the Big Bang, and then light and energy tore outward in every direction. Rhet reached to his sides, fingers curling around phantom holsters only he could feel. He drew. Two fingers lifted. Two soft clicks. Reality flinched.

A fracture burst open behind him like a cosmic bullet hole, jagged and spiraling, rimmed in red and green corruption. Frost detonated across the street. A shockwave of cold blasted outward, racing over pavement, swallowing storefronts and crawling up lampposts. Breath crystallized. Windows cracked. The air itself froze mid-motion.

Then the hoppers came.

They did not emerge. They erupted, streaking through the tear like shards of living shrapnel, twisting and shrieking as they launched themselves at the Viatori lines. The Viatori responded instantly. Order. Perfect, disciplined, synchronized order. Shields locked. Boots planted. Sweep teams pivoted as one. Evacuation units tightened around civilians, moving them with practiced precision. Every motion was clean, controlled, centuries-deep muscle memory.

But chaos did not care. Chaos did not pause. Chaos did not breathe. Chaos hit.

Hoppers streaked overhead in a blur of red and green sparks, too many, too fast, too loud. One slammed into a shield wall, knocking three Viatori back. Another spiraled down like a drill bit, claws screeching across armor. A third burst through a storefront window, showering the street in glass. The sound was everywhere, shrieks and metal and cracking ice and shattering stone, a rising, choking roar that swallowed thought.

The Viatori held. Then bent. Then buckled.

And the chaos kept coming.

Nicholas stumbled backward as the shield dome around the Triad flickered under the assault. A hopper slammed into the barrier overhead, spraying red and green sparks across the street. Anna grabbed his arm. "We have to move." Mel's lavender aura flared copper, then bronze-white as she hurled a mist burst that knocked a hopper off course. Another dove straight for them.

Antonia intercepted it mid-flight, her gauntlet cracking across its jaw and sending it spiraling into a parked car. "Triad," she shouted, voice cutting through the chaos. "Move. Stay tight and move." She knocked another hopper out of the air with her shield, pivoting without losing a step.

The golden armored Viatori tightened their circle, trying to shepherd the Triad toward the armored transport waiting at the end of the street.

But Rhet was not going to let them leave.

He stepped forward, coat drifting like smoke, glass shard eye gleaming. "Leaving so soon," he drawled. He snapped his fingers. The fracture behind him detonated open, a jagged wound in the air vomiting red and green light.

A hopper burst through, bigger and faster, its body twisting like a serpent made of shattered glass and hunger. It dove straight for Nicholas.

The Viatori moved, but not fast enough.

Anna shoved Nicholas aside. Mel screamed his name. Chanotedah was already throwing spheres. One Evanidus sphere arced wildly over the street, bounced off a frozen mailbox, and detonated in a useless puff of mist. "Why do they never go straight?" he shouted, grabbing another. He hurled it with both hands. It clipped a lamppost, ricocheted, and exploded harmlessly against a storefront window. A hopper streaked past his ear, trailing red and green sparks. Chanotedah yelped, ducked, and flung a third sphere straight upward in pure panic. It burst like a firework against nothing at all. "I am helping," he insisted, mostly to himself.

The serpent hopper did not even glance at him. It was locked on Nicholas.

Nicholas hit the pavement hard, the impact knocking the breath from his lungs as the vessel shot from his hand. It skidded across the asphalt in a wild spinning arc, bouncing once, twice, before coming to rest beneath the shattered remains of a streetlamp, its glow flickering like a dying star.

Nicholas scrambled toward it, but the serpent hopper dropped out of the sky like a meteor, slamming into the ground between them. The asphalt cracked under its weight. Red and green sparks hissed off its wings. It lifted its head with a slow predatory click, a sound that felt aimed straight at Nicholas's spine. Its claws dug into the pavement, carving grooves as it crouched.

Nicholas froze. The hopper's body coiled, muscles tightening, glass shard plates shifting like they were sharpening themselves. It was going to pounce.

Anna did not hesitate.

She hit the serpent hopper mid-air, a streak of gold and fire, her body already folding into her oriole form. Feathers burst from her shoulders in a radiant flare. Light wrapped around her like a shockwave. She collided with the creature hard enough to rattle the street. Claws met claws. Teeth met glass fangs. Her wings flared wide, glowing like molten metal as she wrestled the hopper backward.

Mel was right behind her. Her lavender aura snapped outward, deepening through copper into a violent bronze-white blaze. She thrust both hands forward, and a mist burst detonated from her palms, spiraling around the hopper's wings, dragging it off balance just long enough for Anna to seize control. Anna twisted mid-air, slammed the creature into the pavement, and pinned it with a snarl that vibrated through the street.

Nicholas did not wait. He sprinted for the vessel. The world narrowed to a single point of light lying beneath the shattered streetlamp, flickering, pulsing, calling to him. He was inches away when the sky screamed.

Another hopper streaked down like a comet, trailing a tail of red and green sparks that hissed through the frozen air. Nicholas dove, rolling across the pavement as the creature slammed into the ground where he had been standing. The impact sent the vessel bouncing again, farther this time, skittering across the asphalt like a kicked star. It tumbled end over end, glowing brighter with each bounce, until it came to rest beside a burning transport, flames reflecting in its surface like a warning.

Nicholas scrambled to his feet, lungs burning, vision swimming. He ran.

"Nicholas," Antonia's voice cut through the chaos, not a warning but a command.

She did not wait for him to listen.

A hopper dove for Nicholas's back, claws outstretched. Antonia hit it first. Her gauntlet lit with a burst of gold as she slammed into the creature mid-air, blasting it sideways into a parked car hard enough to cave the door in. Shards of red and green sparks scattered across the pavement. She did not even watch it fall. She was already sprinting after Nicholas.

He lunged for the vessel, but Antonia caught him by the back of his shirt, half-lifting, half-shoving him forward with the strength of someone who had trained for war her entire life. "Move," she barked, dragging him through the hail of sparks and frost. "Get to it before they do."

Another hopper swooped low, jaws snapping. Antonia pivoted, firing a Defensio burst over Nicholas's shoulder that detonated against the creature's face, sending it spiraling into the street.

Nicholas stumbled, regained his footing, and dove. His hand closed around the vessel. It pulsed, frantic, terrified and alive.

A hopper shrieked overhead, diving straight for him.

Nicholas did not think. He reached into his belt, grabbed an Evanidus sphere, and slammed it against the vessel.

"Go," Nicholas shouted.

The Evanidus sphere cracked open in his hand, not a burst, not a flash, but a detonation of white-blue light that swallowed the vessel whole. For a heartbeat, everything froze. The light wrapped around the vessel like a cocoon, threads of energy tightening, pulling, folding reality inward. The air hummed. The frost on the street lifted. Even the hoppers hesitated, their shrieks caught in their throats.

And then the world blinked.

The vessel vanished. Not with the familiar flash of teleportation. Not thrown. Not hidden. Simply gone.

The hopper collided with Nicholas a split second later, slamming him backward, skidding him across the pavement. His vision blurred. His ears rang. His ribs screamed.

But none of that mattered because the vessel was gone.

Mel's scream tore through the street. "Nicholas, what did you do?" Anna ripped a hopper off her back, claws glowing. "Where is it? Where did it go?" Nicholas staggered to his feet, chest heaving, blood in his mouth, frost on his lashes. "I don't know," he rasped. "I just needed it gone. I think… I think I sent it somewhere."

Antonia froze mid-strike, eyes wide. "You what?"

Rhet stopped walking. His smile died. The red and green lights around him flickered once, twice, like a glitch in the universe. "Well now," he said softly. "That was a mistake."

Nicholas did not look away. He stood there, bruised and shaking and breathless, but unbroken. "No," he said. His voice cracked, but the words did not. "It was the only thing I could save."

Rhet tilted his head, glass shard eye narrowing. "Oh, cousin. What did you do? That might make family reunions a little tense."

The street seemed to hold its breath.

Nicholas did not look away.

Rhet lifted his hand.

The fracture behind him widened, red and green light spilling out like a wound tearing open. Hoppers poured through in a shrieking swarm, living shrapnel slicing through the frozen air. The Viatori braced. The Triad stood together.

Nicholas wiped blood from his lip, chest heaving, eyes blazing.

Rhet smiled at him, slow, cruel and inevitable.

Nicholas stared back, bruised and shaking and defiant.

"Well," he said, voice rough but steady, "guess I will not have to worry about bringing pie to the next reunion."

Even the hoppers hesitated, just for a heartbeat, as if the universe itself blinked at the audacity.

Rhet's smile twitched. Not gone. But cracked.

Chaos surged.

Hoppers tore through the air, slamming into the Viatori lines. A golden armored soldier fell to his knees, and a hopper latched onto his throat. Another was dragged into the air, screaming, before a sweep team shot the creature down. A third collapsed beside Antonia, armor cracked, breath ragged.

Nicholas, Anna, and Mel fought back-to-back. Nicholas hurled a Defensio burst that shattered a hopper mid-air. Anna slashed through another with glowing talons. Mel's lavender aura flared copper, then deepened into bronze-white as she blasted three more off their feet.

But they were tiring. Fast.

Nicholas's arms shook with every Defensio burst. Anna's oriole form flickered at the edges, feathers dimming. Mel's aura sputtered between lavender and burnished copper, frantic and unstable.

And the Viatori were losing ground.

Not all at once. Not in a clean collapse. But in violent, shuddering swings, like a pendulum on a hallway clock fighting gravity. One moment, they surged forward, shields locking, boots digging into the frost-slick street, pushing the hoppers back in a burst of golden force. The next moment, the swarm hit back twice as hard, slamming into the line and driving them several feet in the opposite direction.

Forward. Back. Forward. Back.

Each swing was shorter. Each recovery, even slower. Each push costs more than the last.

A hopper tore through a soldier's leg, dropping him instantly. Another ripped a shield from a Viator's grip and hurled it across the street. A third slammed into the golden perimeter with such force that the entire formation buckled, the crack echoing like a snapped bone.

The pendulum swung again, but this time the Viatori did not regain the ground they lost.

Nicholas felt the world narrowing around him. The vessel was gone. The Viatori were falling. The hoppers were closing in, red and green sparks raining down like corrupted snow. And the pendulum was about to swing one last time.

Then Rhet stepped into the center of the street. Not fast. Not slow. Simply with the kind of inevitability that made the world rearrange itself around him. His single spur clicked once against the frost-cracked pavement, a sharp metallic note that cut through the chaos like a blade.

Somewhere in the wreckage of a shattered shop, a clock, half frozen and half broken, answered with a single toll. Low. Hollow. Final.

Everything stopped.

Hoppers froze mid-air, wings suspended in arcs of red and green sparks. Viatori halted mid-strike, blades inches from their targets. Even the fracture behind Rhet seemed to hold its breath, its jagged edges trembling as they feared him.

Rhet stood loose-hipped in the street, boots planted in a gunslinger's stance. His coat drifted around him like fog rolling off a river at dawn, slow and ghostly, untouched by the wind. He tipped his hat back with two fingers, glass shard eye glinting.

"Well now," he murmured, voice soft as dust on old wood. "Ain't this a picture?"

Nicholas, Anna, Mel, and Antonia, bruised and bloodied but unbowed, stood together in the center of the street. The Viatori flanked them on both sides, forming a battered wall of gold and steel, still cutting down the few hoppers twitching at the edges of the freeze.

From the shattered storefront to their right, Chanotedah peeked out, eyes wide, clutching an Evanidus sphere like it was a stress ball he regretted picking up.

Nicholas's heart pounded. Anna's claws glowed. Mel's aura burned white. Antonia lifted her shield, jaw set.

Rhet smiled, slow, dangerous and inevitable.

"Let us finish this."

CHAPTER 33

Rhet did not move like a man. He moved like a fracture given form. One heartbeat, he stood still, hat tipped back, single spur glinting, coat trailing behind him in slow, smoky folds that moved independently of the wind. His glass-shard eye gleamed with cold amusement, catching the streetlight in a way that made it look alive.

The next moment, reality buckled. A shockwave erupted from him, green and yellow at its core, streaked with red filaments that writhed like living hairs, rippling outward in a warped halo. The air bent around it. Streetlights bowed. The pavement rippled like water struck by a stone. Nicholas did not even have time to brace.

The shockwave hit him like a fist from the sky, hurling him backward as if gravity had suddenly chosen a new direction. His feet left the ground, his stomach lurched, the world spun. He hit the pavement hard, the breath ripped from his lungs in a single, brutal exhale. And Rhet kept walking, slow, measured, inevitable, as if the shockwave had been nothing more than him clearing his throat.

Anna surged forward in her oriole form, claws blazing with white-hot light, a streak of gold and fury cutting through the warped air. Rhet did not brace. He did not flinch. He did not even look at her. He flicked two fingers, and gravity inverted. Anna's wings snapped open in instinctive panic as her body was yanked upward like a puppet on a reversed string. She slammed into the underside of a fire escape with a metallic crack that echoed down the street.

Gravity snapped back. Anna dropped like a meteor, hitting the pavement hard enough to rattle the frost. Her glow sputtered, feathers dimming, breath knocked from her lungs. Mel did not hesitate. She thrust her hands forward, releasing a burst of lavender-bronze mist that spiraled outward like a living storm.

Rhet did not dodge. He did not shield. He simply stepped into it. The moment his body breached the mist, Mel felt it, that impossible, buzzing tension, as two magnets forced together the wrong way. Her aura shoved outward instinctively, mist recoiling in a shimmering halo around her. The air vibrated. Her teeth rattled. Her pulse stuttered.

Rhet smiled, and the polarity flipped. The repulsion snapped into attraction so violently that it punched the breath from her lungs. Her aura lurched inward, dragged toward him as if the universe had suddenly reversed its charge. Her mist followed, not drifting, not collapsing, but slamming toward Rhet in a spiraling rush of lavender, copper, and bronze-white.

The collision was not physical. It was energetic, a shockwave detonating inside her chest, ripping through her ribs like a silent scream. Her mist shattered, not in a burst, not in a scatter, but like confetti at the bottom of a kaleidoscope, fragments spinning in impossible patterns, refracting light into a thousand tiny shards before collapsing into nothing. Mel staggered, choking on air that suddenly felt too thin.

Rhet walked out of the kaleidoscope of her broken mist, coat drifting like river fog, single spur clicking once against the pavement. His glass-shard eye gleamed. "Cute trick," he murmured. "Try another." He kept walking, coat drifting, spur clicking, eye bright with cold delight.

Mel's aura flickered violently, sputtering like a candle in a storm. Nicholas staggered upright, ribs screaming with every breath. "Stop," he shouted. The word cracked across the battlefield like a thunderclap, sharp enough to make even the frozen hoppers twitch in the air.

Rhet paused. Nicholas planted his feet, shoulders squared, fists trembling. He dragged in a breath, reaching for the Continuum the way Lazer had taught him to reach for his resonance, the way no thirteen-year-old should ever be able to do. It rushed into him like cold fire, flooding his lungs, his limbs, his bones. He was not ready. He was not trained. He was not old enough. But he stood anyway, a child facing a cosmic wound.

Rhet tilted his head, amused. "You think you can stop me, boy?" Nicholas did not answer. He did not blink. He did not breathe. He simply held his ground. Rhet flicked two fingers. A shard of fractured resonance tore toward him, ruby at first, then twisting, refracting, turning emerald green as it neared Nicholas's aura, as if it recognized something in him and changed its mind mid-flight.

It struck, and it did not slice cleanly. It fought for every inch, like a butter knife sawing through a pork chop, grinding, pushing, forcing its way through layer by stubborn layer. Nicholas's aura sparked and flared, bending around the shard, refusing to give, refusing to break. Nicholas screamed through clenched teeth, the sound ripped from somewhere deeper than pain, but he did not fall.

The shard pushed harder. His aura splintered, cracks spiderwebbing through the light around him. Then it broke through. The emerald shard punched into him, not piercing flesh, but shoving his entire being backward and upward, as if it had hooked into the core of him and yanked. His feet tore off the ground. His spine arched. His breath vanished.

With it, Rhet jerked forward, dragged by the same resonance tether, as if the attack had linked them, bound them, made them two ends of the same cosmic thread. For a heartbeat, they hung there, suspended, Nicholas and Rhet, boy and monster, fulcrum and fracture, light and corruption, balanced in midair as if the universe itself had paused to weigh them on an invisible scale.

The moment stretched, held, judged. Nicholas's aura flickered like a dying star. Rhet's glass-shard eye blazed with emerald fire. The tether hummed between them, vibrating with a sound too low for ears and too ancient for language. Then the shard released. The tether snapped. Nicholas was flung backward, crashing into the pavement with a force that rattled the frost and cracked the asphalt beneath him.

Rhet staggered, just a half-step, just a hitch in his stride, but for the first time, his coat did not drift like fog. It snapped, whipped, as if the universe had slapped him. And the Viatori surged.

They were not simply holding the line now. They were fighting for every inch like a piston in a cosmic engine on the verge of seizing. Their shields slammed forward in perfect unison, a wall of gold and steel blazing with resonance. Hoppers hit them like a living avalanche. The line buckled, shoved back an inch, boots scraping across fractured asphalt. The Viatori roared as one and drove forward again, reclaiming that inch with sheer will and centuries of discipline.

Back and forth, forward and back, Order and Chaos locked in a brutal, grinding rhythm, a piston driving the battle's heartbeat. Every Viator's Cura joined the assault beside their partner, hands raised, voices harmonizing in a battle-call that vibrated through the bones of the street. Miniature bursts of white-gold resonance rained down, tiny white-gold explosions popping like Fourth of July firecrackers, scattering sparks across the battlefield.

The creatures shrieked, twisting midair, shaking off the bursts like gnats at a summer picnic, but even irritation from a creature of Chaos was dangerous. A Viator stumbled. Another's shield cracked. A third was dragged half a step out of formation before two more hauled him back into place. The line held, barely, but the pressure was building, the rhythm tightening, the piston straining. One more swing, one more push, one more heartbeat, and everything might break.

At the center of the line, Antonia planted her shield. She did not brace. She did not strain. She planted. The ground beneath her boots cracked outward in a spiderweb of golden fissures, as if the street itself recognized her and bowed under the weight of her stance. Her aura flared, not bright, not loud, but deep, a molten gold that hummed like a cathedral bell struck underwater.

A hopper lunged for her throat. Antonia did not lift her shield. She shifted her weight, just a fraction, just enough. The hopper hit the invisible pressure around her, a wall of force so dense it folded the creature midair, snapping its wings like brittle leaves before it crumpled at her feet. Another dove from above. Antonia raised her eyes, only her eyes.

Her aura pulsed once, a low, resonant thrum that rippled through the Viatori line like a heartbeat. The hopper froze mid-dive, suspended for a breath, then slammed sideways into a streetlamp with bone-shattering force. The Viatori felt it. The Triad felt it. Even Rhet's glass-shard eye flickered.

Antonia stepped forward, shield still planted, voice low and steady. "Hold the line." The piston surged again, this time with her. The Viatori did not stop. They fought harder, weapons humming, armor glowing, voices rising in harmonic battle calls that made it sound as if the bones of the world were singing.

Nicholas felt it. Anna felt it. Mel felt it. They were not alone. The Viatori were not just protecting them; they were fighting with them, burning themselves down to embers if that was what it took to hold the line. But Rhet kept advancing. He lifted a hand. A ripple of sickly green and red energy tore through the street, cracking asphalt, shattering windows, ripping through the Viatori formation with a shockwave of pure wrongness.

Anna and Mel were thrown off their feet, skidding across the pavement. Nicholas dropped to his knees, every muscle screaming as he crawled toward them. "Anna. Mel." Anna lifted her head weakly, her gold aura flickering like a dying star. Mel reached for him, aura sputtering between lavender and pale copper. Nicholas reached back. Their hands met.

The world fell away. Not in violence. Not in pain. In a soft, impossible pull, like the tide drawing them backward through time, gentle and absolute. The battlefield dissolved. Heat replaced cold. Salt replaced smoke. Light replaced chaos.

Suddenly, they were sitting on the beach again, the first time. But it did not feel like a memory. It felt present, alive. The salt air brushed their faces with deliberate warmth, as if greeting them. The sand beneath their legs was not just warm; it held them, cradling their weight like an old friend. The ocean murmured, steady and ancient, each wave rolling in with the slow, patient rhythm of a heartbeat older than the world.

The butterflies rose from the mist in shimmering swarms, blue, gold, white, drifting around them like living fragments of light. This time, they did not simply appear. They approached. They circled. They gathered. They hovered close, wings brushing their skin with the faintest whisper of warmth. The chord hummed beneath everything, in the sand, in the air, in their bones.

Nicholas inhaled sharply. Anna's eyes widened. Mel whispered, "We are here." But they were not. The beach was not a place. It was a presence, a threshold, a memory with gravity, a moment that had been waiting for them to return. Beneath the warmth, beneath the beauty, beneath the butterflies' glow, something in the air trembled, as if the beach itself knew what was coming next.

They were still on the battlefield, Viatori shouting, hoppers shrieking, Rhet stalking toward them with murder in his eyes, yet the beach wrapped around them like a memory made real. The chord pulsed once, twice, stronger. Mel did not touch Nicholas or Anna; she did not have to. Her aura flared outward, a trembling lavender-bronze halo that wrapped around all three of them, drawing resonance into long, shimmering threads. The air around them thickened, humming with resonance.

Above the Viatori line, something moved. A shape, a presence, an eagle made of red and green mist soared over the battlefield, wings beating with the rhythm of Chaos itself. Its cry split the air, sharp enough to rattle the shields below. The Viatori braced.

Before the eagle could dive, a silver lion erupted from the mist behind the Triad, massive and radiant, its mane rippling like liquid moonlight. It leapt skyward with a roar that shook the frost from the rooftops. The two forces collided midair, mist against light, Chaos against Continuum. The lion slammed into the eagle, knocking it out of the sky in a burst of red-green vapor. It landed beside the Triad, shoulders heaving, silver eyes fixed on Rhet.

The battlefield and the beach overlapped, salt air mingling with smoke, warm sand bleeding into cracked asphalt, butterflies swirling through falling debris like stardust. The chord pulsed again, a deep, resonant thrum that vibrated through their bones. Nicholas gasped as something cold struck his palm, not from between their bodies, not from the beach, but from the battlefield.

Across the chaos, Antonia hurled the last Evanidus sphere, her arm cutting through the air with perfect precision. The sphere streaked toward him, trailing a ribbon of molten gold. Nicholas caught it against his chest, breath hitching. Anna's eyes locked on his. Mel's aura tightened around them, drawing more resonance, more light, more everything. The butterflies spiraled upward, forming a luminous vortex above them.

Rhet froze mid-step, glass-shard eye flickering. "No," he snarled. "Not this. Not now." Nicholas whispered, voice raw, "Now." Anna braced. Mel steadied the flow of her aura. The lion growled low beside them, its silver fur bristling.

The chord pulsed again, louder, brighter, unstoppable. They lifted with it, guiding it, delivering it. The Triad hurled the sphere. It left their hands as a streak of pulsating light, a comet ripped straight from a rainbow, carried forward by a spiral of butterflies whose wings beat in perfect harmony with the chord thrumming through the air.

The sphere struck Rhet in the chest. The world split open. A burst of color erupted outward, not a flash, not an explosion, but a spectrum stretched to eternity. Ribbons of red, gold, lavender and blue spiraled into the sky, bending around buildings, painting the battlefield in impossible hues. For a moment, everything was color. Everything was light. Everything was the chord.

Then the spectrum collapsed. All that infinite color snapped inward, folding into a single point, a blinding, white-hot star burning in Rhet's chest. The air screamed as a fracture tore open through him, not behind him. His body bent around it, folding inward like paper caught in a vortex.

Rhet clawed at the air, at the pavement, at reality itself. "You do not… you do not know… what you have…" The fracture pulled harder. His coat whipped violently. His limbs twisted as if gravity had forgotten how to hold him. His glass-shard eye flickered, then shattered into dust.

His body folded once, twice, a third time, impossibly collapsing along invisible seams. Then he fell through himself, vanishing into the fracture that had opened inside his own chest. One final flicker of ruby and emerald light. The fracture snapped shut.

Silence followed, not relief, not release, but the kind of silence that feels like the world is waiting to see what happens next. The butterflies dissolved into mist. The salt air faded. The beach slipped away like a dream that knew it was not allowed to stay.

Nicholas exhaled a thin, trembling breath. Anna's shoulders sagged, her gold aura guttering. Mel's aura flickered once, then dimmed to a faint, exhausted shimmer. The three of them collapsed together, not like children fainting, not like warriors falling, but like stars burning out, their bodies folding as the last of the Continuum finally released them, unceremonious, uncontrolled, unconscious.

The Viatori rushed toward them, boots pounding the fractured street. Antonia reached them first. She dropped to her knees beside the Triad, shield still strapped to her arm, golden fissures still glowing faintly beneath her boots. Her breath caught, not from fear, but from awe and something dangerously close to relief.

She leaned over them, arms bracing the ground on either side, her voice barely more than a tremor. "I have you." Not shouted. Not declared. Whispered like a vow. A promise that she would see to the end.

Around her, the Viatori slowed, then bowed their heads, then took a knee, one by one, armor clinking softly as they lowered themselves in a ring around the fallen Triad. Not out of protocol. Not out of command. Out of reverence, out of recognition, out of the quiet, collective understanding that they had just witnessed the impossible and survived because the three exhausted members of the Triad stood against a cosmic wound and did not break.

And the Triad did not hear any of it. They had already passed out.

CHAPTER 34

The lion appeared from the chaos of light and matter, its silver mane rippling like moonlit fire. It stepped through the settling haze of the battlefield and into the ring of kneeling Viatori, its presence bending the air like heat over stone.

The Viatori didn't rise. They bowed their heads deeper.

The lion lowered itself beside the collapsed Triad—Nicholas, Anna, and Mel folded together, breaths shallow, bodies slack. It wrapped its shimmering energy around them. Silver light curled protectively over their shoulders, their backs, their tangled limbs.

Then, with a single sweep of its luminous tail, the lion parted the circle.

A seam opened beneath the Triad—soft, silent, like a curtain of mist parting.

The lion nudged them gently, guiding their unconscious bodies toward the light.

And the three of them slipped through the seam, lifted by the lion's energy, carried into the glow without ever waking.

One moment, they lay collapsed on the ruined street—limp, unconscious, the last echoes of the harmonic chord still trembling through the air.

The next…

They landed in Nicholas's room.

The familiar walls. The soft lamplight. The scattered books. The rumpled blankets.

The Council stood around them; Bharati, Lazer, Paloma, Asiza, and Chittaswarup all looking as if they had aged a decade in a single hour. Like Mel, several wore the subtle insignia of Sustentets, the stabilizers and anchors who served throughout the Conclave.

Antonia was already on the floor.

She had slid down the wall beside them, knees pulled to her chest, shield still strapped to her arm. Her back pressed against the plaster, her eyes fixed on the Triad with a vigilance that didn't waver. Not once. Not for a moment.

She didn't speak. She didn't sleep. She simply kept watch. The seam closed. And the room fell silent.

They slept for two days.

The Council checked on them in shifts, speaking in hushed tones, their faces tight with something that wasn't quite relief. Something fractured. Something unspoken.

But Antonia never left the room.

She stayed on the floor, back to the wall, knees drawn up, exhaustion carving shadows beneath her eyes, but her gaze never strayed from the Triad. She watched them breathe. She watched them heal. She watched them live.

On the morning of the third day, Nicholas stirred.

Then Anna.

Then Mel.

They blinked awake; groggy, disoriented, sore in places they didn't know could hurt.

Antonia rose in a single, fluid motion; not dramatic, not showy, but with the quiet strength of someone who had been waiting for this moment with every breath.

The Council gathered behind her.

"Oh, our heroes awaken," Paloma said with a smile that didn't reach her eyes.

"You saved the realm," Bharati added, voice warm but strained.

"You did what none of us could," Asiza said, hands clasped too tightly.

Lazer stood behind them, arms crossed, jaw set. Pride radiated from him, but so did worry.

Antonia stepped forward. Her voice was steady, controlled. "You're safe now."

But even in their exhaustion, the Triad felt it.

Not a word. Not a look. A shift.

A crack running beneath the Council's polished surface, thin as a hairline fracture in glass but spreading. A tension coiled behind their praise, sharp enough to taste. A ripple of unease that moved through the room like a draft under a closed door. A fear not of what the Triad had done…

…but of what they might become.

Nicholas exchanged a glance with Anna. Anna with Mel. Mel with Nicholas.

They didn't say anything.

They didn't need to.

Antonia saw it—the overwhelm, the instinct to escape the tightening ring of Council eyes. She stepped subtly between the Triad and the others, her stance casual but unmistakably protective.

"Give them space," she said, not unkind, but with a firmness that left no room for debate.

The Council hesitated. That was all she needed.

Antonia angled her body, creating a narrow path behind her—a quiet invitation. Nicholas caught it first. Anna followed. Mel slipped in last, her shoulder brushing Antonia's arm in silent thanks.

Without a word, Antonia shifted just enough to block the Council's view as the Triad moved past her. They didn't run. They didn't rush. They simply walked—steady, silent—out the door, down the hall, and into the sunlight.

Antonia didn't turn to watch them go.

But she stood there, a quiet sentinel, until the Council finally exhaled.

They walked to their beach.

The path felt different now; quieter, heavier.

But when they reached the shoreline, everything felt right again.

The lake shimmered. Dragonflies skimmed the surface, wings catching the light in iridescent flashes. Loons called from somewhere across the water, their voices echoing like distant memories.

Their driftwood log waited for them.

Nicholas approached his usual spot, the towel still draped over it from their last visit; untouched, unmoved, preserved in the one place time could never touch them, no matter how violently the outside world unraveled.

Nicholas lifted the towel.

And froze.

There, resting exactly where he always sat, was the vessel whole, unbroken, healed. Its surface glowed faintly, pulsing with a soft, steady rhythm, the same rhythm that had thrummed through the Triad when the harmonic chord ignited.

As the glow brightened, Nicholas felt something tug at the edge of his awareness. A shimmer of color flickered in the corner of his vision. He turned and saw Mel standing just behind him, the lake-light brushing her skin in soft lavender and gold.

And on her thigh, where there had once been a single dolphin tattoo, three now swam in a slow, spiraling dance.

Silver. Gold. Lavender.

Their bodies glimmered as if lit from within, weaving around one another in a perfect triad, their motion syncing with the pulse of the vessel. Nicholas blinked, breath catching. The dolphins weren't static ink. They moved, not wildly, not theatrically, but with the gentle, tidal rhythm of something alive. Something awakened.

Something changed by the chord.

He watched them circle once more, the silver leading, the gold following, the lavender drifting closest to Mel's pulse point,

Nicholas didn't speak. He didn't need to.

Anna gasped. Mel covered her mouth with both hands. Nicholas reached out, fingertips trembling, and touched the vessel.

Warm. Whole. Safe.

Whatever had happened after Nicholas sent it away, the vessel had returned whole.

The Triad sat together, the vessel between them, dragonflies dancing over the water, loons calling in the distance. For the first time since the battle, they breathed easily.

The realm was quiet. The vessel was safe. And the Triad was whole.

EPILOGUE

Nirvana was quiet.

The lake shimmered in the late afternoon light, dragonflies drifting lazily over the water. Nicholas sat on the driftwood with Anna and Mel, the vessel resting between them like a heartbeat made visible. They did not speak. They did not need to.

A soft ripple moved across the lake, not wind, not water, but something older. Something that had been waiting. Nicholas felt it first, a tug, a pull, a quiet summons threading through the air like a memory he had not lived yet.

Anna straightened. "You feel that."

Mel nodded. "It is not danger."

"No," Nicholas whispered. "It is time."

A seam shimmered open at the edge of the shoreline, patient and expectant, the way a door waits for someone who already knows they must walk through it.

Antonia stepped out.

She was not armored. She was not carrying her shield. She looked like someone who had been awake for days and would stay awake for days more if that was what the Triad needed. Her longer brown hair, usually pulled into a tight ponytail above razor-short sides, had fallen loose and flopped to one side, strands escaping in uneven arcs that softened the sharp lines of her face. Ash from the battle still clung to her clothes, streaking her denim jacket and dark shirt in pale smudges, as if the fight had followed her all the way here and refused to let go.

Her gaze softened when it landed on them.

"It is time," she said quietly.

Anna's breath caught. "For Nicholas?"

Antonia shook her head. "For all of you."

Mel frowned. "What does that mean?"

Antonia stepped closer, her boots sinking slightly into the sand. "The realm is safe for now. The danger is gone. But Nirvana cannot hold you the way it has."

Nicholas swallowed. "Because we need to age?"

"Yes," Antonia said. "You need to grow, to become who you are meant to be. And that can only happen in timelines where time moves forward."

Anna's voice trembled. "Then we go with him."

Antonia's expression softened with something like sorrow. "Not this time."

Anna blinked. "Why not?"

Antonia turned to Anna. "You have another charge waiting for you in a different timeline. Your bond with Nicholas remains, but a Cura's active charge can change once a Viator no longer requires constant protection. Someone else needs you now."

Anna's breath hitched. She did not argue. She understood.

Mel looked between them, her jaw tightening. "And me?"

Antonia placed a hand on her shoulder. "You return to the Council. They need you now more than ever. The division is widening. You are the only one they might listen to."

Mel exhaled shakily. "So that is it. We are splitting up."

"Not splitting," Antonia said. "Expanding."

The seam behind her brightened.

And someone stepped out.

Chase. More weathered. Steadier. His eyes widened the moment he saw Nicholas, as if he were looking into a mirror that remembered more than he did. Nicholas stood. Chase did too. They met halfway, the seam's light casting both in the same glow. Anna covered her mouth. Mel's eyes filled. Antonia looked away, giving them the dignity of the moment.

Chase spoke first, voice soft. "Ready to come home."

Nicholas nodded. "Yes. I think I am."

Anna threw her arms around him, fierce and trembling. Mel followed, pressing her forehead to his, their breaths mingling in a silent promise.

"You come back to us," Anna whispered.

"You better," Mel added, her voice cracking.

Nicholas smiled, small and tired but real. "I will."

He stepped toward the seam. Chase reached out a hand. Nicholas took it.

The lake shimmered. The vessel pulsed once. Dragonflies rose in a glittering cloud.

Nicholas looked back one last time.

Anna stood tall, the responsibility of her next charge already settling across her shoulders. Mel squared her shoulders, the mantle of Council responsibility settling over her like a familiar cloak. Antonia stood behind them, a silent sentinel, her presence steady and unyielding, the quiet guardian who had carried them through every fracture and would carry their memory into every battle yet to come.

He stepped through.

The seam closed.

Nicholas stepped through.
The seam closed behind him.
And for the first time since the clock shop, he was going home.

Made in the USA
Monee, IL
04 November 2026

67382306R00157